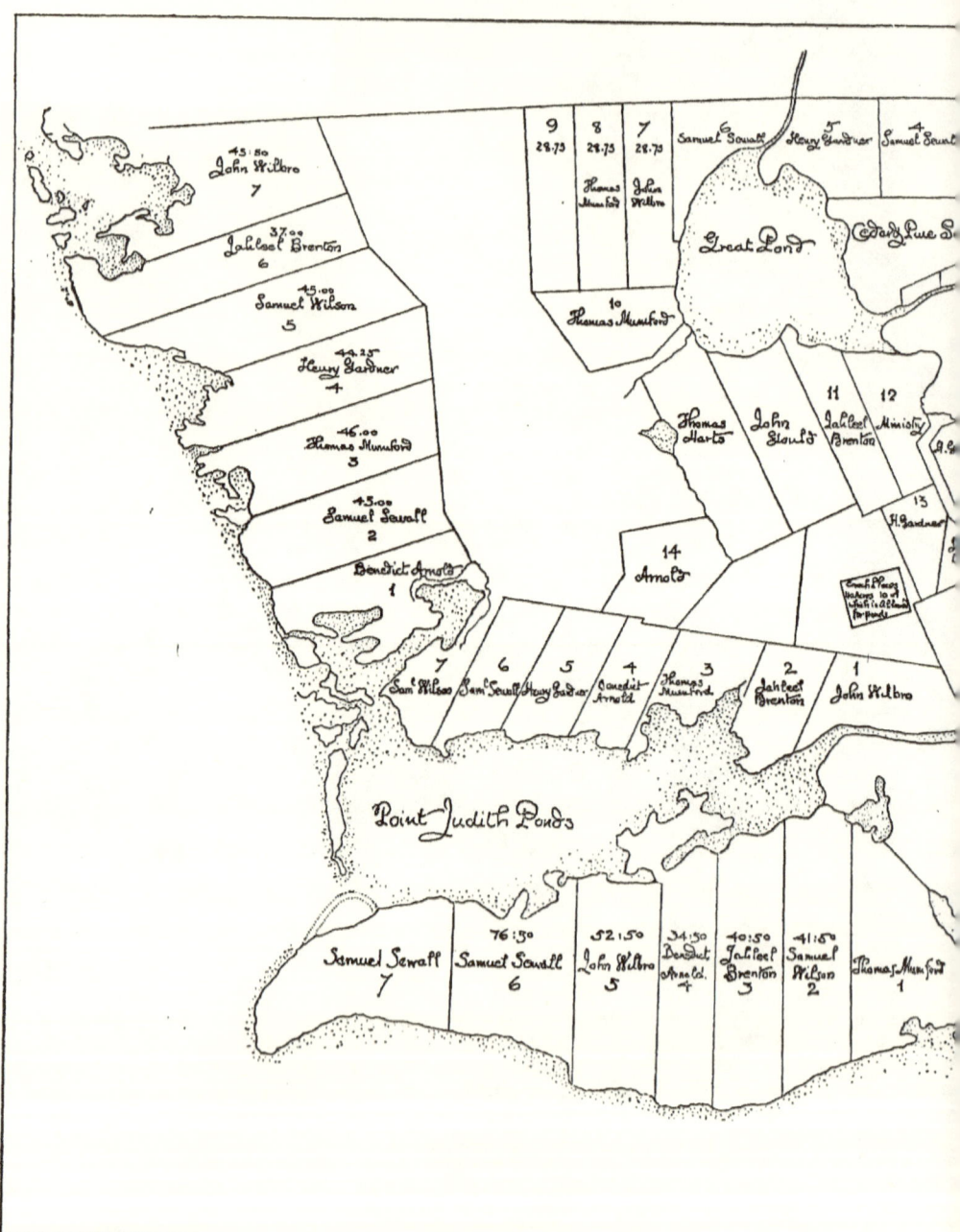

This is a true copy of the Draught of Pettaquamscutt Purchase which was delivered to me John Mumford Surveyor. True Copy of the Draught of Petaquamscut Purchase as on file ia. Martin Cler.

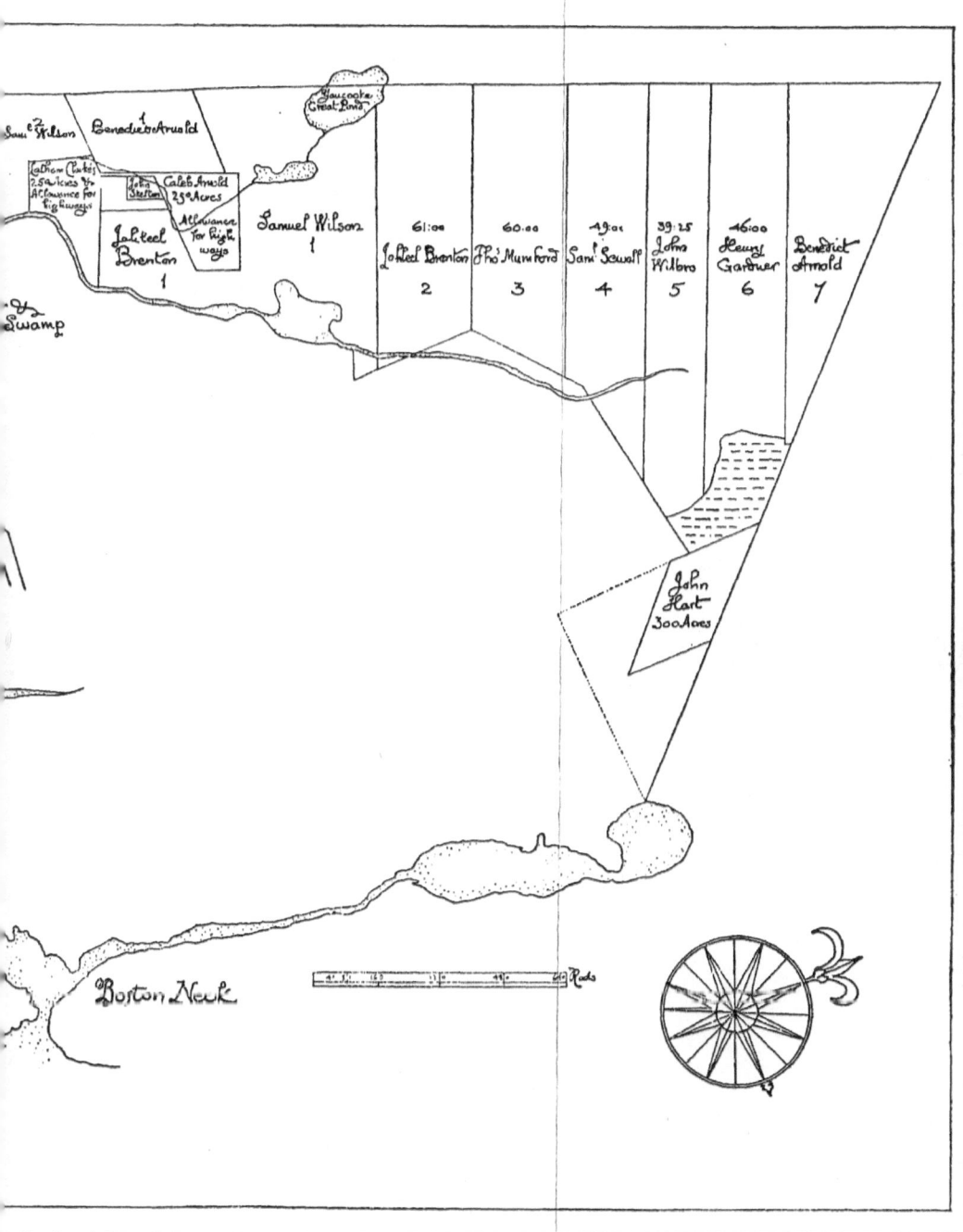

y Richard Ward, Recorder & was taken & compared this 21st Day of April 1724. Attested per
e Case: Joseph Torrey vs George Mumford tried in the Superior Court in March 1733. Teste

From copy in Rhode Island Historical Society. Atlas, vol. 11, p. 6.

Rhode Island Land Evidences

VOLUME I
1648–1696

ABSTRACTS

Southern Historical Press, Inc.
Greenville, South Carolina

This volume was reproduced
from a personal copy located in
the Publishers private library

All rights reserved. No part of this publication may be reproduced,
stored in a retrieval system, transmitted in any form, posted
on the web in any form or by any means without the
prior written permission of the publisher.

Please direct all correspondence and book orders to:
SOUTHERN HISTORICAL PRESS, Inc.
1071 Park West Blvd.
Greenville, SC 29611

Printed Providence, RI 1921
ISBN #978-1-63914-628-4
Printed in the United States of America

Preface

In Rhode Island, the land records are kept by the various towns and not by the counties, as in Massachusetts. This has always been true of this State, even when for a time the Colony government kept a record of land transfers.

There are now in the office of the Secretary of State, four ancient volumes called Rhode Island Land Evidence. They contain a great variety of deeds, a very few of Providence, many from Newport and many from the various parts of South County—some, such as Roger Williams' deed to Richard Smith, from territory where there was no town government at all.

The deeds are not arranged chronologically and often early deeds are recorded with later instruments relating to the same piece of land, apparently to strengthen the title. Probate and other legal records are also contained in these books.

Two other volumes of early colonial records, the "Rhode Island Colony Record, 1646-1669," and the "Records of the Island of Rhode Island, 1639-1646," also contain land evidences.

Although a few of these deeds have been printed in full and in abstract, the mass of this material has been available for study only at great cost of time and effort. Over a year ago the group of gentlemen, whose names follow, determined to do something towards bringing these deeds before students and historians in a reasonably convenient form:

Edwin A. Burlingame	Norman M. Isham
Frederick D. Carr	Charles D. Kimball
William C. Dart	Walter H. Kimball
William C. Greene	Howard W. Preston
	Henry D. Sharpe

These gentlemen contributed the funds for abstracting the records in the first volume of Land Evidence.

This work was done by Miss Dorothy Worthington.

Miss Worthington's manuscript was turned over to the Rhode Island Historical Society for publication, the cost of which has been paid for out of the "Special fund" contributed by:

R. Livingston Beeckman	Frank W. Matteson
H. Martin Brown	Jesse H. Metcalf
Alfred M. Coats	Stephen O. Metcalf
Samuel P. Colt	Paul C. Nicholson
Charles J. Davol	Samuel M. Nicholson
Michael Dooley	Frederick S. Peck
Mrs. Robert H. I. Gammell	Mrs. Frank A. Sayles
William Gammell	Henry D. Sharpe
Mrs. C. Oliver Iselin	George L. Shepley
Charles D. Kimball	Robert W. Taft
Webster Knight	William A. Viall
Henry F. Lippitt	John Carter Brown Woods

The book which the Society now publishes is the oldest of these four books of Land Evidences. It consists of 445 pages, each about 7½ by 11½ inches, the writing upon which is enclosed, at the top and on both sides, with an ink border line which may possibly once have crossed the bottom also. The rectangle of manuscript is 6 1/16 by 11¼ inches. The paper has a water mark, an urn with an elaborate finial ending at the top in a crescent.

There is no ancient title now to be seen, as the old fly leaves have disappeared.

The old binding also has perished and the book has been rebound, with the following title on the back:

RHODE-ISLAND
LAND RECORDS
. . . .
1648 to 1696

Norman M. Isham,
For the Committee.

Abstracts from Volume I of the Rhode Island Land Evidences in the State Archives

[1] [Blank.]

[2] This present Deed or writinge made in the Fower and Twentith yeare of the Reigne of our Soverraigne Lord Charles .....Wittnesseth, That wheras there is a percell of Land Contanninge Forty Acres of Land bounded on the West End by the Highway on the East side of the mill, on the North Side by Joshua Coggeshalls Land on the South side by the Land of Mr William Jefferey, and on the East End by the highway to the Comon as alsoe another percell of Land Containinge two acres more or less lyinge on the west side of the said mill higway bounded on the North and West by the land of James Rogers and on the south by Mr. William Jeffereys land and East on the aforesaid highway, which said two percells of Land.....being the proper Inheritance and possession of James Rogers of Newport in Rhode-Isl. in the province of providence in New-England. The said James Rogers.....doth.....sell the said two percells of Land..... unto Richard Knight of the same Towne..... In Wittnes whereof the Sayd James Rogers hath sett to his hand and seale this prsent sixteenth day of January. Ann. Dom. 1648. in the presence off us   The marke
                                                   I R
William Dyre Gen. Recordr   James Rogers
I doe promise and ingadge my selfe to make the fence that hath been in Controversy betwixt Richard Knight and my selfe betwixt this and March next and to maintaine the same for ever.
Witnes my hand hereunto the Sixth of June 1650
    Wittnesses
    Peter Talmann   William Jefferey
    Nathanell Britten

Newport the 8th day of February 1648.....I Richard Knight of Newport doe.....inverce and ingage to my wife Sarah Knight that I will not sell.....any of that Tract of Land latly bought of James Rogers and Robert Griffin but doe.....Intaile it upon her and my heires forever, but Especialy to her and my Eldist sonn if any and in case wee have no sonn to my Eldist daughter to be my and her proper heire after my death and if a sonn he shall have it at The age of one and Twenty yeares if I have left my beinge in this life, and if noe sonn then the Eldist daughter shall have it at Sixteene yeares of age provided alwaies that the thirds of the Land and the best and convenientest roome in the house is to be my wifes, duringe her life, and then to returne to the heire .....But if there be more then one Sonn the daughters are noe heires soe long as any of the male be liveinge, but if noe sonn or sonns or if the sonn or sonns die without Ishue, then the Eldist daughter then livinge shall be the Right heire, But this is more Largely declared that if the Eldist sonn dye without Ishue the next shall enjoy it, But if the first have children whether sonns or daughters and alsoe the rest that are herein appointed to be heires, And this have I done the day and yeare above written, to avoyd strife because my sonn in ole England shall have nothing to doe herein nor have any Right to any Land of mine in New-England. In testimony hereof I put to my hand this day and yeare aforesaid.

Signed in the
pressence off   Richard Knight
John Downeing
  his **X** marke
Robert Spink
X his marke

'[3].....I Cogamaquoant one of the chiefe Indian Sachims or prince of the Narragansetts in the Collony of Rhod-Island .....have for.....Tenn pownds in peage Eight the peny in hand by me the aforesaid Cogamaquoant Received from Richard Knight & Henry Halls both of the Towne of New- port.....wherwith I the sayd Cogamaquoant doe.....dis-

charg the said Richard Knight and Henry Halls of all debts
.....I.....doe.....sell.....unto the said Richard Knight
& Henry Halls their heires.....a certain percell of Land
Scittuate and lyinge in the aforesaid Narragansetts Cuntry
neere or adjoininge unto the Land Formerly Sould by me unto
Mr. John Porter and Mr Samll Wilbore &c at pettacomscutt
and is by Esteemation two Miles Square be it more or less
beinge butted and bounded as Followeth Vizt. on the East
side from a place called in Indian Qumatumpick, southward
to a place called chippachuat and soe westerly to a place called
Quowachauck and from thence northward to a place called
Winatompick and soe to extand from thence upon a straight
line unto the first boundery,.....to be Houlden of our Royall
Soverraigne Lord Charles the Second.....not in Capett nor
by Knights service but in comon Soccage after the manner of
East Greenwich in the County of Kent.....Further I the
said Cogamoquant doe.....bind myselfe.....in the sum
or Bond of Five hundred pounds Starl of good and lawfull
mony of England or to the vallew therof that the Land mentioned in this deed is a good Reall and firme Estate unto the
said Richard Knight and Henry Halls.....and that the said
land is cleere and free from all intailments deeds of sale leases
mortgages and all other alienations of what nature or kinds
whatsoever.....and to cleere and remove or cause to be
removed at or before the first of march next after the date
hereof Every Indian or Indians Inhabiting there on and not
to suffer for the future any Indian to dwell or plant upon the
aforesaid Tract.....this ninteenth day of January and in
the yeare of our Lord god one Thousand Six hundred Sixty
and fower.....

in presence of
John Archer
The marke of
X
Alse Archer
Richard Bulgar

The marke of
X
Cogamagooant
The marke of Wotomer
X   an Indian
Cobsounk his marke
X   an Indian

[4] Noumto. Univrsi, prputs me Henrycum Button de Buckland in Com. Southt Armr teneriet fermiter obligary Nicholas Easton de lymington in Com. prd Tanner in ducentis libris bonet Legati monete angt Soluend eidem Nicholas Easton aut suo certo aturnato Executor vealassigna suis ad qua quidem solucoriem bene et fidelit faciend obligo and hered Executor et administrator meos firmiter prputs Sigillom eo sigillat dat visisimo sexto die Junu Anno Regnie dm nor Jacobi dei grat angli fraunce et hiberni Regis fidei defensor & decimo quarto et stotie Quadragesimo Nono 1616. [Know all men by these presents that Nicholas Easton of Lymmington in the County of Hants, Tanner, holds and formally binds me, Henry Button of Buckland in the County aforesaid, Gentleman, to the sum of two hundred pounds of good and lawful English money to be paid to the said Nicholas Easton or his authorized attorney, executor or assignee, to the good and faithful execution of the payment I bind myself, my heires, Executor and Administrator, formally in witness whereof I affix my seal, given the 26th of June in the fourteenth year of the reign of our Lord James by the grace of God, King of England, France and Ireland, defender of the Faith,......1616.]

The Condicon of this obligation is such that if the above bownded Henry Button.....soe long as he the said Henry Button his heires or assignes shall or may lawfully in joy..... the prfitts of certaine Copie hold lands in pennington in the County of South t. specified.....and agreed upon betweene the said William Dolinge Elizabeth his wife and Nicholas Easton of the one part and the said Henry Button of the other part dated the day of the Date hereof.....shall well and truly pay yearly the sum of Eleven pownds of Lawfull English mony.....
in the pressence of

Henry Button

Edward Button   Edward Keiylway
Thomas Hurst   Edmund Barnes.

[5].....I John Porter of pettacomscutt in the Collony of

Rhod-Island.....for.....the sum of Four hundred pownds starling.....paid by Richard Smith of Newport in the Collony aforesaid merchant.....have.....sold.....unto the said Richd Smith.....a certaine percell of Land lyinge and beinge within the bounds of the Towne of portsmouth, on Rhod-Island in the Collony aforesaid Containinge by Esteemation two hundred and forty Acres more or less Bounded on the north by Land now or late in the posession of Mr William Baulston or his assignes, on the west by the sea, on the south by Land now or late in the posession of Thomas Hazard or his assignes, and on the east by the Comon, together with all and Singular the houses.....In wittnes whereof I the said John Porter have hereunto sett my hand and Seale (as alsoe Horrud porter the wife of me the said John porter .....the six and Twentith day of September.....Anno. Dm. 1671

John porter

in the pressents of
(the word Baulston
being Interlyned)
Francis Brinley
John Almy
Richard Baily

    I Hurrud porter doe consent to the bovesd Deed and doe Release all my Right intrest and Title in the abovesaid premises Notwithstandinge my jointure or Dower made me by my now Husband before Marriage with me. Wittnes my hand and seale this thirty day of Sept 1671

Wittnes.....
Samuell Wilson
Georg X Hicks
  his marke
Georg X Gardner
  his marke

The mark of
Horad Porter
X

[6]   This Indenture made the Eighteenth day of October in the ninth yeare of the raigne of our Soverraigne Lord Charles .....Betweene Henry Tew of Maidforde in the County of North'ton yeoman of the one part and William Clarke of priors Hardwicke in the County of Warr. yeoman of the other

part Witnesseth that for and in Consideration of a marriage by the grace of god shortly to be had and Sollemnized Betweene Richard Tew Sonn and heire apparant of the said Henry and Mary Clarke one of the Daughters of the said William Clarke and for the sum off Twenty pounds of Lawfull mony of England by bond scured to be payd by the said William Clarke unto the said Henry Tew upon the last day of May next Ensuinge the date off these pressents. And for the sum of one hundred and Twenty pounds of Lawful mony England by Bond secured to be paid by him the said William Clarke to him the said Richard Tewe upon the Nine and twentith day of Septembr which shall be in the yeare of our Lord god one Thousand Six hundred and Forty.....It is hereby Mutualy covinnated.....that he the said Henry Tew..... shall.....be seised of.....that Messuage, Tenement, Close and one yardland; and halfe yardland.....Scituate.....in the Towne parish and Feilds of Maidforde aforsaid, And now in the possession Tenure or occupacon of the said Henry Tew, ...and of and in all that Cottage.....now in the Tenure or occupacon of Nicholas Carey,.....and of and in all that other Cottage.....now in the Tenure or occupacon of Nathaniel Shen.....To the only proper use of the said Henry Tew for and during the tearme of his Naturall life, And Emediatly from and after his decease to the only proper use and behoofe of the said Richard Tewe.....And for touchinge and Concerninge the said Messuage yardland and half.....To the only use and behoofe of the said Henry Tewe for and during the Terme of seven yeares.....(if the said Henry shall soe long live), And Emediatly from and after the end or other detirminacon of the said Tearme of seven yeares to the only use and behoofe of the said Richard Tew.....[7] In Witnes whereof the parties to theis pressents have to theis pressent Indentures interchangeably sett their hands and seales.....

Sealed and Delivered   Henry Tewe
in the presence of
  William Leeke
  Samuell Leeke
  John Maior

..... Whereas there is found wanting in a certain lott laid out by mr Noise and some others to John Rathbone and Edward Vose which should have been two hundred and Tenn Acres, And falling short six score and tenn acres. Therefore Know yea that I John Williams Aturney to John Greene Aturn. to the Guardians of the estate of the late John Alcock of Roxbury phissission deceased havinge by their order in Aprile last past ordered me to deliver the said Rathbone and his partner what land shall be found wantinge to them in some Convenient place in the Comon land at Block Island; Therefore Know yea that I have layd out to the said Rathbone sixty Acres of land on the East side of Mill River butting and boundinge with the land of Samuell Deringe south one hundred & Eighty Eight Rod long Buttinge to the sea on the East A hundred and fower Rod to the land of Samuell Hagbourne north a hundred and Twenty fower Rod soe to goe downe to the Mill Brooke Thirty five Rod in Bredth, till it comes to the Land of Samuell Hagbourne and to have a highway through James Sands yard over the mill Brooke soe to run as a drift way through the land of the said Rathbone two Rods wide along by mr Hagbournes Reaves and Dodges land to the now Harbour on the East Side of Block Island. In wittnes whereof I have hereunto sett my hand this Eleventh day of October 1671.   John Williams
Wittness
　Robert Guthrey
　Trustram Dodge

..... Wee whose names are under written doe aprove and allow of John Williams act in delivering John Rathbone that land that Joines to Samuell Derings great lott (formerly sold to Samuell Hagbourne) for his Sixty or Sixty five Acres of land wantinge in his great lott in the South end of Block Island. Wittnes our hands Octor 18; 1671.
　　　　　　　　　　　Samll Dering **X** his marke
　　　　　　　　　　　Henry Neale **X** his marke
　　　　　　　　　　　Phillip Wharton

..... That I Samuel Derin doe Resigne up all my Right Title and intrest to the percell of Land Given to John Rath-

bone (for Sixty five acres of Land missinge in his great lott)
to the Heires of John Alcock and the Company belonginge to
Block Island as wittnes my hand this 18th day of October 1671.
Wittness   his marke
  John Williams   Samll Derin
  Henry Neale
     his marke

[8].....I Mary Dering vid the late wife of Samll Dering
Sometimes of Braintree in the County of Suffolke yeoman,
Deceased, for and in consideration of the considerable sum of
one hundred Forty and five pounds of currant silver mony of
New England.....received of Mr. James Sands of Block
Island.....doe.....sell.....to James Sands, his Heires.....
all that Tract of Land that was the Land of my late deare
Husband, Samuell Deringe aforesaid at that time when he
made a Lease of the same Lands Anno. 1669 Aprill the First
.....Scituate lyinge and beinge in Block Island in the Collony
of Rhod-Island.....Alwaies saveinge and Reserveinge the
said Lease.....to the Grantees or Leasee.....untill the full
time and tearme therein mentioned.....It being formerly by
my said deare Husband lawfully purchased of mr John Alcock
late of Roxbury phisician deceased.....the Lease aforesaid
to Trustram Dodge Senr, Trustram Dodge Junr and William
Dodge.....And further I the said Mary Deringe Doe further
sell to the said mr James Sands all that part of the stock of
Cattell and other Utencills of Husbandry mentioned in the
Lease of the first of Aprill 1669 with all the increase.....In
wittnes wherof I the said Mary Deringe have hereunto put my
hand and affixed my seale 11 : 9 mo : Anno 1671.
  in presence of us   Mary Dering
    Cornelius Fisher   her marke **X** seale
    Samuell Hunting

[9].....This Deed.....bearing date the two and Twentieth
Day of Sept.....1671 betweene William Brenton and Benedict Arnold of Newport on Rhod-Island Merchts John Hull of
Boston.....Mercht, John Porter Samll Wilbur Samuell Welson and Thomas Mumford of the Collony of Rhod-Island

.....of the one part and Robert Hassard of portsmouth in the Collony of Rhod-Island &c Shipp-wright on the other part .....That wee the said William Brenton.....in consideration of the sum of Five and Twenty pounds starll.....paid by the said Robert Hassard.....have sould.....to the said Robert Hassard.....two peecis of percells of Land Containinge by Esteemation five hundred & sixty Acres.....in the Narragansitt Cuntry or Kings province.....one percell.....beinge five hundred Acres more or less is bounded on the north by a highway on the East by Saugawatuckett River on the south partly by land belonging to Edmund Shearman & Samson Shearman and partly by a high-way on the west by Land layd out to the purchassers, the other percell of the said Five hundred & sixty Acres beinge Sixty Acres more or less is adjoyninge to Two Hundred and fifty Acres which the said Robert Hassard purchased of John Sanford.....Only Excepted that is at any time hereafter any Minneralls shall be Discovered in the said percells of Land or Either of them the said Minneralls shall be devided into Eight equall shares or parts seven wherof shall be and remaine to the use of us the said William Brenton, Benedict Arnold, John Hull, John Porter, Samuell Wilbur, Samuell Welson, & Thomas Mumford, and the other Eight part to the use of the said Robt. Hassard.....wee have hereunto sett our hands & seals.....
in the presence
off

  John Albro   William Brenton
  John Winchcombe   Benedict Arnold
                                   John Hull
                                   John Porter
                                   Samuell Wilbur
                                   Samuell Welson
                                   Thomas Mumford

.....Robert Hassard to Georg Brownell. Robert Hassard of Portsmouth.....Nine pounds.....Georg Brownell of Portsmouth.....one-third part of three hundred and Tenn Acres of Land lyinge.....in the Narragansett Cuntry in that Tract belonginge unto the purchassers of Pattacomscutt and is by them already Layd out two hundred and fifty Acres of the said Three hundred and tenn beinge by me purchased of John Sanford the other sixty beinge granted and Layd out thereto by the.....purchassors.....Twenty-fourth Day of Novembr.....1671

Wit.   Robert Hassard.

  John Sanford.
  Gidion **X** Freeborne
     his mark
  Joseph Samson

  .....Robart Hassard.....ye first day of June 1698 Acknowledged ye Above written.....

                                                         Joseph Sheffild Ast:

[10]   Robert Hassard to Gidion Freeborne.

.....Robert Hassard of.....Portsmouth.....Eighteenepounds.....Gidion Freeborne of.....Portsmouth.....two third parts of Three hundred and Tenn Acres.....the other third.....I haveing sold unto George Brownell,.....Lyinge.....in.....that Tract belonginge to the purchassors of Pettacomscutt.....Two hundred and fifty Acres.....being by me purchassed of John Sanford.....Twenty fourth Day of Novembr.....1671

Wit.   John Sanford   Robert Hassard
      Joseph Samson
      George **X** Brownell
          his marke

[11]   Samuell Hubbard—Land Recorded.

Samuell Hubbard of.....Newport.....posession of.....Land containge Twenty fower Acres.....within.....Newport is bounded North, with the Land of Nicholas Wiles and a lane throug his land to the Comon East by the River Called Stony River, South by the land of mr. Walter Cunnigrave and part by the Land of mr. Walter Clarke West by the High way twelve Rods.....Twenty fower Rods by the land of Andrew Langworth with All.....dwelinge or mansion housis Barnes and outhousis ardins orchyards.....15th Day of Aprill.....1672.

John Sanford G. Recorder.

Trustram Dodge to Peter Georg.

.....Trustram Dodge.....seventy pounds.....paid by Peter Georg Samuell Dearing and John Williams Inhabitants of Block Island.....do.....grant.....all my Land.....upon Block Island lately bought of Thomas Terry.....Thirty Acres.....with all.....housing chattells movable goods..... upon my lands.....sixteenth day of Aprill.....1666
Wit.   Trustram Dodge

Willi Reves
X
his marke
William Nightingall

[12]   Peter Georg to John Williams.

Peter Georg of Block Island do assigne.....all the Right .....unto John Williams of Block Island.....15th day of November 1668:

Peter X George.
his marke.

Nicholas Easton Land Records.

.....Nicholas Easton was granted: 300 Acres for his farme and 20 cowes grass with 25 ackers of Cow-pasture and fower ackers of a home Lott—Upon the 5th day of February..... 1644 the old freemen of Newport were called together for the Dispotion.....of the Towne Land undispossed of..... finding not above sixty acres left:.....agree.....that he should have that percell.....at two shillings per acre..... his farm to begin on the East side of the mill pond in the midst of the Valley and soe on in a straight line to Extend Eastward to the marked trees at Stony River and by that Rivers side to the Falls and from thence by the virge of the hill to the sea to the Edge of the Rocks and soe bounded by the sea South and West to the midle of the hill between the Issueing out of the pond and the Carte way, and from thence about by the pond side to the afore-said valley: lickwise on the southwest side of the pond Bounded by the high-way on the back-side to over against the house and soe by marked trees unto a small tree over against mr Brentons line and by that line through the swamp unto the verdg of the pond, a part of mr. Brentons marsh interveaning, as alsoe two Acres of pasture and one Cowes hay lying neere Aquednock point with his home lott and six acres of upland and six acres of Fenceinge Copes lyinge betweene mr Bracys Farme and Henry Bulls meadowes.....which.....Land is layd forth for his proportion of 369 Acres alowed him by order with 20 also by order allowed for the mill in proportion of acres .....The neck at Sachueast 140 layd out to mr Easton 50 to Robeson 40. to Edward Andrewes 25. sold to mr Easton .....amounting to the number of 389 acres

      Joseph Terry Towne Clerke
      1662 December: 5

[13] Mr. Easton is to fence his Farme in wholy except mr Brentons Fence betwene them and the line betweene the high-way that goeth downe to the pond and the beach bordering ther upon and the medow ther in also Robert Feild and John Anthony is to fence off their ground and the Comon is to Fence upon them

      Joseph Terry
      1662 Decemr: 5

To James Barker 40 Acres lyinge on the north side of a percell of Land which was measured to mr Easton of all 150 acres with the Rocks and was desined by him for his 100 Acres alowed him for his part of the Mill Land wherof mr Easton allowed him 40 acres and the allowance for Rocks the rest is by consent layd down for Comon and both this and all James Barkers is bounded on the East end on the Brooke on which mr Hutchinsons &c. but James Barker is .....bounded on the north by Nicholas Cotterill.....
1662 Decembr 6

      Joseph Terry Towne Clerke

 John Tripp to Joseph Tripp.
  .....John Tripp of.....portsmouth.....Senr. Shaft Car-

penter.....granted.....unto Joseph Tripp of Dartmoth in the Collony of plymoth.....one quarter share of Land lying ....within.....Dartmoth that is.....one fowerth part of one whole or intyer.....portion of Land belonging to one purchassor it being the one halfe of that Land which..... John Tripp bought of John Alden of.....Duxbury.....to be holder as of his Majhie his manner of East Greenwich ....third day of May.....1671
Wit. John Tripp.
   William Hall Junr.
   William Hall Senr.

[14] Tomas Kent—ratification of holdings.
.....Thomas Kent.....of....portsmouth.....Eigh acres ....granted by the Towne of portsmouth Unto Stephen Wilcooks and lyinge.....in.....Towneshipp of portsmouth ....Established.....22th of May 1662.....promisses are Ratified.....The 14th day of June 1672
                        John Sanford G. Recorder
  Assigned to Witt Hall—Lawrence Gonsalles.
.....Lawrence Gonsalles of pequemins in ye County of Albemarle in ye province of Carolina Taylor by the Authorety and power of a Letter of Aturny from my father in law Tho. Kent of ye province afore. sd. doe by these pressents assigne this in written deed unto Witt. Hall of portsmo. on Rhod Island in ye Collony of Rhod:Island.....I say Assigned to the sd. Witt Hall junr.....17th of June 1672
Wit. Laurance Gonsalles.
  Hugh Persons   Icobed Potter
  Peleg Tripp   Henry Matteesson.
  Thomas Kents Letter of Aturney to Laurance Gonsalles.
.....Thomas Kent of Pequemins in the County of Albemarle in the Province of Carolina plantr.....doe Constitute .....Laurance Gonsalles.....my true and Lawfull Aturney .....to manage all such affairs wherein my selfe, am..... Conserned at Rhod-Island.....Twenty Eight of March One Thowsand Six hundred seventy-two.

Wit.
   Samuell Pricklove
   Robert **X** Paine.
      his marke.
   William **X** Charles
      his marke

              Thomas **X** Kent
              his marke

[15]   Letter of Aturney to Samuell Nicholson.
.....Joseph Nicholson Thomas Nicholson and Elizabeth Nicholson (now wife of Nicholas Andrewes) the Children of Edmund Nicholson, of Marble-head, in the County of Essix, in the Colleny of Massachusetts, Fisherman deceased have Assigned.....our.....brother Samuell Nicholson of Marblehead.....Fisherman to be.....our.....Lawfull Aturney.....and receive of mr Peleg Sanford of Newport..... as Executor of the Last Will and Testament off Francis Simpson of Newport.....seventeenth day of June.....one Thowsand six hundred seventy & two.
Wit.
   Hilliard Veren Senr.
   William Dounten.

            The marke off—
          Joseph **X** Nicholson.
          Thomas Nicholson
            The marke off—
          Elisabeth **X** Andrewes

   Peter Eastons Receipt.
Newport—27th of July 1672
Received off—Edmund Calverly by the appointment of Mary which was the wife of Richard Pray of Providence for her centance at the Court of Tryalls held at Newport.....the sixt of May-1672 Pray received tenn pounds in Boston silver which was to acquitt her of beinge twice whipt for her fact done. Received by me
Wit.   Peter Easton. Treasurer
   John Greene Asistant
   Edmund Calverley

[16]   John Tripp to Peleg Tripp.
.....John Tripp.....of Portsmouth senr in....Rhod-Island ....grant.....unto my second sonn Peleg Tripp a fourth part of a share Lott.....lyinge.....at the place.....called Acassett within the Towne of Dartmoth, in the jurisdiction of new plymouth.....together with all.....uplands, medowes, woods, timbers, watters.....to be houlden of his Majestie of England.....as of his manner of East Greenwich, in the County of Kent.....not in Capitt nor Knights service by the rents.....thereby due and of Right accustomed .....only it is provided that.....Peleg Tripp shall hereafter .....sell the.....part.....of Land it is to be sould unto me.....or my heires.....Eight day of Septr.....1665
Wit.   John Sanford   John Tripp
       Samuell Sanford.

[17]   Wm. and Anne Coddington to Nicholas Easton. Rhod-Island.
.....William Coddington and Anne Coddington his wife doe sell unto Nicholas Easton.....a percell of Land lyinge .....in the.....Towne of Newport.....Contanninge by esteemation Thirty two Acres.....which is boundinge..... North by the way to the great Swamp, South by the Land of William Dyre, West on the Sea, and East by the Land of .....Nicholas Easton which he purchassed of John Clarke and others.....17th day of the 4th moth 1672.
Wit.   Wm Coddington senr.
   Danll. Gould   Anne Coddington
   Ednd Thurston   X
   Wm. Brinley

[18]   Thomas Loveday Letter of Aturney to Wm. Barcker
.....Thomas Loveday Cittison and Goold smith of London .....Have made William Barcker of the Citty of New Yorke upon Long Island beyond the Sea my....Aturney.....and in my name to.....receive.....from Nathanill Johnson of Newport in Rhod-Island in the parts beyond the seas Merchant all such sums.....of mony as are due.....five and Twentieth day of July Anno-Dom. 1671

Wit.   Thomas Loveday
   Peter Floger
   Robt. Merrifeild
       Quod attestor
   Rich Stonebill   Nots. Pub.cus
   Richard Cornell to Gersham Wodell
.....Richard Cornell of Cornebery upon Long-Island have received of Gersham Wodell in Portsmouth upon Rhod-Island satisfaction.....from all bills.....21th of June 1672
Wit.   Thomas Cornell   Richard Cornell
     Lawrance Gonsalles

[19] William Minnion to Edward Inman and John Mowry.
......William Minnion of Punkkipage.....Collony of the Massachusetts Bay.....have Freely given.....Edward Inman and John Mawry of Providence.....two Thousand acres.....bounds,.....lyinge from loquiset northward, the first bound is a chestnutt on the south marked on fower sides at the first indian Feild on Wessukkuttomsuk hill runninge a mile due North and then upon a line to Ummohtukkonit takeinge in all the Medow and soe to run to Nipsharuck, and soe to the Indians ground, and soe to a champ of pines called the Key, and soe to the springe called Wessukkattomsuk, to the chestnut tree above mentioned, and soe to the Patuket river Northward and on the end of the mill North to Patukit River.....Fourteen day of May 1666
              the marke **X** of William Minion
              the marke **X** of Joseph William
                Mynions Coson
Wit.
   Daniell Abbott
   John Steere.
   William Manannion to Edward Inman.
.....William Manannion Indian livinge at Punkapoge (alias paliene).....Twenty pounds.....paid by Edward Inman late of Providence, hath given.....Five hundred acres..... bounded at Wewesapinset, and from thence upon a straight line to Umstococonnet, and from umetocconnet to the Midle

of a great seader swamp to a Butten tree and from thence runs to Potucket river almost North there bounded by a walnutt tree, and these are the bounds of the last purchassed Lands comonly called.....Wansaakitt hill,.....thirteenth of May......One Thousand six hundred and sixty & nine
Wit.   William Manannion X Marke
  Samuell Goston Junr
  Jonathan Blisse.

[20]   King Philip to Edward Inman.
.....Wee King Phillip Joseph Manannion Totoroms widdow named Kewapam & William Manannions Uncle called by the name of Jeffery.....Release unto.....Edward Inman..... of Providence.....thirteenth day of May.....one Thousand six hundred and sixty and nine
Wit.   King Phillips X marke
  Samuell Gorton Junr
  Jonathan Blisse.

[21]   Edward Inman to James Blakmor.
.....Edward Inman & John Moory....., yeomen.....have for.....a Valuable Consideration.....paid by James Blakmor and John Bukman of Rehoboth in.....New-Plymouth, ...a full sixt part.....of Land that wee bought of William Mininion.....Bounded as followeth, the first bounds beinge a chessnutt tree marked on fower sides at the first Indian Feild to the South on Wesukuttomsuk hill runninge a mile due north, and then upon a line unto Unmotaktonct, takeinge all the meddow and soe to run Nipsachuit and to the Indian ground, and soe to a clump of pines called the Key and soe to the spring at Wessuktonsuk and soe to the Wessuktonsuk to the chessnutt tree above mentioned, and soe to Patuckett River,.....tenth day of October.....one thowsand six hundred seventy and two.
Wit.   Edward Inman
  William Carpenter   John Moory
  John Johnson

[22]   Edward Inman to James Blackmor and John Bukman
.....Edward Inman.....yeomen.....paid by James Black-

mor and John Bukman of Rehoboth.....New-Plymoth.....
sell a full sixt part.....purchased of William Minninion of
Punkapoge the whole tract of Landed bounded.....at Wewe-
supinsit, and from thence upon a straight line Ametococomett
and from Ametococomet to the midle of a great seader swamp
to a Butten tree and from thence to Patukett River almost
North three hundred by a walnutt tree, this Land comonly
knowne by the name of Wansuket hill,.....tenth of October
.....one thousand six hundred seventy two.....

Wit.   Edward Inman
  William Carpenter
  John Johnson

[23] Edward Inman to William Bukland,
.....Edward Inman and John Moory yeomen.....paid by
William Bukland, Joseph Bukland, and Benjamin Bukland,
.....of Rehoboth.....New-Plymoth.....a full sixt part of
a tract of Land.....William Minionion sold Edward Inman
and John Moory: the whole tract of Land that Edward
Inman and John Moory purchassed is Bounded as followeth,
the first bounds beinge a chesnut tree marked on fower sides
at the first Indian Feild on the South, one Weskutomsuk
hill runninge a mile due North and then upon a line unto
Unmoktakconitt taking in all the meddow and soe to run to
Nipshankuk, and to the Indians ground, and soe to a clump
of pines called the Key and soe to the spring at Wesukuttomsuk, and soe Wesukuttomsuk to the chesnutt tree above-
mentioned and soe to patuket River,.....tenth day of October 1672.....

Wit.   Edward Inman
  William Carpenter   John Mowry
  John Johnson

[24] Edward Inman to William Bukland
.....Edward Inman.....of Rhod-Island.....yeoman.....
paid by William Bukland Joseph Bukland and Benjamin
Bukland of Rehoboth.....New Plymoth.....a full sixt part
of the.....Lands.....he purchassed of William Mininion
the whole Tract of Land beinge bounded,.....at Wewesupin-

sit and from thence upon a straight line to amettococomet and from amettococomet to the midle of a great seader swamp to a Butten tree and from thence to patucket River, almost North there bounded by a walnutt tree this Land comonly Knowne by the name of Wansukett, hill.....tenth day of October in the yeare of Our Lord one thousand six hundred seventy & two   Edward Inman
Wit.
   William Carpenter
   John Johnson

[25]   Letter of aturney from John Alcock to John Williams. .....Overseers and Guardians.....mr. John Alcock Deceassed:.....considering.....accounts of severall Inhabitants of Block-Island..........hereby order.....John Williams.....to demand.....full satisfaction of the several .....23th February 1668.
Wit.
   John Leveret   Wm Davis
   Peter **X** George   his marke
   Edward Ball

                        Richard Russell
                        Ann Apalsgrave her marke
                        Edward Rawson
                        John Hull

   Thomas terry to John Acres.
.....thomas terry of Block-Island.....yeoman.....paid by John Acres of.....Block-Island.....One hundred and Fifty acres of Land.....upon Block-Island, adjoyninge to the Land of Samuell Staple on the North on the sea to the Southwest, and Joyninge to mr. Phillip Wharton on the South-Easterly exceptinge one acre and so to run East in the Land of Thomas Terry till it makes up the Complement of one hundred and Fifty acres,.....Fifth day of Aprill.....1670
Wit.   Thomas Terry
   Lyman Ray
   Jno Williams
   John Acres to John Williams.

Received of John Acres of Block Island.....Twelve pound in sheepe and catle upon.....publick charges of halfe a share of Land that did belong to Edward Vose.....30th of October 1672
Wit.   X me John Williams
   Emanuell Woolsey
       hi.
   Turinut X Rose
       marke

Edward Inman—John Mowry Land Recorded.
.....Edward Inman and John Mowry both of.....providence.....Right posession of.....Land by them purchased of an Indian called William Minion,.....containinge two thousand acres.....lyinge from Logiussett Northward. The first bound is a chesnut tree, on the South marked on four sides, at the first Indian feild on Wessukkutomsuk hill runinge a mile due North, and then upon a line to ummolutukkonitt, takeinge in all the medow, and soe to run to Nipsharuck, and soe to the Indians ground, and soe to a champ of pines called the Key, and soe to the springe called Wessukkatomsuk to the chesnutt tree above-named, and soe to the patuckitt river—Northward and on the end of the Mill north to patuckitt river,.....together with all.....dwellinge houses, Barnes,.....are hereby ratefied by law made 22th of May 1662.....fourth of February 1672
                                      John Sanford Recorder.

[27]   Wm. Dyre to Henry Dyre.
.....William Dyre of Newport.....Gent.....granted to my sonn Henry Dyre into that part of my Farme lyinge at the northerly and there of: to witt, from the Stone Ditch, as alsoe from the tree where my sonn Mahers Tobacco house stood, from the Cave to and by that tree upon an Equi distante line from the said Stone Ditch downe unto and through the swamp unto mr. Coddingtons line by the brooke (the fence is equally devided).....percell of Land....so,..... bounded with a free Egress ingress and regress to and through

the Land of my sonn Samuells.....but in case my sonn Henry should have Isue only Femailes then my sonn Samuell .....after the death of the said Henry shall Give one hundred and fifty pounds starllinge the eldest to have a double portion the rest an equall dividend of the Residue, but if only one .....all to her &c besides the Valluation of the....houssinge .....thereon built.....the Land to return to.....Samuell .....7th day of July 1670. William Dyre.
Wit.
  The **X** marke off.
  Robert Spinke.
  John Furnell.
[28] Award of John Easton to James Barker about Henry Palmer and Stephen Sebeere.
....
Thirdly Wee do Award.....Stephen Sebeere shall acknowlidge unto Henry Palmer.....done ronge unto him and his wife in sayinge that his wife is a witch.....
Fourthly Wee do award. Henry Palmer. acknowlidge..... that he hath done Ronge in callinge.....Stephen Sebeere French dog and french Roug.....19th day of Nov. 1672:
  John Easton
  James Barker
  Land Recorded of John Vahan. [Vaughn]
.....John Vahan of.....Newport.....percell of Land..... containinge seventy-nine acres and two thirds of an acre..... bounded, Northward partly upon the Land of mr Joshia Coggeshall and part upon the Comon Eastward upon the Comon, Southward upon the Comon and high-way westward upon the Sea, was purchassed Sixty acres of Ralph Earll..... thirteene acres of John Fairefeild six acres and two thirds of William Lytherland, together with all.....dwellinge..... houssis.....Ratified by a law of the 22th of May 1662..... this present.....16th of Aprill 1673.
[29] Land Recorded of John Vahan.
.....John Vahan.....of Newport.....peaceable posession of.....Land lyinge.....in.....Newport.....Eight Acres

.....bounded North-wardly and Eastwardly upon the Comon South-wardly upon the Scoole Land Westwardly upon the Land of mr John Clarke, the.....Eight acres....was part of it purchassed of mr Samuell Wilbore and part of Robert Bennitt.....Eight Acres.....with all.....dwellinge..... Ratefyed by the law of 22th of May 1662.....16th day of Aprill 1673.

John Vahan to his sonn John Vahan.

.....John Vahan of Newport.....yeoman.....sonn John Vahan.....grant.....Eight acres....Newport....bounded Northwardly and Eastwardly upon the Comon Southwardly upon the Scoole land Westwardly upon the Land of mr John Clarke.....with all.....the dwellinge or mansion houssis Barnes.....sixteenth day of Aprill.....1673:

Wit.
  John Sanford
  Tyler X Pearce
    his marke

John Vahan
X
his marke

[30] Land Recorded of Thomas Burgis

.....Thomas Burgis.....of Newport.....two tracts..... one Containinge.....Forty-Fower Acres.....bounded on the East and South by Land of Robert Taylor, on the West by the Comon on the North by the Land of John Wood the other beinge a percell of meddow is lyinge in these meddowes comonly called Sachuest Meddowes and is.....bounded on the East or south-east by Robert Taylors on the south and westerly by a Creeke where the salt watter floes.....with all .....dwellinge or mansion housis.....According to a Law of the Collony made 22th of May 1662.....Ratified.....5th day of May 1673

Richard Knight to Laurance Turner.

.....Richard Knight of Newpt.....sum received.....sell unto Laurance Turner of the afore-said Towne Fower Acres of Land.....bounded.....on the West with the Land of Richard Knight, and to begin at a dead tree next to the Land of the said Laurance Turner at the South-west corner, and soe to Range to a Liveinge tree on the North-west Corner,

and from thence downe to the high-way as the fence runs
.....which Fence the said Laurance Turner his heirs.....
to maintaine forever.....and doth binde him selfe that if
.....there Shall be any Damages or Trespass done through
the Defect of the.....Fence.....he shall pay Duble Damages.....to the grieved party provided the.....Lawrance
have tenn daies warninge of the defects.....fifth day of
December......one thousand six hundred fifty and Eight.
Wit.   Richard Knight
  Will Jefferay
  Richard Bulgar

[31]   Richard Knight to Georg Kenrick

.....Richard Knight of Newport.....sell.....unto Georg
Kenrick of Providence.....Twelve Acres.....Bounded.....
to the North with certain Lands of James Weedens, on the
East with the high-way that goeth to the Comon, on the
south with the Land of Lawrance Turners and on the West
with the Land of the said Richard Knight he.....Georg Kenrick also is to leave out two Rods of the said Land lying next
to James Weedens for a High-way, only for the use of.....
Richard Knight,.....Georg Kenrick is to pay.....Twenty
shillinge an acre.....two and Twentith day of December
1656
Wit.   Richard Knight
  Will Jefferay
  Obadiah Hulme

Georg Kenrick—Lawrance Turner.

.....Twenty Eight Day of December.....one Thousand six
hundred sixty and three.....Georg Kenrick Lether dresser
livinge in Newport.....for.....Valuable sum of mony.....
Have.....sold unto Lawrance Turner Senr. Masson of Newport.....Land beinge.....bounded on the East with a High
way that leadith into the Comon On the South with Land in
the posession of Lawrance Turner, on the West with the
Land of Richard Knight, and on the North with a High-way
of two Rod-wide, betwixt the afore-said Land and the Land

of James Weeden,.....with.....one Dwellinge house all out housing, Hovills, Barnes.....
Wit.   Georg Kenrick
  James Barker   Jane X Kenrick
  John Cranston   her marke

[32]   William Jefferays to Lawrance Turner.
.....twenty second of March.....one Thousand six hundred Fifty and three or (54).....sixty seven Rodd or pole in Length and fifty six.....Bredth beinge the Eastern part of the Lands of William Jefferays of Newport.....Bounded on East by the high-way betweene the Land of Clemant Weaver Senr. and the afore-said Lands on the South by a high-way that leadith to the Milne of Newport.....on the North by the Land of Richard Knight and on the West by the Land of.....mr William Jefferays.....sold.....to Lawrance Turner and Tobia Saunders both of Newport.....
Wit.   Will Jefferay
  Mordica X Cranett
        his marke
  Wm Lytherland

Land Recorded of Lawrance Turner and Tobias Saunders. .....Lawrance Turner and Tobias Saunders both of..... Newport Land in.....Newport containinge in lenth sixty seven Rodds and in Bredth Fifty six Rodds.....bounded on the East, and South by high-waies on the West by Land now in the posession of Thomas Waterman formerly belonging to mr William Jefferay. North by the Land of the said Lawrance Turner, by him purchassed of Richard Knight..... together with Dwelling.....rights.....According to a Law made in this Collony the 22th of May 1662.....Ratifyed..... 29th Day of May 1673

[33]   Land Recorded of Lawrance Turner.
.....Lawrance Turner of Newport.....sixteene Acres..... lyinge within.....Newport.....bounded North by the Land lately belonginge to James Weeden and two Rodds Reserved by Richard Knight for a high-way. East is bounded by a high-way, South—by the Land purchased by the said Turner

and Tobias Saunders of mr William Jefferay; West by the Land of Richard Knight, twelve Acres of the sixteene beinge purchased of Georg Kenrick, and fower Acres purchassed of.....Richard Knight.....Land.....with dwelinge..... Deed.....According a Law made in Collony the 22th of May 1662.....Ratifyed.....29th day of May, 1673

    Koshkotap to Thomas Gould.

.....Koshkotap sachim of bassuketukquage in Nanhygansett bay have sold unto Thomas Gould of Newport.....a little Island lyinge betweene Quononogutt and Rhod-Island called by the Indians aquepinoquk and by the English Goulds Island, and have received satisfaction for the same.....28th of March 1657

Wit.   Koshkotap sachim of
  Georg Hamonde   Bassuketukquage.
  John Sassumon   his X marke
  Henry Timberleake
  The marke X of apoowatuk.

  Aquinaumpau to Thomas Gould.

Aquinaumpau haveing been a planter three or four years upon Aquibinauke alias Goulds Island.....Resigne up my Right.....unto Thomas Gould.....15th of May 1660

Wit.   Aquinaumpau X his
  Henry X Timberlake   marke
    his marke
  Georg Hamonde

[34]   Thomas Gould to John Cranston

.....Thomas Gould of Aquidnessett in the Narragansett cuntry.....Twenty pounds me.....paid.....by John Cranston of Newport.....Phisician.....Doe.....sell a certaine Island comonly called.....Goulds-Island and by the Indians named Acqueebenawquck lyinge in the Narragansett Bay.....Twentieth Day of May.....1673

Wit.   Thomas Gould
  John Sanford
  Richard Baily

[35]   John Cranston—Deed Ratifyed.

.....Captn John Cranston.....of Newport.....Phisician.....Beinge.....in full.....posession of the one halfe of that Island called Goulds Island by the English and by the Indians called Acqeebenawquk.....lyinge in the Narragansett Bay and between.....Rhod-Island and Quonogutt Island .....and whereas by Deed of Sale.....of Thomas Gould the other halfe of the said Island (after the Decease of Thomas Gould) shall belong.....unto the said Captn John Cranston.....Deed.....According to a Law made the 22th of May 1673.....Ratifyed.....8th Day of July 1673

John Cooke to Robert Gibbs.

.....John Cooke, of portsmouth on Rhod-Island.....yeoman,.....Twenty pounds.....to me.....paid.....Robert Gibbs (now Inhabittinge at punkatest in.....New Plymoth) .....Doe sell.....three fower parts of a share.....beinge In New Jersey at the place Comonly.....caled portapeage .....Fifteenth day of July.....1673

Wit.   John Cooke
  John Sanford   his X marke
  Francis X Brayton
      his marke

Deed of John Cooke to Robert Gibbs anulled.

This Deed mad from John Cooke unto me Robert Gibbs, ...sale beinge made voyde by mutuall agreement & the originall deed-Returned.....24th of January 1674

Wit.   Robert Gibbs

[36]   Thomas Burge to

......Tho. Burge......of Newport......for......Eleven pounds Five Shillings in New England Silver.....to me paid by John Cooke of.....Portsmouth.....sell.....the one sixt part of a whole.....share of Land Lyinge......in.....Dartmoth.....New-Plymoth,.....at the places Comonly called Acushnett Ponagansett Acockssett and places adjacent in the said Towne-shipp both in uplands and Meddows.....To Bee Houldon of his Majtie of England.....as of his manner of East Greenwich in the County of Kent.....and not in Capitt nor in Knights service by the Rents and services thereby due and Law accustomed.....Two and Twentith Day of August 1671

Wit.   Thomas Burge
  John Sanford
  Richard Hart
  Joseph Anthony

[37] Jonathan Atherton to Richard Smith.

Jonathan Atherton of Dorchester.....Massachusetts Collony .....sonn and heire to 'Humphrey Atherton of.....Dorchester Deceased.....For.....the sum of Fifty pounds mony in England, and one hundred pounds in New England Mony .....paid by Richard Smith of Narragnsett in the Kings province.....have.....sold.....unto Richard Smith..... Land lyinge souther-most in the great Neck Comonly Called Boston Neck in the Narragansett Cuntry.....adjoyninge to the harbour Comonly Called Pettacomscutt harbour, beinge a whole share of that purchase and is about 'seven hundred acres of Land.....now in the posession of George Croft my Tennant. Together with all.....houses, out-houses, Barnes, Stables, edeffices, gardens orchards Fences Comons.....three and Twentith day of July.....1673

Wit.   Jonathan Atherton
                    ....24th of July 1673 Jonathan
                    Atherton.....owned the above written
                    ....William Coddington Dept. Go.
Frances Brimley
Richard Updick
Edmund Oliver
    The marke of
Elizabeth X Geratt

[38] Richard Smith to Joseph Terry and Richard Baily.

.....Richard Smith of Newport.....Mercht.....for.....a Valuable sume of mony.....paid.....by Joseph Terry and Richard Baily both of Newport.....Doe sell.....Four acres lyinge at the pond side in.....Portsmouth.....second day of March.....1671

72

Wit.   Richd. Smith
   John Collins
   Francis Simson

[39]   Gersham Cob to Thomas Lawton.

     Gersham Cob.....of New-Plymouth.....for.....five pounds sta. to me.....paid by Thomas Lawton of portsmouth in Rhod-Island.....doth.....sell.....All.....my.....Land at a place Comonly called puncketert Neck lyinge.....against Rhod-Island.....the said neck, Medowes belonginge unto the said neck.....which was given unto me by my Gran father James Hurst Deceassed.....with all.....wood, watters.....thereunto belonginge.....unto.....Thomas Lawton.....To be howlden of.....the King as of his manner of East Greenwich.....Fifth day of June.....1668

Wit.   ......Gersham Cob
   Thomas Doty
   John Smith **X** Senir
       his marke
   Wm. Crow

Gersham Cob.....acknowlidged the above written.....
Tho. Southworth Asist.

[40]   William Nelson to Thomas Lawton.

     .....William Nelson Senr. of New-plymoth.....for.....five pounds Starll.....paid by Thomas Lawton of portsmouth on Rhod-Island.....Sell.....All.....Land that I have at a place Comonly called puncketest Neck.....and.....Medowes.....and the Court Grant by which I have Right to the said Neck.....To be Holden of.....the King as of his manner of East Greenwich in the County of Kent within the Rhelme of England.....fifth day of June.....1668

Wit.
   Thomas Doty
   John Smith **X** Senr
       his marke
   Wim Crow

William Nelson
Martha **X** Nelson
   her marke

William Nelson and Martha his wife..... acknowlidged the above-written .....Tho Southworth Asistant
   5th of June 1668.

[41]   Alice Bradford to Thomas Lawton.

.....Alice Bradford Wid.....of New-Plymoth.....for....five-pounds stall. to me.....paid by Thomas Lawton of Portsmouth.....Doth.....sell.....All....Land that I have at a place Comonly called Puncketest Neck.....beinge against Rhod-Island.....To be Holden off.....the King as of his manner of East Greenwich in the County of Kent within the Rhelme of England in free and Comon Sottage, and not in Capitte, nor by Knights Service by the Rents and Services there of and thereout due and of Right Accustomed, to the only proper use and behoofe of.....Thomas Lawton..... fift day of June.....1668.

Wit.
   Jonathan Sparrow
   Wim Crow.

Alice **X** Bradford
   her marke

   Mrs. Alice Bradford came.....before me & acknowleged .....the Above.....to be her.....Deed.....

                    Thomas Southworth
                         Asistant.

William Crow to Thomas Lawton.

.....William Crow of New-Plymouth.....for.....five pownds starll.....to me.....paid by Thomas Lawton..... have.....sold.....two Necks of Land that lyeth against Rhod-Island comonly called Punketest Neck and Sopowett Neck that is uplands or medow lands.....To be houlden of .....the King as of his manner in East Greenwich..... twelfth day of February one Thowsand six hundred sixty and eight

Wit.   Wim Crow
   Jonathan Barnes
   Jaber Howland

[42]   John Brigs to Thomas Lawton.
.....John Brigs Senr of Portsmouth on Rhod-Island.....Yeoman.....for.....mony.....received from Thomas Lawton.....doe.....sell.....two purchassers proportion.....of Land.....lyinge.....in the Neck of Land called Puncketest lyinge Eastwards of Rhod-Island.....To be Holden of his Majtie of England.....as of his manner of East Greenwich .....Nineteenth day of February.....1668.
Wit.   John **X** Brig's Senr
   John Almy   his marke
   Jos. Holderbe

[43]   Thomas Southworth.....of Plymouth.....five pounds to me paid by mr John Almy.....of Portsmouth on Rhod-Island.....Merchant.....doe.....sell.....all my share of Land Granted to the Towne of Plymoth afore-said bearinge date Anno Dom. one Thowsand six hundred Forty-nine lying over against Rhod-Island.....comonly called.....Punkateaset and places adjacent both upland and Medow.....as it is bounded in the Record of the Court for the Jurisdiction of Plymoth.....bearinge date 1653.....To be Holden.....of .....the King.....Eight of March.....1668
Wit.   Thomas Southworth
   James Coal Senr
   Nathaniell Morton

John Almy to Thomas Lawton.
.....John Almy of Portsmo.....absolutely assigne.....this Inwritten Deed.....unto Thomas Lawton.....Twentith day of September.....1671 .
Wit.   John Almy
   his **X** marke
   Anthony Emry
   William Hall

[44]   Thomas Morton to John Almy.
.....Thomas Morton....of Plymoth.....yeoman.....that

for.....five pounds.....paid by mr John Almy.....of Portsmouth.....have.....sold.....All my share.....of Land granted to the Towne of Plymoth.....bearinge date Anno Dom one Thowsand six hundred forty nine lyinge over against Rhod-Island.....att a place called.....Punckateeset ....bounded in Record of the Court of New-Plymoth bearinge date 1653, both devided and undevided, That which is Devided.....belonging unto me beinge the one halfe of a lott.....layd out to me.....and Richard Foster deceassed beinge in number the 35 lott.....To be Holden of.....the King.....Eight of March.....1668

Wit.   The **X** marke of
   James Coal Senr.   Thomas morton
   William Bassitt

John Almy to Thomas Lawton.

.....John Almy.....of Portsmo.....have received full satisfaction.....for.....promisses contained in.....Deed, And doe.....surrender the same.....unto.....Thomas Lawton.....Twentith day of Septr.....1671.

Wit.   John Almy
   The **X** marke of
     Anthony Emry
   William Hall.

[45] Andrew Ringe to John Almy.

.....Andrew Ringe.....of Plymoth.....for.....five pounds .....to me.....paid by mr John Almy of Portsmouth..... doe.....sell.....all my share.....off.....certaine Tract of Land granted to the Towne of Plymoth.....bearinge Date Anno Dom. one Thowsand six hundred Forty nine, lyinge over against Rhod-Island at a place comonly called..... Punckateeset.....as it is bounded in the Record of the Court for the Jurisdiction of Plymoth bearinge date 1653.....one halfe a lott.....layd out to me.....and Gabill Stallowell beinge in number the Eight lott. To be Holden of.....the King as of manner of East Greenwich.....Eight day of March.....1668

Wit.   Andrew Ring
  Georg Watson
  James Browne
  Andrew Ring Acknowlidged the above-written.....before me   Thomas Southworth Assistant

  John Almy to Thomas Lawton
.....John Almy of Portsmouth.....have received full satisfaction of Thomas Lawton.....for.....promisses contained in the inwritten deed.....and surrender the same..... Twentith day of September.....1671.
Wit.   John Almy.
  his X marke
  Anthony Emry
  William Hall

[46] John Jourdaine to Thomas Lawton.
.....John Jourdaine of Plymouth.....Taylor.....for.....sum of five pounds and odd mony to me alredy paid by.....Thomas Lawton of portsmo.....Doe.....sell.....all my share.....of Land granted to.....Plymoth.....bearinge date .....one Thowsand six hundred forty nine lyinge over against Rhod-Island.....at a place comonly called.....Punckatessett.....bounded in the Record of court for the Jurisdiction of Plymoth.....bearinge date 1653.....one halfe of a lott....layd out unto me.....and Jacob Cooke beinge in Number the one & thertith Lott.....To be Holden of.....the King as of his manner of East Greenwich..... eight of March.....1668
Wit.   the marke
  James Browne   of John X Jourdaine
  Georg Watson
John Jourdan acknowlidged the above.....
                         Thomas Southworth Assistant
  Samuell Dunham to John Almy.
.....Samuell Dunham.....of Plymoth planter.....for.....fower pounds to me.....paid by mr John Almy of Portsmoth .....yeoman,.....doe.....sell.....a certaine Tract of Land granted to.....Plymoth.....bearinge date.....one Thow-

sand six hundred forty nine lyinge over against Rhod Island
.....at a place comonly called.....Punckateeset.....
bounded in the Record of the Court for the Jurisdiction of
Plymoth bearinge date of 1653.....beinge one halfe of a lott
.....layd out to John Dunham Senior my father late deceased and my brother Jonathan his sonn beinge in Number
the seventeenth Lott my.....Father his halfe thereof.....
given unto me.....To be Holden of.....the King as of his
manner of East Greenwich.....Eight of March.....1668.
Wit.   Samuell Dunham
   Georg Watson
   Jabez Howland.

                The marke of X Abigall Dunham sole
                Executrix.....of John Dunham her
                husband.....

                                the marke of
                                Benem X Prat
                                Daniell Dunham
Abigall Dunham Acknowlidged.....above.....before me
                        Tho. Southward Asistant

[47]   John Almy to Thomas Lawton.
.....John Almy.....of Portsmouth.....have received full
satisfaction of Thomas Lawton.....for all.....promisses
.....in this within written Deed, and doe.....surrender the
same.....Twentith Day of September.....1671
Wit.   John Almy
     his marke
   Anthony X Emry
   William Hall.
[48]   John Richard to John Almy.
.....John Richard of.....New-Plymoth in the Collony of
New-Plymoth.....for.....sum of five pounds starll.....
paid by John Almy.....doe.....sell.....all.....Land that
I have in a neck of Land comonly called Punketest Neck
lyinge against Rhod-Island.....beinge the one halfe of the
Seventh Lott and is Eleven acres.....To be Holden as of
.....the King as of his manner of East Greenwich.....

Eighth day of June one Thowsand six hundred seventy one.
Wit. John Richard

John Miller
Wm. Crowe

Acknowlidged before Tho. prence Govo.

John Almy to Thomas Lawton.

.....John Almy of.....Portsmouth.....have received full satisfaction of Thomas Lawton.....for all.....promisses contained in.....deed.....Twentith day of September.....1671
Wit. John Almy

  his X marke
Anthony Emry
William Hall

[49] Randall Houlding to Anthony Paine.

June 2th 1645.....Randall Houlding of Portsmouth.....in the Nanhigansett bay.....doe sell unto Anthony Paine of the same Towne one percell of Land containinge one hundred Acres.....butting to the North upon the Mill Swamp neer unto.....Portsmouth, borderinge to the south upon the Lands of Ralph Earll—and the Lands of John Roome close adjoyninge to the East of the afore-said hundred acres bordering to the West upon the Lands of William Freeborne....
Wit. Randall Houldon

John Warner
William X James
       marke
Joseph Wilbore

Rose Weeden to Mathew Greenell.

.....Rose Weeden.....of.....Portsmo.....for the sum of Therty pounds.....doe.....sell.....unto Mathew Greenell of the Same Towne......a certaine percell of Land.....Fifty and three acres.....beinge within the Bounds of.....Portsmouth.....being bounded westerly with Land late in the posession of Nathanill Browninge, Northerly and Southerly by the Comon, Easterly by the Land of.....Mathew.....

with.....housinge,.....seventeenth day of December.....
one Thowsand six hundred seventy and three

Wit.   Rose X Weeden
  John Heath   her marke
  William Hall

[50] John Paine to Sarah Hannah and Anna Paine. .....Jno Paine of Boston.....Mercht.....upon.....marriage with Sarah Parker.....did receive a Considerable..... Estate by the Gift of my.....Father in Law Richard Parker of.....Boston Genta.....and Did Give.....unto my..... wife.....a certaine Estate in Lands and housses for.....her and my thre children Sarah Hannah and Anna Paine..... before it was delivered.....it pleassed.....God,.....sixteen hundred Sixty Six January 25th to take my.....wife unto him Selfe.....I.....Request.....Nathanill Paine of Rehoboth in.....Plymoth and Joseph Taynter of Watertowne .....Mattachussetts.....in trust to accept this.....Estate .....but for the Sole.....use.....of these.....thre children and theire next heires.....I.....Have Given,.....unto Joseph Taynter and Nathanill Paine Yeomen.....That Norther-most part of Prudence Island poyntinge towards Providence and soe Runninge Southerly to the fence goeinge Cross the.....Island devidinge between the Lands Lett unto John Smith, and those lett unto William Allin,.....The Bay or waters surrowndinge it on all other sides.....containinge six hundred Acres.....with buidings.....it is.....in the power of me.....upon the payment of Three Thousand pounds of Mony of New England to the use.....of my thre children.....to purchase the above.....Lands.....Twenty day of July sixteen hundred sixty and nine.

Wit.   Jno. Paine
  Ed Page and Willia. Howard.
    .....In pressence of John Smith John Snooke and
    William Allin.....19th August 1673
    John Smith X his marke
      William Allin
    John Snook X his marke

[52]   Mathew West—Land Recorded.
.....Mathew West of.....Newport.....Taylor, beinge.....
in.....posession of a certaine percell.....of Land containinge Forty Acres.....lyinge within the bounds.....of Newport, and.....bounded Northwardly by the land of John Crandall, Southwardly by the land of John Thornton, Eastwardly and Westwardly by the Comon which.....said Land formerly belonged unto John Roe and Edward Browse,.....with all Dwellings or mansion houses Barnes, Outhouses, Fenceings, Gardens, Orchyards.....This.....Deed.....doth .....declare.....hereby Ratifyed accordinge to a Law made .....the 22th of May 1662.....Recorded 28th day of March 1674

John Sanford.

Thomas Ward—Land Recorded.
.....Thomas Ward of Newport.....Merchant.....beinge .....in.....posession of a.....percell of Land Containeinge .....tenn Acres.....within the bounds.....of Newport,..... is.....bounded North and West partly by a Ditch beteene the Land of William Coddington Esquir. and the said Land and partly by the Comon, on the South, by the Lands of Captn John Cranston, on the East by a certaine peice of Comon called Bakers Swamp, which.....Land was by..... Thomas Ward purchassed of Mary and William Timberlake., All which.....Land.....with all dwellinge or mansion houses, Barnes, Out-houses, Fences, Gardens Orchards..... This.....doth.....declare.....hereby Ratifyed according to a law made May 22, 1662.....17th of June 1674

John Sanford

[53]   Joseph Wise to Deacon William Parke.
.....Joseph Wise of Roxbury in the County of Suffolke in New-England.....for.....Twenty five pound in mony & corne & catle.....paid by Deacon William Parke of the Towne.....abovesd.....doth hereby.....sell.....the..... .....halfe part of six hundred Acres of Arable Land medow & pasture.....beinge in the Towneshipp of Providence butted by the Land of Thomas Borden North, by the Land of Henry

Fowler South by the Land of Hugh Bluett East by the Towne land West. which sd. six hundred acres.....the said Wise purchassed of William Feild & Henry Fowler.....the moety hereby convayed is.....one halfe of six hundred acres if it be more, or 300 acres certaine, if the same be less.....and to be the Northerly end.....of.....Tract.....to be devided by an Easterly lyne before the first of October next, at fowerteen daies warninge.....seventh day of June.....one Thowsand six hundred seventy one.

          Joseph Wise (Senr.)
.....there is a mistake in the South bounds being said upon the land of Henry Fowler it must be said in the Records upon the Land of Joseph Wise Senr. which is soe agreed upon by Joseph Wise.....And Samuell Williams.....for his father Deacon William Park.....

Wit.   Joseph Wise Senr.
 Thomas Harris Senr.   Samuell Williams.
  the marke of
 John X Allin
 Joseph Dardley
 Tobias Davis
.....the said William Park is to have the one halfe of Privileges.....in.....Providence which.....Joseph Wise purchassed of mr John Sayles.....the sd purchasser shall have noe more meddow than lyes exactly on.....northerly side of lyne.....
Joseph Dudley
Nathanill Seuer

[54] Thomas Gould to John Cranston
.....Thomas Gould of Aquednessett in the Narragansett Cuntry.....did by a.....Deed of Bargaine.....bearinge date the Twentith day of May.....1673.....sell Unto John Cranston of Newport.....physician the Island called Goulds Island and by the Indians named Acqueebenawquck.....beinge in Narragansett Bay.....only Reserveinge unto my selfe the one halfe of.....Island For.....the Tearme of my Naturall life.....for.....Valuable satisfaction unto me.....

paid.....twelfth day of May.....1674
Wit.   Thomas Gould
   Joseph Toney
   Ireh Bull
   Richard Baily

[55]   John Cranston—Land Recorded.
.....Captn. John Cranston of.....Newport.....phisician by.....Due purchass.....from Thomas Gould of Aquednes-sett.....beinge in.....posession of a certaine Island lyinge.....betweene Rhode-Island and.....Quononoqutt, and..... Knowne to the English by the Name of Goulds-Island, to the Indians......Aqueebenaquck......now......every part of.....Island beinge within.....posession of.....Captn John Cranston.....with all Dwelling or mansion houses Barnes.....Orchyard.....premisses.....according to a Law made.....the 22th of May 1662.....are hereby Ratifyed..... Recorded 24th day of June.....1674.
   William Weeden—Land Recorded
.....William Weeden.....of Newport.....beinge in..... posession of Land lyinge within.....Newport.....sixty Acres.....bounded Northwardly by the Land of Joseph Card, Eastwardly partly upon a drift Way to the Land of Joseph Card, partly upon Land of James Rogers and partly upon the mill pond; Southwardly upon the Land of John Bliss and Westwardly partly upon the Land of Joseph Torrey and partly upon the Land of mr Bendedict Arnold Only this is Reserved for publick use the Liberty of a Driftt-way two Rodd wides through the said Land for all persons that have occassion to pass.....that way to and from Newport, All of the.....Land.....with all Dwellinge or Mansion housis, Barnes,.....Orchards, Gardens.....and all.....Rights..... according to a Law made the 22th of May 1662.....are hereby Ratifyed.....Recorded 30th day of June.....1674.
                                        John Sanford
[56]   Joseph Card—Land Recorded.
.....Joseph Card of.....Newport.....beinge in.....Law-full posession of.....Land.....lyinge within.....Towne

of Newport containinge Sixty acres.....bounded, Eastwardly partly by the Land of James Rogers, and part upon the Mill river Southwardly partly upon the land of William Weeden and part upon the Land of Mr Benedict Arnold Westwardly partly upon the said mr Arnolds land, part upon the highway and part upon tenn Acres of Land given to Jo Card and now in the posession of his mother—Northwardly partly upon the said tenn Acres and part upon the Land of mr. Peleg Sanford or mr William Brenton.....with all dwellinge or mansion houses, Barnes,.....Orchards, Gardens.....All .....promisses according to a Law made the 22th of May 1662 are hereby Ratifyed.....Recorded first day of July 1674

John Sanford

Agreement betweene Walter Clarke and Mrs. Francis Vahan

Articles of agreement.....betweene Walter Clarke of Newport.....and his mother mrs Francis Vahan.....agreed upon also by.....the Gaurdians of.....Walter Clarke (his brother in law) mr Barker and Captn Cranston.....Walter Clarke.....hath.....setled upon him.....the dwellinge house where in mrs francis Vahan now lives with the yards Garden and Orchard.....and the grass plat which lyeth next to the sea before the house, and the Barne with the litle barne Feild, and great Barne Feild, and the ground comonly called the Meddowes buttinge upon mr Eastons ground, mr Brentons Ground lately bought of Goodman Champlin. Goodman Clintons Land and mr Arnolds; and.....sixty acres..... lyinge by Marmaduke Wards Land: Which houseing and .....Woods.....is declared to be the Inheritance of..... Walter Clarke.....the halfe of the house comonly called .....the Stronge Walter house, wherein Goodman Moone now lives with the Land thereto belonginge is to be sold by mrs Francis Vahan to pay debts:.....the Land called..... the farme buttinge upon mrs. Coggeshalls Farme, and Goodman Bulls with the swamp buttinge upon Goodman Bulls, and Marmaduke Wards meddows,.....is to remaine with the

said mrs. Francis Vahan for she.....and the rest of the children, which she had by her husband Captn Jeremiah Clarke.....The houseinge which Captn Cranston now lives in with the Land..... is to be.....Captn Cranstons.....The .....Land which mr Arnold bought of Captn Clarke is to be confirmed.....by Deed from.....Walter Clarke.....
Eighteenth of January 1656
Signed by   Francis Vahan   John Cranston Gardian
            James Barker Gardian   Walter Clarke

[57]   John Clarke to Richard Smith.
.....John Clarke of Newport.....phisician.....For..... the Sum of Twenty pounds starling unto me.....paid.....by Richard Smith of Newport.....Merchant,.....doe.....sell .....Land lyinge.....in.....Newport.....and late.....in the posession of Francis Binley.....bounded.....on the north.....by.....Land now in the posession of me....., on the West by the Sea or harbour of the said Towne of Newport, and on the South and East by certaine high-waies, the said land.....granted Exetndinge from the said Land now in my posession on the North untill it come fower foot to the Southward of the Warehouse thereon Erected, on the South where it meets with the.....highway belonginge to the said Towne, and is in bredth from the.....Land belonginge unto me on the North to the.....high-way on the South fifty fower Foott.....seven and Twentith day of April.....1674
Wit.   John Clarke
   John Salmon
   Richard Baily

[58]   Samuell Wilbore to Hannah Clarke.
.....Samuell Wilbore of.....Portsmouth of Rhode Island .....there was Granted and layd out to me.....By order of the free-Inhabitants of the said Towne for which the Treasurer is paid.....a certaine percell of Land beinge..... Sixty-two Acres.....beinge within the.....Towne-shipp of portsmo......bounded......southwardly......with the Land of Thomas Lawton and William Freeborne Eastwardly with a high-way between the said Land and

Burtons Lands, and a high-way betweene the said Land and Ralph Cowlands land, Eastwards Northerwardly with a hig-way between the said Land and Gyles Slocums Lands Westwardly with the Comon,.....doe.....Give, ...my.....Daughter Hannah Wilbore alias Hannah Clarke, and to my.....sonn in law Latham Clarke her Husband.....Twenty day of Aprill.....1666.
Wit. Samuell Wilbore
  Caleb Arnold
  Margrit Porter

Receipt for mony paid by Samuell Wilbore
Where as it is ordered that for every acre of Land that is impropriated two shills. is to be paid in to the Treasury..... have Received of Samuell Wilbore six pounds Eight Shillings .....for sixty fower Acres.....Layd out to him on this side mr Sanfords.....Received by me.....21t of Aprill 1658 .....6£-0-0
                       William Baulston Treasurer
                             for Portsmouth

[59] Samuell Wilbore to Latham Clarke.
.....Samuell Wilbore of Portsmo. on Rhode-Island.....doe .....give.....my,.....son in law Latham Clarke.....three peeces.....of Land Contaninge in the whole Five hundred Acres.....beinge in the Narragansett Cuntry or Kings Province,.....is part of.....Land there of which I..... with.....others are a Joynt.....purchasser....., one percell of the said five hundred acres.....granted beinge a house lott lyinge at Pettacomscutt containinge.....Therty acres.....bounded on the South by the Minnerall land on the West by a high way on the North by Land now in the posession of me.....and on the East by a high-way or foot path, an other percell of the said five hundred acres.....containeth.....Two hundred and Twenty acres.....and is the one halfe of fower hundred and forty acres granted unto me by the purchassers lyinge about a mile & a halfe Northerly from Pettacomscutt.....the other halfe beinge my sonn in law Caleb Arnolds which I have given unto him, the said

fower hundred and forty acres.....to be Equally devided both upland and Meddow between my.....sonns in law Latham Clarke and Caleb Arnold,.....Latham Clarke is to have the first choyce and the Remainder of the said five hundred acres.....is Two hundred and Fifty acres, being the half of five hundred acres granted unto me by the purchassors but not as yett Layd out, the other half beinge my Sonn in law Caleb Arnolds which I have given unto him, the said five hundred acres.....last mentioned.....to be Eaqually devided both upland and meadow between my.....sonns in Law Latham Clarke and Caleb Arnold,.....Caleb Arnold is to have the first choyce:.....fourteenth day of October 1671
Wit.   Samuell Wilbur
  John Heath
  William Correy

[60]   John Greene to Thomas Lawton.
.....John Greene Junr.....of Warwick.....have sold unto Thomas Lawton of Portsmouth on Rhode Island Six hundred acres of upland.....beinge appointed by the purchassers..... of Warwick to be layd out for me as yett undevided.....I have sold the said Land lyinge at the Southwest end of Warwick.....for the sum of sixteen pounds.....28th day of November 1654
Wit.   John Greene Junr.
  Mathew Bridgman
  Thomas Greene.

Agreement between Thomas Lawton and John Almy.
Puckatest, the 17th day of March 1673
.....Mutually agreed.....between Thomas Lawton and John Almy both beinge proprietors and part owners.....of the.....neck of land called punckatest,.....there hath been difference between.....Lawton and Almy in Refferance to their.....claimes.....in the said Neck of Land,.....Almy hath had of.....Lawton some hundreds of Rayles and a Carte the same are.....acquited.....And.....for the Future.....Lawton is to have and.....make use of.....for

.....seven yeares from.....the date here of.....the Sixt part of.....Punckatest.....

Wit.   Thomas X Lawton
  Constant Southworth   his marke
  John Sanford.   John Almy
  John Champlin releaces Negro Salmerdore.

.....thirtith day of.....March.....John Champlin heire to John Gard Deceased.....did declare that he gave his Negro Salmerdore his Freedom.....forever.....Newport on Rhode Island   Walter Clarke Asistant.

[61]   Joseph Carpenter to Abyah Carpenter

.....Joseph Carpenter of Muskeeto Cove In Longe-Island within the Collony of.....James Duke of Yorke,.....have made an Exchainge of Lands with my Brother in Law Abyah Carpenter of Pawtuxet in Rhode-Island Collony.....Lands which I Exchainge.....is all.....Lands and Comonage which Fell to me by my wife.....from her father, And alsoe a therd part of my Lands which lyeth betweene Paseaunsa Cove and Pawtuxett River, And.....Five pounds.....Oyster bay.....Eight day of June.....one Thowsand Six hundred Seventy & three.....

Wit.   Joseph Carpenter
  Matthias Harvy
  Nathanill Coles.

Edward Robinson to Samuell Billing.

.....Feb. the twenty thurd.....one Thowsand Six hundred Eight.....Edward Robinson of Newport.....for Valuable Consideration.....sold unto Samuell Billing.....of Newport.....Land lyinge within.....Newport.....neare the line betweene Newport and Portsmouth Contaninge.....Eight acres one thurd.....lyinge on the North side the Land of Samuell Billinge yt was bought of Thomas Wood, bounded on the East by the Comon Seventeen pole to a small shrub oake, on the North by the Comon fower score pole to a small black oake beinge marked for the two Corner trees on the North side all which.....Land.....granted me.....by the

Towne of Newport.....
Wit.   Edward
  Richard Tew   his **X** marke
  James Barker   Robbyson
  Edward Smith and James Barker—bounds changed.
January.....27 at a quarter meetinge it was Ordered upon a Request of mr Richard Tew that mr Edward Smith and mr James Barker should remove the bounds of the land bought of Wood leaving out as much.....at the North-east corner as they take in from the Comon at the North-west corner.
                X me Marke Lucar To. Clerke
.....to certify.......that accordinge to order made the 27th of January 1657 wee have taken 31 Rod from the North-east corner of Mr Tews land and laid out 31 Rod to the North-west corner, this 2 of February 1657
                                    Edward Smith
                                    James Barker

[62] William Brenton to Thomas Ginings.
.....19th of March.....one Thowsand six hundred Fifty nine.....William Brenton of Newport Marcht, for.....full satisfaction.....hath.....sold unto Thomas Ginings of Portsmouth on Rhode Island.....Eight Acres.....in..... Portsmouth.....bounded on the South by the land of..... Thomas Ginings lately Gyles Slocums Land, On the North by the land of Henry Pearcy lately Nicholas Brownes land, on the East and West by the Commo.....with.....all..... houses fenceings,
Wit.   William Brenton
  William Baulston
  William Dyre Senr.
  Thomas Ginings Senr to Thomas Ginings
Thomas Ginings Senr.....of Portsmouth on Rhode Island .....doe for.....One hundred pounds starll.....make over unto my sonn Thomas Ginings my Now dwellinge house and sixteen acres of Land.....sixteen day of July.....1674
Wit.   the marke **X** of Thomas
  Peter Talman   Ginings Senyor
  Richard Bulgar

I ann Ginings.....aprove of all the above.....

Ann Ginings

[63] Richard Smith to John Brigs.
.....Richard Smith of Narragansett.....for.....Twenty five pounds.....received from John Brigs of Narragansett have......sold.....the land formerly belonginge to Rubin Willis which I bought in England from his father and Mother William and Sussanah Hixe.....havinge order from Rubin Willis to make sale of same, it lyinge.....in Narragansett Cuntry contaninge.....Fifty seven Acres.....bounded on the East by five-hundred acres of Land not layd out as it is in the North ward purchass, On the West bounded by the Comon, on the North with the high-way, on the South by the lands of Samuell Waite,.....Eleventh day of January.....1672

Wit.   Richd Smith
  Henry X Teeppitts
    his marke.
  John Greene

[64] Awawsunks Sachim to James Barker & Caleb Carr
.....Awaswunks Sachim Squa of Surronet and Wawweeyowitt her husband, and Amos alias Samponock their sonn, ...for Sixty pounds starllinge.....paid.....by James Barker Senior and Caleb Carr Senior both of Newport.....have sold.....their.....Land lyinge.....at Succonett.....wheither.....upland, meddow, pasture, wood-grounds, Marches, ...Creeks, Coves, Watterings, Wayes,.....Nine & twentith day of September.....One Thowsand six hundred seventy Fower

Wit.

  John Greene   Awawsucks X her marke
  Tho Jeffery   Amos X alias Samponock
  Machemowenin X alias
  Interpreter his marke   his marke
  James Sweet   George the Indian
  Interp X his marke

.....Thirtieth day of Septem: 1674 Awassuncks and Sampoonock her son.....owned the above-written.....Newport.....

Walter Clarke Asist.

This Record.....not a true Coppy.....Truly Recorded in the 69th page of this Booke.

[65]   Joseph Carpenter to Stephen Arnold.

Joseph Carpenter.....of Muskeata Cove neer Oyster Bay on Long Island.....Formerly Inhabitant on the south of Pawtuxet River within.....Warwick.....For.....mony.....paid.....me by my uncle Stephen Arnold of Pawtuxet within.....Towne-shipp of Providence.....Have with.....consent of my Father William Carpenter.....of.....Pawtuxet.....doe.....sell.....unto.....uncle Stephen Arnold, ...one halfe of all my.....Lands.....on the South side of.....Pawtuxet river, Exceptinge only my dwellinge house, lott and pasture and meddow adjoyninge to it.....beinge at the place of the.....Pawtuxet River called the wadeinge place.....lyinge on the north side and west end of a Cove comonly called.....Paseunkett Cove (within.....Towneshipp of Warwick.....) all within a fence and on a Neck reachinge Eastward to a place called.....Shuppaquansett, the southern part boundinge with the.....Paseunkett Cove, The Genl. fence boundinge the West-ern part of the.....Land and the Northern part.....bounded by.....Land of Stephen Arnold.....And alsoe halfe of all the meddow which.....William Carpenter.....bought of Mathias Harvie formerly of.....Warwick.....which is scittuate.....on the head and on the North side of.....paseunkett Cove it reaching to and takeinge a place called Shuppaquonsett. Alsoe.....one halfe of a Corne mill standing upon.....Pawtuxet River and at the Falls of the.....River together with the furniture.....belonginge and one halfe of the dwellinge house belonginge to the .....mill, as alsoe a percell of meddow adjoyninge to the.....mill and dwelling house lyinge Westward from.....mill and dwelling house it boundinge on the south part with the.....Pawtuxet River, and on the North part with a Lott .....belonginge to the heires of Zachary Roades formerly

.....of Pawtuxett, the Mill dwelling house and meddow is on the North side of the.....Pawtuxet River within..... Towne-shipp of Providence. Alsoe one acre of Land..... beinge from the.....Pawtuxett River and at the East end of.....William Carpenter his.....Six Acre share of Land lyinge in that.....Land called Pawtuxet great Neck, and is the Sixt Lott Northward from the.....Pawtuxett Falls, Alsoe fower Shares of Land in Pawtuxett little Neck,.....which Neck is.....on the Eastward and Northward side of the mouth of.....Pawtuxett River at the Isuinge of the..... River into the sea; The which Fower shares of Land..... was posessed with by my.....Father William Carpenter, ...each one Contaninge.....one acre and a quarter a peece.....three of them lyinge together in one percell bounding on the North with the Land of.....Stephen Arnold one the South with Land belonginge to the heires of Zachariah Roades on the West with.....meddow belonginge to the Surviver of Richd Watterman formerly.....of Providence, and on the East with the Salt River, the other share lyinge more southward and boundinge on the north part, with the Land of William Arnold of.....Pawtuxet and on the south with Land belonging to the heires of Zechariah Roades on the East part with the salt water on the West with the River that runneth from the.....Falls.....I.....Binde my selfe..... at all times to save.....Stephen Arnold.....from any claime .....which.....may arise.....through Hannah my now wife.....second day of September.....One Thousand six hundred seventy Fower.
Wit.
  Silas Carpenter
  William Carpenter junr
.....William Carpenter of Pawtuxet
Doe.....assent unto.....the above-said
                        Joseph Carpenter
                        William Carpenter Senr.
                        The marke of **X** Ana
                        Carpenter

[67]   Stephen Burton to Francis Brayton
.....Stephen Burton (Eldist sonn of Stephen Burton of..... London Merchant.) sonn and heire unto the deceased mr. Thomas Burton late.....of Portsmouth on Rhode-Island .....I.....by.....due right.....from my.....Father..... Stephen Burton......by deed.....all the lands.....formerly belonginge.....to my.....Gran father Thomas Burton,..... and for.....three pounds five shillings New-England silver, to me.....paid by Francis Brayton of.....Portsmouth Senr .....doe.....sell,.....Land formerly belonginge unto my .....Gran father, given and granted unto him by the freemen of.....Portsmouth,.....fower Acres.....lyinge within the said Towne on the hill side and over against the Comon pound .....bounded North, East, and South by the hig-way and Comon and Westerly by the land now in the posession of John Archer,.....fower, and Twentith day of July—1671
Wit.   Stephen Burton
   John Anthony
   John Sanford
   Joseph Anthony
         .....wee.....were personally present and did see
      mr Stephen Burton.....make delivery of.....land
      unto Lt. Francis Brayton.....by turff and twig.....
      24th of July 1671
                     John Anthony   John Sanford
                     John X Cooke   Joseph Anthony
                        his marke

[68]   John Greene to William Carpenter.
.....John Greene Junr.....Warwick.....Have sold unto William Carpenter of Pawtuxet in Providence.....all my right in the little neck of Land layinge below Pawtuxet Falls, ...all my right in that place comonly called the Vinyard, ...alsoe my right of Land as yett undevided from Packassett river Eastward downe to the Sea together with all the previleges of water.....20th of November 1658
Wit.   John Greene
   Ezekel Holyman
      his X marke
   Christopher Unthanke

[69] Awawsunck to James Barker and Caleb Carr.
.....Awawsunck Sachim Squa of Succonett and Wawweeyowitt her husband and Amos alias Samponock their sonn.....for.....sixty pounds Starling.....paid.....by James Barker Senior and Caleb Carr Senior both of Newport..... have.....sold.....all our Land Lyinge.....at So Succonett .....be it upland, meddow, pasture, wood grounds, marshes, ...with all.....Creeks, coves, waterings waies.....nine and Twentith day of September.....One Thousand six hundred and seventy four

Wit.
  John Greene
  Tho Jefferay
  Machemowenin
  Interpreter X alias George
      his marke   the Indian
  James X Sweet Interpreter
    his marke

                        Awawsuncks X her marke
                        Wawweeyowit X husband of
                          Awawsuncks his marke
                        Amos X alias Samponack
                          his marke

On the 30th day of September 1674.....Awawsuncks and Sampononck her sonn.....owned the above written..... Newport.....   Walter Clarke Asist.

[70] Cakochawhunt to James Barker and Caleb Carr.
.....Cakochawhunt alias Simon Eldist sonn of Awawsuncks Sachim Squa of Suaconett.....whereas my Mother Awawsuncks.....with my Father Wawweeyowitt and my Brother Samponock alias Amos.....did.....sell unto James Barker and Caleb. Carr.....all.....Land belonginge unto them..... lyinge.....at Succonett.....I.....doe.....willingly consent to.....Deed..... sixth day of November One Thousand six hundred seventy and four

Wit.   Cakechawhunt X alias Simon
  John Greene   his marke
  Tho. Jefferay

[71]   Wm Dyre—conserning High Wayes.
High Wayes Layd out by mr Nicholas Easton mr John Clarke and my selfe
In the Towne of Each Side the eight rod Lotts a way of 6 poles wide with a way of 2 rod wide between each fower.
A High-way of 2 rod wide as farr as Gardners house lott and then one from the water side up to over against Havilands house soe to mr Coggeshalls farme A way crossinge the way by Tobies house lott up to the way that goes to mr Brentons farme principally layd out for the accommodation of the Land that did accomodate the house Lotts from Harry Bulls house Lott to the said way An other drift way up to the Southmead Medows of 2 poles wide Running 2 poles between Robinsons Lott and Jeffereys lott
An other high-way from the Entrance of mr Coggeshalls farme to goe to castle hill and soe leadinge to all the Lands and Comons upon the neck wch. way was layd out by us to the brooke that came downe by Aplegates plaine the rest is not detirmined as yett where to runn—A Highway from the Towne layd out of 2 poles wide to Wi. Dyres Farme and soe to lead to the lands on the north side of the Towne virt the medows, mr Coddingtons Cow-pasture the Artillery Garden mr Clarkes land and Willia. Dyres Land, and soe by Wim. Dyres medow; a way into the land that the said Dyre bought of Aplegate to fetch off the wood of that land for the Townes use which Land was layd forth by Captn Clarke and mr Robert Jefferays as alsoe by them was the wood reserved and the way appointed only for that use
A High-way appointed, from the Towne at the Corner of mr Barkers ½ acre lott to goe to the grass and medows in the pond and to the beach wich way way was 2 pole wide to run along betweene the Land of mr Coggeshall, Clarke, Jeffereys on the west side, and the land layd out to mr Easton and others on the East side
A High-way betweene the Lott of John Lawrance, and Marmaduke Ward of 2 pole wide leadinge to mr Coddingtons lands, only the way betweene Wilbor land and Bakers, and

Richardsons was above 6 pole to goe to Wanemetonony hill and soe by the foot of the hill into mr Coddingtons farme, and soe through that to the Lands layd out at Earlls wiggwam comonly calld Pocassett high way

A High-way at the east end of Wards land to goe by mr Brentons land to green end and the lands layd forth that way, and soe a highway of 10 pole broad to the said mill brook soe for as these lands were layd out to Greenman &c, and from that way was another way to goe downe to the mill.

A hie way appointed to goe from out the Night Comon through mr Brentons farme to the Mill for 2 Rod wide, and the be layd out where was most convenient for horse or cart.

A hie-way appointed and layd out to go up by mr Fosters house lott to mr Bracys farme and to the lands layd out on the South and Eastern side there of and a drift way appointed to South Mead Medows as proper only therto.

A hie way layd up from the Mill to Joseph Clarkes and soe on the fore side of those lands downe to the Comon beyond mr Barkers that on the east side of the Brooke being about 20 pole at the North end thereof Cross the way from the Mill at the end of mr Brentons mens lotts and between Captn. Clarkes land now in the posession of Goodm Weavor went the hie way towards the great Comons, and by the side of mr John Clarkes Joseph and Thomas Clarkes lands &c being on the east side thereof went the hie way of six poles broad to mr Eastons Farme, and from that layd out to John Anthony on the south and John Lawton on the North went downe and was laid out a highway of six poles broad downe to Stony River to meet with that way on the West ends of mr Barkers lands and soe came into the Comons at the Rocks and from that way was layd out to each neck and medows and beach.

There was a way alsoe layd out on the east side of Greenmans land that butted upon the Penfold Richardson lying on the other side wch way was to goe to the Penfold being layd out to mr Brenton

A hie way lickwise to goe up on the northe side of the layd to Andrews which way went to the Hermitage and these lands thereabouts from out of which way went downe to the high way to mr Hutchinsons Lands but for which hieways was appointed and layd to the lands about & adjoyninge to Sachuis brook.....refer.....to Record of lands in these parts layd out by mr Robert Jeffereys, whose fenceings were appointed by mr Jeffereys Captn Clarke and my selfe.....I doe declare in my observation two or three impedimts

First mr Coddington in that his way that goes to the Artillery Garden & buryinge place he hath sett neer sixty pole of Fencing upon the hie way six foot at least at the North end 2ly Richard Tew hath not only turned the part of the hie way out of his proper place but hath incrocht upon and inclossed upon thre rod of the way and halfe a pole upon part of the rest. Lett them therefore that knowes any injury in this kinde put it downe.....soe shall wee avoyd hipocrisy dissemulation, bark biteinge and secrett wolveish devoveringe one of another,.....lett all that love the light come forth to the light and show their Deeds soe saith

.....to be a Record   Will Dyre
from the simple and honist
intent of my hart & soule
this 15th Feb. 1654

[73] Thomas Clarkes Will.
Newport.....28th Day of July 1674
The Will.....of Thomas Clarke Senior liveinge at Newport .....my Lands upon this Island with the houseings Fenceings.....to my brother Joseph Clarke.....Lands at Quononoqutt Island.....unto my cussin William Clarke sonn of my brother Joseph Clarke.....my househould-stuff.....to my brother Joseph Clarkes wife Margrett Clarke.....the stock upon My Farme which William Clarke injoys when his time is out is to be distributed amongst my brother Joseph Clarkes Children eaqually only William Excepted:.....there is due from my brother John Clarke for.....service.....when he was gon for England twelve yeares.....providinge for.....John Clarkes stock.....in which time was reared twenty horse kinde and about nine-score sheepe; and one hun-

dred acres of Land purchased at Quonnonoqutt, a quarter share at Miscomocutt and tenn acres.....at Aplegates Neck upon this Island, for which I demand.....Twenty pounds a yeare, and.....out of this.....my will.....is that it be equally devided betweene my brother Joseph Clarkes children.....to see this.....performed.....I choose mr Obadiah Holmes and John Salmon both of Newport.....

Wit.   Thomas **X** Clarke
   Walter **X** Cunygrave   his marke
     his marke
   James **X** Rogers
     his marke
   George Hamonds

Walter Cunigrave and James Rogers tooke.....oath this Eighteenth of December 1674 to be the last Will.....of the Deceassed Thomas Clarke, before me,
                                Wim Coddington Govor.

The Names of the Children of Joseph Clarke of.....Newport that are livinge this 19th of December 1674

{ Joseph Clarke   { William Clarke   { Mary   { Sarah Clarke
{ John Clarke   { Susanah   { Joshua Clarke { Thomas Clarke
                                                       Kary Clarke
                                                       Elizabeth Clarl

[74] Thomas Lawton—letter of aturny to Daniell Lawton .....Thomas Lawton of Portsmouth upon Rhode-Island .....Yeoman, Have.....Constituted my.....sonn Daniell Lawton of Portsmo.....Yeoman, to be my.....Aturney .....fifth day of June.....One Thowsand Six hundred Seventy and foure.

Wit.   Thomas **X** Lawton
   John Newton   his marke
   John Hayward Scr.
.....acknowlidged by Thomas Lawton.....June the 5th 1674 before me   Edw Ring Asistant

[75] Sarah Reape to Leonard Smith
.....Sarah Reape of Newpt.....Widdow.....for..... Twenty and three pounds Sterling.....paid.....by Leonard

Smith.....for.....two peeces.....of Land lying in..... Providence.....Ninty acres.....my Husband purchased of John Acres in.....1661.....I.....sett my hand.....one and Thertith day of March One Thousand six hundred seventy and foure
Wit.   Sarah Reape
  John Hullme
  Richard Baily

[76]   Gidion Freeborne—Land Recorded

.....By order of the Towne of Portsmouth.....10th of 12th month 1639.....Given.....unto William Freeborne..... One hundred and Forty Acres of Land.....Eighty Acres .....Layd out.....Westwardly upon the sea Northwardly upon John Walkers side line Eastwardly partly upon the Comon, and partly upon the Land granted.....unto Randall Houldon, and Southwardly upon the Comon,.....in..... Will.....of.....William Freeborne he hath given Unto his sonn Gidion Freeborne all the said Land.....Exceptinge that part.....Formerly.....Given to his Daughter Sarah Brown(ell—[worn away]).....Eighty acres.....Ratifyed
.....   John Sanford

  William Freeborne—receipts.

14th of the 5th month 1639

.....for every Acre of Land impropriated two shillings shall be payd into Treasury.....received of Goodman Freeborne two pounds tenn shillings and tenn pence
                        by me. Jo. Coggeshall Treasr.
.....for every Acre of Land that is impropriated two shillings is to be payd into the Treasury.....Received of William Freeborne. Fower pounds seven shillings two pence which with monyes.....payd.....is in full for one hundred and twelve acres of Land granted.....25 of January 1657
                                      4: 07: 02
                            William Baulston Treasur.

[77]   William Freeborne—Land Recorded.

.....by.....Grant.....of Portsmouth.....and purchase from others William Freeborne was.....posest of.....percell of Meddow and Upland contaninge Fower acres and a halfe.....lyinge in.....Portsmouth.....bounded Northwardly by a high way to the Springe Neere mr Baulstons Meddow, Eastwardly by the Creeke and Cove neere John Sanfords Meddow, Southwardly by the Land now in the posession of Thomas Cornell Westwardly by the high-way and Comon, And.....William Freeborne in his.....will..... haveinge, Given.....the said Lands.....unto his sonn Gidion Freeborne.....The said Land.....Ratifyd.....

John Sanford.

Boston in Massachussetts Bay.....

.....there was an agreement of Eighteene persons to make purchass of some place to the Southward for a plantation whether they Resolved to Remove, for which end some of them was sent out to Veiw a place for them selves and such others as they should take in to the liberty of Freemen and purchassers.....upon their Veiw was purchasst Rhod-Island. with some small neighbouring Islands and previleges of grass and wood of the Islands in the Bay, and Maine adjoyninge, ...the saile of the.....purchass from the Indians hath ever since byne in the hands of William Cottinton Esque.— which beinge a great trouble to the afore-said purchassers and Freemen I.....doe.....promiss to deliver the said Deeds .....with what Records is in my hands.....14 April 1652
Wit.   Wim Coddington,
   Robt. Knight.
   Georg Muning

[78] Wm Brenton to Joseph Browne

.....William Brenton of Tanton.....New-Plymoth..... Esqui.....unto my sonn in law mr Joseph Browne of Charletowne.....Massachussetts, and my daughter Mehetabell (his wife).....have given,.....All yt my farme on Rhode-Island, formerly in posession of mr John Gard deceassed called Midlford,.....bounded Northwardly with the land of Mathew Borden, Eastwardly with the sea, Southwardly with the land of Thomas Cooke senior and Westwardly with the Comon, the Land of John Cooke and Anthony Shaw,.....about two hundred and fifty acres.....and all my peece of Land on Quononoqutt which I purchased from Serjant James Rogers being one hundred and twenty acres.....and one sixteenth part of all my Land at Natticot on Merrimack River, being Eight Thowsand acres in the whole,.....with all houses, fences, Barnes, buildings,.....and alsoe two breeding mares, and one hundred breeding sheep.....18th day of August..... 1674

Wit. William Brenton
  Jahleel Brenton
  John Winchcombe

[80] William Brenton of Newport—Will

.....William Brenton.....doe make.....my Eldist sonn Jahleel Brenton my Executor.....I doe give unto.....Jahleel.....all my two farmes at Hamersmith now in posession of John Rathbon, and all the houses fences Barnes Buildings .....with the Marshes and Upland in Newport Neck thereunto belonging, and one Eight part of all my Land at Natticot on Merrimeck River, being.....tenn Thousand Acres,..... and fower oxen and working steers two breeding mares, and one hundred breeding sheepe.....unto my son William Brenton.....my farme.....in posession of William Case and all houses,.....barnes,.....with.....adjaycent swamp .....one Eight part of my.....Land at Natticot, two breeding mares and one hundred breeding sheep:

.....unto my son Ebinezer Brenton.....all my Neck of Land Called Mattapoissett now in posession of Jared Bourne senior, with all houses,.....Barnes,.....and one sixteenth part of my Land at Natticot, and one hundred and fifty pounds in Currant Cuntry pay a paire of oxen two breeding mares Eight Cowes and hiffers and one Bull

.....unto my Daughter Sarah Brenton.....my farme at Quononoqutt now in posession of Michall Kaly with all the houses,.....Barnes,.....and one sixteenth part of my Land at Natticot two Breeding mares and one hundred breeding sheep.

.....unto my Daughter Mehetabell Brenton.....all my farme formerly in posession of mr John Gard deceassed (now to be called.....Midlford) with all houses,..... Barnes,.....and my peece of Land on Quononoqutt lying Northward of my.....Land in posession of Michall Kaly which I bought of Serjant James Rogers,.....about one hundred and Twenty acres,.....and one sixteenth part of my.....Land at Natticot, two Breeding Mares and one hundred breeding sheep.

.....unto my Daughter Abigall Brenton.....my farme..... bought of mr Elisha Hutchinson of Boston, and.....Bakers farme, and one sixteenth part of.....Land at Natticott, and all houses,.....Barnes,.....two breeding mares and one hundred breeding sheep:

.....unto my son in law mr Peleg Sanford.....one Eight part of my.....Land at Natticot, and all my Right title and interest in Elizabeth Islands, and the Gay head and Land adjaycent thereunto, and all the Debts Due to me in the Island of Barbados.....

.....unto my sonn in Law mr John Poole.....one Eight part of my.....Land Natticot:

.....unto my.....friend Major Generall John Leveret Esquire.....one sixteenth part of my.....Land at Natticot.

.....unto my.....friend Captn John Cranston.....one sixteenth part of my.....Land at Natticot.....unto my..... friend mr George Shove Pastor of the Church at Tanton..... one sixteenth part of my.....Land at Natticott.

.....unto my Cussin Philip Sandy.....one hundred acres of my.....Land at Natticott.

.....unto Michall Kaly.....one hundred acres of my..... Land at Natticot.

.....unto John Winchcombe.....two hundred acres of my .....Land at Natticott

And the overpluss of my.....Land Natticot (if any be) I leave to be disposed of.....towards a stock for.....my children.....And I.....appointe my.....son in law mr Peleg Sanford.....Guardian over my.....sons Jahleel,

William and Ebinezer, and my.....daughter Abigall,.....
until they come to the age of Twenty & one yeares unless.....
Abigall be married before.....that age,.....unto my son in
law mr Peleg Sanford two therd parts.....And to Captn
John Cranston.....one therd part, of the whole debt and
damages.....due to me from the Estate of George Bliss of
.....Newport.....

.....unto my Sister Kathrine Cooks Children to be paid
within a yeare and a day after my decease (if demanded)
twenty pounds in stock at Currant prices.....

.....unto my Sister Christian Sandys children tenn pounds
.....in stock.....

.....unto mr George Shove.....five pound in Currant Cuntry pay:

.....unto my Grand Childe John Poole.....tenn pounds in
Catle at Currant price.

.....unto Seath Shove.....twenty shillings in currant cuntry pay.

.....unto Elizabeth Shove.....Twenty Shillings.....

.....unto James Bell of Tanton.....forty shillings.....

.....unto John Winchcombe.....five pound.....

.....unto Michall Kaly two therds—and to his wife one
therd of fifteen pounds due from him to me for Land granted
to him at Pettacomscutt.

.....unto Rachill Wilkison.....a young cow or a two yeare
old heiffer at Mattapoissett and five pounds in Currant Cuntry pay.

.....unto my Negro Abraham four pounds.....

.....unto my Negro Antonia forty shillings.....

.....unto my Negro Rose therty shillings.....

.....unto my Negro Zipporah twenty Shillings.....

.....unto my Negro Samson tweny shills.....

.....unto my Indian Edom twenty shillings.....

.....Remainder of my Estate.....to be devided between all
my children.....in case my.....negros Abraham and Antonia.....demeane themselves.....obedient.....at the Expiration of five yeares after my decease be sett free,.....and
.....shall give.....them five pounds.

.....unto mr Roger Williams of Providence twelve Ewes or Ewe lambs and a wether sheep.

.....appoint.....my.....son in law mr Peleg Sanford, Captn John Cranston and mr George Shove.....my Overseers,.....unto each of them.....Five pounds............

Ninth day of February one Thowsand six hundred seventy and three.   William Brenton

Signed.....
  William Harvey
  Georg Macey
  John Richmond

Newport.....13th day of November 1674.....appeared before me William Harvey George Masey and John Richmond.....

                          William Coddington Govr.

[84]   Inventory of William Brentons Estate.

	£	sh.	ds.
.....farmes and houses at Hamer-smith in posession of John Rathbon, and Lands..... and the stock.....given to my son Jahleel —	2600		
.....farme in posession of William Case and .....stock.....given to my son William —	1100		
.....farme and houses at Mattapoisett in posession of Jared Bourne senr. and stock .....given unto my son Ebinezar — — —	1150		
.....farme and houses in posession of Michall Kaly and.....stock.....given to my Daughter Sarah — — — — — —	650		
.....farme formerly in posession of mr John Gard deceased and.....Land on Quononoqt. with stock.....given unto my Daughter Mehetabell — — — — — — — —	650		
.....farme and houses bought of mr Elisha Hutchinson—and farme called Bakers farme and stock given unto my Daughter Abigall —	600		
.....houses Land & wharfe in Newport —	1200		
.....Land at Natticott on Merrimack River	800		

......260 acres.....Land in the North part

	£	sh.	ds.

of Quononogutt — — — — — —   300
.....houses and Land in.....Tanton — —   300
.....my Intrest in.....land at Narragansett
and Pettacomscutt — — — — — —   300
.....part of Elizabeth Islands — — —   40
.....70 horses and mares young and old.....
besides what is dispossed of by my Will 3li
head — — — — — — — —   210
.....34 head of Cattell in custody of my
teeneants.....at 3li head— — — — —   102
.....1100 sheep in the hands of my Tennants
.....at 6li 13.3 4 — — — — — —   366 13 4
.....my quarter part of the Ketch dove —   150
.....my therd part of the Ketch Industry —   50
.....all my house-hold goods — — —   200
                              Tottall is — 10768 . 13 4

Wit.—20th of August 1674
   William Harvey   William Brenton.
   John Winchcombe

[85] William Brenton Esqur. of.....Newport.....late deceassed (in.....Tanton.....).....in his.....Will..... appointed.....his son Jahleel Executor, and Peleg Sanford Guardian.....I doe hereby give full power.....unto..... Jahleel Brenton and Peleg Sanford.....ninth day of December 1674
                                       William Coddington Go.

[85] John Anthony to Richard Tew.
.....4th day.....8th month 1642.....John Anthony of Portsmouth.....Planter.....have.....sold unto Richard Tew.....of Newport.....three percells of Land.....within the bounds of Newport.....Eastward from Newport Mill within a tract of Land called the great inclosure,.....Fifty acres.....Fourty of it was given me by Towne Grant tenn given me as beinge a servant at my first cominge bounded on the Nor by the Comon or hie-way to Sachuest, on the west by the high-way to Sachuest, on the South by the Land of Nicholas Easton, on the East by the river called Maidford

river, alsoe one percell of Salt Marsh lyinge at the West end of Sachuest Marshes containinge Eight acres.....bounded South-East and Nor with the naturall water bounds, on the West by the high-way on the beach leading to Sachuest Comon, alsoe an other percell of salt marsh lyinge on the other side of the water Eastward called.....Lubbars pound contaninge about one acre and a halfe, bounded East and West by the great Rocks, on the south by.....the water.....
Wit. John Anthoni
  Susanah **X** Anthony
     her marke
  Joseph Lad

[86] John Layton to Richard Tew.
.....John Layton of Newport have sold to Richard Tew..... 30 acres.....Lyinge.....within the situa The Land of John Peckham on the north side Maidford river on the East the hie-way South and West 6ei.13.4 to be paid.....one halfe in hand the other at May,.....which will be.....1643 then to be paid in swine.....as two men Shall prize them.....
Wit. The marke **X** of John Lation
  James Weeden Richard Tew

Henry Tew—Land Recorded.
.....Henry Tew (sonn and heire of Richard Tew late) of .....Newport.....(deceassed).....two.....percells.....of Land lyinge.....within......Newport.....Eighty Acres..... bounded.....the one percell North by the hie-way East by Maidford alias Stony river South by land in the posession of Mathew Boomer, West partly by the hie-way and partly by lands in the posession of Mathew Boomer and Peter Easton, the other percell is bounded North by the Land of John Peckham senr. East by the.....Maidford river south and west by the hie-way which.....two percells.....were purchassed by.....Richard Tew of John Anthony and John Layton.....with all mansion houses, Barnes,.....fenceings, Orchards, Gardens.....According to a Law made the 22th of May 1662 promisses are hereby Ratified.....Recorded .....15th day of January.....1674
                        John Sanford.

[87]   James Barker to Richard Tew.

.....James Barker of.....Newport Yeoman.....have..... sold unto Richard Tew of.....same Towne yeoman, one percell of Salt Marsh lyinge on the East side the hie-way to Sachuest. bounde on the South by the land of Owin Williams on the East by Richard Tew on the north by the River..... two Acres.....

Wit.   James Barker
   William Waight
   John Cotterill

Thomas Painter to Richard Tew.

.....Thomas Painter.....in Newport.....for.....sum..... Received of Richard Tew.....in Newport.....have sold .....my now dwellinge-house and the halfe Acre of Land .....belonginge on which it stands,.....granted by the freemen of Newport to Edward Andrews.....bounded on the West by Maidford River, and on all other sides by the Comon, together with a percell of Marsh lying neere Sachuest beach, bounded on the South by the Comon beach, on the East by John Crandells Marsh Northerly by the river or chanell, Westerly by the beach, both.....percells I bought of Owin Williams.....Eleventh day of March.....1663 or 1664.....

Wit.   The marke of Thomas X Painter
   Thomas Harris Junr.
   Marke Lucar

[84]   William Jefferays Will

.....William Jefferay of Newport.....Gent.....unto my Eldist daughter Mary Greene the wife of John Greene of Newport.....Lands.....beinge in Blackman Street neere the Citty of London which Lands.....were given me by..... my Mother Audry Jefferay late of Chittingly in.....Sussex which Lands are now, out at lease to.....Tennants which pay rent 18th.....a sufficient part reserved for.....my wife Mary Jefferay.....unto my sonn Thomas Jefferay all the remainder of my Estate in Old England.....unto my daughter Sarah the wife of James Barker of Newport.....five pounds in silver.....unto my two daughters Priscilla and

Susannah Jefferay all my Land and houseinge.....25 acres
.....lyinge.....in.....Newport.....Constitute my Daughter Mary Greene my Executrix.....my wifs two Breatheren John and Danill Gould over-seers.....Eight day of December 1674

Wit.   Edward Greenman   William Jefferay
       John Salmon

[85] Cagananaquoant to William Coddington.
Newport.....Aprill 17th 1657.....Caganaquoant Indian and a Cheife Sachim and Comandar of the Indians of Narragansitt and Quononaqutt Island.....for.....Gifts.....received .....and for.....one hundred pounds Sterlling.....doe .....make.....sale of.....the Island Quononaqutt..... unto William Coddington Esquire & Benedict Arnold (senior) Both of Newport.....

Wit.   Caganaqutt **X** his marke
  Fra: Brinley
  Hugh Bewitt
  Mattackis **X** (alias) Newcome.
         his marke

[86] Cachanaquoant to Benedict Arnold.
.....Cachanaquoant a chief sachem and comander of all Indians of Narragansitt and Quononaqutt Island.....for .....Twenty pound sterlinge in good peage and Cloth..... received.....doe.....deliver unto Benedict Arnold of Newport.....a small Island called.....Acquedneessuck: or in the English Island, which is.....in the Bay of Narragansitt neere.....unto &.....upon the West side of the Island called Quononaqutt.....which I sold.....17th of Aprill one Thowsand Six hundred Fifty seven.....22th day of May in .....1658 at Warwick.....

Wit.   Cachanaquoant **X** his marke
  James **X** Sweete
       his marke
  X Awashaws
the marke of
the **X** marke of

Wamppapawgat alias
Neesoalkagg.

  Caskottape to Wm. Coddington.

.....Caskottape and Wequaquaniutt cheife Sachims of the Nanhigansetts Cuntry and owners of Qinoniquocke and Aquidnesicke Islands.....doe.....sell.....unto mr. Randall Houlden William Coddington Esquire mr Benedict Arnold and mr William Brenton,.....for one hundred and fifty and five pounds in peage.....18th of July 1659

Wit.   Caskottape X his marke
  Walter Todd   his X marke
    his X marke   Wequaquinuit
  John Smith Masson
  The X marke off
  Sankhequahim
  John Sassumon
  house X
    his marke
  the X marke
    of moake
  the X marke
    of Weskonssas
  the X marke of
    Potucke

[87]   Quisaquance to William Brenton.
Warwick the 25 of July 1659

.....Quisaquance Cheife Sachim of the Nankygansett, have sold.....two-Islands of Quononoqutt and Aquednessett..... unto mr William Brenton mr William Coddington mr Benedict Arnold mr Richard Smith senr and Caleb Carr.....for..... sixty pounds.....

Wit.   The marke of X
  Thomas Greene   Quisaquance
the marke of X William Eaton
the marke of X Awashouse
the marke of X Saukequaskne.

Randall Howldon to Benedict Arnold.

.....Randall Howldon of Warwick.....have received of Benedict Arnold of Newport and mr Brenton of the same .....one hundred fifty five pound in peage & for the two Sachims Wequaganuett and Kaskatape and sixty pounds for Quissuckquansh the Cheife Sachim.....for.....Quononaqutt and the Island called Dutch Island.....alsoe..... have Received for all my.....Troubles.....about the premisses made to.....other Indians as House and the rest..... one hundred Thirty and six pounds Eighteene Shillings and Eleaven pence.....at the rate of peage Six a penny..... 23th of March 1659

1660

Wit.   X me Randall Howldon
  Gregory Dexter
  William X Vahan

[88] Towasibbam to William Brenton

.....Towasibbam Indian.....petty sachim of Quononaqutt, ...have for.....Five pound sterlinge in peage.....given my.....aprobation for the posession of.....Quononaqutt Island as Sold by the cheife-sachims of Narragansett unto mr William Brenton, mr Coddington, Benedict Arnold and all .....purchassers.....of said Island and Dutch Island..... the.....five pounds.....Received.....one halfe of mr Brenton and the other of Benedict Arnold.....24th January 1660.

Wit.   Towasibbam his
  John Cranston   X
  Peleg Sanford   marke
  Benedict Arnold Jur.

mem. Towasibbam 22 s. & 6 d. more in peage afterwards besids, the five pounds.....

[89] John Crandall to John Crandall

.....John Crandall senior.....unto.....sonn John Crandall of Newport.....have given.....all.....my goods, Chattells, Debts, household stuff.....and.....have putt my.....sonn in.....posession of all.....promisses by the delivery unto

him of one shilling in silver currant mony.....of England
.....Third day of October.....1670
Wit. John Crandall
   William Weeden
   Richard Baily
   Walter Clarke to William Brenton.
.....1657.....seventeenth day of May.....Between Walter Clarke of Newport.....and William Brenton of Boston Merchant.....Walter Clarke was posessed.....of Land.....as heire.....to his.....Father Jeremiah Clarke.....and instated in them by his mother.....(now wife to William Vahan).....one percell.....lyinge in Newport, between the streets and the sea or harbour.....bounded on the West side by the sea or harbour, on the south by the land of..... William Brenton lately purchased of Jeffery Champlin, on the East side by the streete, and on the north end by the Land of John Cranston, which is one pole or pearch broad, & the north side there of is to run upon a due range, answeringe to the line hedg or fence which is upon the end of the Orchard of Walter Clarke soe that the.....Land is bounded just one pole bredth within the.....Range, exceptinge from the west side of the two graves unto the streete on the East side..... with an other percell of Land lyinge at the East end of the said William Brentons Land beinge the house Lott of Jeffery Champlin lately purchassed by.....William Brenton..... which.....Land is bounded, on the West side partly by the .....said Lott soe farr as the marks upon the fence Stands partly upon the Land of Robert Carr, and partly by the Land of Benedict Arnold and upon the South Side is bounded upon the way leads up to the highest percell of Land bought of the said Jeffery (to which the said way of two poles wide from the streete was.....impropriated).....on the east bounded by the Land last mentioned and on the North side by the land of the said Walter,.....which.....Land.....Walter.....doth.....sell.....unto.....the said William.....
Wit. Walter Clarke
   William Baulston

the marke of **X**
   William Vahan
   Will. Dyre
   .....as Guardians to the said Walter.....
   doe confirme.....Deed of Sale.....
                              John Cranston
                              James Barker

[91]   Richard Sisson to Peleg Sanford.
.....Twenty fourth day of September.....one Thowsand six hundred and sixty.....Richard Sisson of Portsmouth on Rhode Island.....Hath.....sold unto Peleg Sanford of..... Portsmouth all right.....in Quononoqutt Island and Dutch Island, which was his owne share and two Three hundreth shares, which he.....bought of William Hall and Thomas Manchester.....

Wit.   Richard **X** Sisson
   John Sanford   his marke
   Samuell Sanford

Thomas Manchester to Richard Sisson.
.....Thomas Manchester of Portsmouth in Rhode Island .....Have sold.....unto Richard Sisson of the same Towne .....one Three hundreth part of Quononoqutt Island..... with one three hundreth part of Dutch-Island.....sixt day of July.....One Thowsand six hundred fifty and eight.

Wit.   The marke of
   John **X** Roome   Thomas **X** Manchester
      his marke
   Ralph **X** Earll junr.
      his marke
   William Hall

[92]   William Hall to Richard Sisson.
.....William Hall of Portsmouth in Rhode-Island.....doe .....sell unto Richard Sisson of same Towne.....one three hundred part of.....Quononoqutt,.....with one three hundred part of Dutch-Island,.....sixt day of July.....one Thowsand six hundred fifty and Eight

Wit.   William Hall
    John **X** Roome
      his marke
    Thomas **X** Manchester
       his marke
    Ralph **X** Earll junr
      his marke

Thomas Mumford to Peleg Sanford

.....Thomas Mumford of Pettacomscutt.....and Sarah Mumford his wife for.....Twenty five pounds currant pay of New England.....paid by Peleg Sanford of Newport.....doe.....sell.....One Thowsand Acres of Upland and Meddow.....which.....is lyinge.....within the.....limitts of the Purchass of Pettacomscutt...Fifteenth day of March 1667.....

Wit.   Thomas Mumford
    Walter Clarke
    Jireh Bull

[94] William Brenton to Peleg Sanford.

.....25th day of March 1670.....William Brenton of.....Tanton.....Collony of New-Plymoth Esqr.....give.....unto my sonn in law mr Peleg Sanford.....of Newport.....one peece.....of Land.....in.....Newport.....bounded.....on the East by the hie-way or Strand Street soe called, and North upon the Land of Captn John Cranston, and is to Extend from the Southward part of.....Cranston Land adjoyninge upon the.....Strand Street or high-way three Compleate Rodds and soe to Runn downe upon a direct straight line into the sea or harbour and westerly to runn into the.....sea or harbour soe farr as my intrest title there in is .....25th of March.....1670

Wit.   William Brenton
    Elizabeth Brenton
    John Winchcombe

Boston July 3th 1702

    John Winchcombe.....before me one of her Majtty Justice of ye peace.....did see mr William Brenton signe.....

                                Jury Corom

Aron Davis to Peleg Sanford.
.....five and twentith day of February.....1672:73.....
.....Aron Davis of Newport.....Mason, have for.....twelve acres and a halfe.....within.....Newport.....to me gianted made over and Delivered; Bargained,.....and delivered up to Peleg Sanford of.....Newport Merchant, a certaine percell.....containinge Fifteene acres.....in Newport.....bounded on the East end by the Comon and on the west end by land lately belonginge to Tho. Watterman on the North side partly by the Land of John Vahan and part on the Comon, and on the South side by Land belonginge to William Brenton Esqr. which.....Land.....with all houses.....Orchards.....Gardens,.....doe.....bargaine,.....and deliver up unto.....Peleg Sanford.....the same.....and doe.....acquitt.....Peleg Sanford.....for the above-mentioned twelve acres and halfe of Land.....acknowlidging the Receipt thereof,.....

Wit.   Aron Davis.
  Hugh Mosher
  John Greene
  Edward Richmond

Aron Davis upon the 14th of Aprill 1674 acknowlidged the above-written   Nich. Easton Gov.
        .....Mary Davis.....Declared.....she.....asented unto the act of her husband.....
                                        The marke of
                                        Mary X Davis

[95]   Thomas Waterman to
.....Fower and twentith day of February.....1672-73.....
Thomas Waterman of Aquidnessett.....Weaver, have with the.....consent.....of my wife Hannah Waterman, For .....five and thirty pounds sterllinge.....paid.....sold.....unto Peleg Sanford of Newport.....tenn acres.....within .....Newport.....bounded on the East by land of Aron Davis and on the West part on the hie-way and part on the Land of Robert Moone, and on the North by the Comon, and

on the South part by the Land of William Brenton Esqr.....
pt on the Land of the said Robt Moone

Wit.   Thomas X Waterman

  John Coggeshall Senr   his marke

  Caleb Carr

The 24th da. of February 1672.....Thomas Waterman.....
did acknowlidge.....   John Cranston Dept Gov.

[96] William Brenton to Peleg Sanford.

.....William Brenton of Newpt.....Esquire Now Resident in the Towne of Tanton.....for.....one hundred pounds sterlling currant pay.....of Rhode Island.....paid unto me by Peleg Sanford of.....Newport.....have sold.....all that percell share.....beinge in.....Newport.....contayninge Twenty Five Acres.....bounded.....North or northerly upon the Land of Peleg Sanford lately purchassed of Aron Davis, and the Land of Robert Moone. East or Easterly upon the Comon, South or Southerly upon the Land of Joseph Card and West or Westerly upon the high-way,..... To be holden of his Majtie as of his manner of East Greenwich.....Twenty fifth day of September.....1674

Wit.   William Brenton.

  John Almy

  Jahleel Brenton

[97] freemen of Newport to John Sanford.

.....at a quarter meetinge of the free-men of.....Newport .....thirtith of Aprill, one Thowsand six hundred Seventy and three, Wee...for.....Four pounds fifteene shillings and Eight pence.....paid.....by mr John Sanford of Portsmouth.....have sold.....a peece of Land lyinge.....in..... Newport.....Containinge foure Rods square, and bounded .....on the South.....by land now or late in the posession of John Odlin, on the West.....by the Land lately sold by the Towne to Peleg Sanford, on the north.....by a hie-way of two Rods wide, on the East.....by the broad street or Comon Roade.....Given under my hand.....29th day of September 1674

Wit.   Weston Clarke
Nicholas Carr   Towne Clerke.
John Odlin
free-men of Newport to Peleg Sanford.
.....the free-men.....of Newport.....the twenty Eight day of January one Thowsand six hundred seventy and three..... for.....Five pounds currant pay paid unto Captn Richard Morris up the account of the.....free-men.....Have..... sold.....unto.....Peleg Sanford.....Land lyinge in..... Newport.....Containinge Foure Rods Square.....bounded .....on the south.....by Land lately sold by the Towne to John Odlin on the West.....by the Comon or hie-way on the North.....by A hie-way of two Rods wide between the said Land and the Land of Edward Thurston on the East by Land now or late in the posession of John Sanford..... These are by an order of the free-men made the thirtith of July 1673.....to confirme unto.....Peleg Sanford.....the Land above-mentioned.....twenty Ninth day of September 1674

Wit.   Weston Clarke Towne Clerke
Nicholas Carr
John Odlin.

[98]   John Sanford to Peleg Sanford.
.....John Sanford of Portsmouth.....for.....seven pounds Sterll—currant pay of the Collony.....paid unto me by Peleg Sanford of Newport.....doe,.....sell,.....Land..... Lyinge.....in.....Newport.....beinge four Rod square .....bounded.....on the South.....by the land now or late in the posession of John Odlin, on the West.....by the land lately sold by the Townesmen of Newport unto Peleg Sanford on the North.....by a hie-way of two Rods wide on the East.....by the broad street that goeth downe the..... Towne.....second day of February.....1674
Wit.   John Sanford
  Francis Brimley
  Caleb Carr
  Covinnant betweene Peter Easton and Henry Stevens

Anno. Dom. 1652 October the 13th.

.....there is a Covinnant Betwene Peter Easton and Henry Stevens both of.....Newport.....Henry hath bought a percell of Land of.....Peter boundinge on Richard Tew his Land on the North side and east end, and on the said Peters Land on the south twenty pole wide from Richard Tew and bounds on the hie way at the West end,.....Henry Stevens doth Engage himselfe.....to.....maintaine such a fence round that.....Land, as may Secure.....Peter.....from any Cattell that may.....pass thereby, and Consideringe there is twenty pole at the East and which Richard Tew is to..... maintaine for a percell of Land.....Richard had of..... Peter Henry doth Engage himselfe.....to.....maintaine twenty rod for.....Peter in an other place, Peter hath alowed Henry 18 months after the date hereof before he make it, there is likewise a ditch on North side of this Land alredy made for which ditch Henry doth Engage himselfe to make as many Rods of Ditch in an other Convenient place where Peter shall appoint him, within eighteene months after the date hereof.....

Wit.   Peter Easton
   Richard Knight   Henry Stevens
   John Shelden

[99]   Indenture between Owin Williams and Mathew Boomer .....Indenture made the twentith day of May.....sixteen hundred fifty and Eight.....Owen Williams off Newport .....have.....made over unto Mathew Boomer of the same place.....Land beinge the one Moyety or halfe a percell of Land by me bought of mr James Barker.....the north part thereof beinge in bredth fifteen poles north and south, and in length twenty one pole and six foott East and west..... Mathew Boomer doth.....binde himselfe.....alwaies to maintaine a.....fence.....in the line on the North side..... of the whole length.....against the land of mr Barker, likewise.....on the east end thereof the whole length of that moyety against the land of mr Barker,.....two pole and five foot of fence adjoyninge to the north end of the fence at the

west end of this moyety against the Land of mr Barker so that noe Trespass or damage may at any time come to him .....and if any damage be thereby to pay full Value of it the moyety.....when it shall be devided the partition fence Boomer shall make.....the West halfe which is next the hie-way and Williams.....the east halfe next mr Barkers Land.....

Wit.   Owin Williams
  James Barker
  Marke Lucas

John Sayles to Stephen Arnold.

.....John Sayles of Providence.....Have.....sold unto Stephen Arnold of Pawtuxett.....one hundreth twenty five acres of upland.....scittuated within.....Pawtuxett..... which.....was formerly bought by.....John Sayles of Thomas Slow now of.....Providence, which.....Thomas Slow formerly bought of John Greene now of.....Warwick ....bounded northwardly with the meddows of Richard Watterman, Roger Williams, William Arnold, William Carpenter, And South East with the.....meddow of the said John Sayles (which he bought with.....the upland of..... Thomas Slow, and on the South with upland (now Comon) .....John Sayles.....shall have free Cartage of hay from his.....meddow through the.....one hundreth twenty five acres of upland.....fourteenth day of August 1659

Wit.   Jno Sayles
  Resolved Waterman
  Henry Reddocke
  Henry **X** Follers marke
  Robert Williams

[100]   William Arnold to Stephen Arnold.

.....William Arnold.....of Pawtuxet.....doe give..... unto my sonn Stephen Arnold.....a percell of meddow which was of a share formerly layd out unto Thomas Olney, the which I bought of him.....lyeth on the North Side of the.....Pawtuxett River, and is bounded on the South with the said River and on the West with Papaquinepoag and

Mashepog River and the North and North east with the Comon, And alsoe.....an acre and halfe of Land where his house and houseinge standith.....and alsoe my share.....in the Island called the Viniard which is on the North side of Pawtuxett River, by his meddow and land Runninge Round most part of it, And alsoe.....Land upon the Neck in quantity Soe many acres as is contayned in any one of the Lotts .....layd out by the thirteen in the same Neck of Land from Pawtuxett Falls Northward and the said Lands is next adjoyninge on the North Side of the afore-said Lotts and it is bounded with the affore-said Lotts on the South side and on the North side with land now in the hand and use of Zacheriah Rhoades on the West a Swamp, on the East with the Salt watter and Watermans Meddow and it is Six acres .....fourth day of Aprill.....1663.

Wit.   William Arnold.

    Zachery Roades
    The marke off **X** William Ward

Zachery Roades to Stephen Arnold.

This 18th of Aprill 1663

.....Zachery Roades.....of Pawtuxett.....doe.....grant, ...unto Stephen Arnold of.....Pawtuxett.....one hundred acres of Land which.....Lyeth.....on the North side of Pawtuxett River.....

Wit.   Zachary Roades

    John Sheldon
    John Piner

[101]   Naw-naw-nanten-new to Stephen Arnold.

.....Naw-naw-nantennew-alias-Qua-noanck-hett the Eldist-sonn now liveinge of Myantenomye my father and that he was the chiefe-Sachim of the Nanegansett bay.....and all the Teretoryes.....belonginge, And by power.....I am the cheife survivinge sachim.....doe.....pass over unto Stephen Arnold.....of Pawtuxett.....Land lyinge.....on the south side of Pawtuxett River.....the.....River boundinge it on the North from Pawtuxett Falls unto the furthest Wadeinge place in the River at Taskaunkenett on the west and from thence bounded on the south side with a straight line runninge East and by South unto the salt watter and from thence bounded on the East with the salt watter unto Pawtuxett Falls.....I doe ratefy......any former grant.....past over unto Benedict Arnold Either by my father.....or Sockcannanacow Sachim of the Pawtuxett, alsoe I.....Ratefy..... all.....Land that Kekettawekett late sachim of.....Pawtuxett deceased past over unto him by a grant.....bearinge date the Twelfth day of March.....one Thowsand six hundred and sixty,.....Thirty day of July.....one Thousand six hundred seventy and four..................

Wit.   the marke   off
    Samuell Winsor   Naw-Naw **X** noantennew
    William Hopkins   alias Quanochchhett
    Richard Everhden.
    John Cranston to Caleb Carr.

.....John Cranston of Newport.....phisician.....for..... money.....paid......by Caleb Carr of Newport.....have sold.....one halfe of the Island called.....Goulds Island alias Acqueebenawquck lyinge.....in Narragansett Bay..... one and twentith day of Aprill.....1675.

Wit.   Jon. Cranston
    Sampson **X** Battee
       his marke
    Richard Baily.

[102]   Nicholas Easton to James Barker.

.....Nicholas Easton of Newport.....Senior.....James Barker of Newport.....senior did about five and twenty years since, grant unto me.....a.....house lott lyinge..... in the said Towne, which.....house lott did formerly belong unto Robert Feild and is now in my posession......doe...... grant.....unto James Barker.....Land lyinge.....in..... Newport.....bounded.....on the North by land now or late in the posession of Richard Tew.....on the East by Stony river and on the West and south by the farme of me .....beinge about fourscore Rod in length, and twenty Rod in breadth.....containinge..... ten acres.....and is now in the posession of Mathew Boomer.....one and thirtith day of December.....1674

Wit.   Nicholas Easton
  John Cranston
  Richard Baily

[103] Connonicus to Peleg Sanford.

.....first day of May.....sixteene hundred seventy and five.....Connonocus formerly called Maussupp cheife sachim of the Narragansett &c.....doe.....make over.....unto Peleg Sanford of Newport.....A certaine Island (lyinge.....in.....Narragansett Bay,.....by the Indian Natives is called Connockenoquitt, and by the English Rose Island.....

Wit.   The marke off.
  The marke **X** of Woodhemore   **X**
  The marke of **X** Assonquewitt   Connonicus
  The marke of **X** Sawonopansqutt

These are witness as Councellers to the Sachim Connonicus
    English
  Richard Knight
  John **X** Davis
    his marke
  William Dyre.
  Edward Inman—Land Recorded.

Edward Inman now or later.....of Providence.....glover, beinge.....in.....posession of.....Land contaninge five hundred acres.....bounded at We-we-sampinsett, and from thence upon a streight line to Uomstococonnet and from umstococonnett, to the midle of a great seader swamp, to a button tree, and from thence runs to Pawtuckett river, almost North, and there bounded, by a Walnutt Tree, which..... Land was by.....Edward Inman purchassed of an Indian Called William Manannion,.....with all dwellinge or mansion houses, Barnes, Orchards, Gardens, woods,.....according to a law made the 22th of May 1662.....all.....promises are.....Ratifyed.....to be the.....Title.....First day of May 1675:

                                                       John Sanford

[104] Joseph Wise to Caleb Lambe & Stephen Williams
.....Joseph Wise Senr.....of Roxbury in the county of Suffolke.....for.....one hundred and forty pounds sterlling.....paid.....by Caleb Lambe and Stephen Williams both of Roxbury.....hath.....sold,.....one halfe of a farme.....of.....three hundred acres.....with one halfe of the housinge out housinge and fenceinge.....and one halfe of.....every.....inclosure, whether.....areaable or pastureland.....The said farme.....lyinge at a place.....called.....Neuticonquenett within the bounds of Providence,..... and is bounded Northerly by the Land of William Parke Westwardly by the Comon Southerly by Neuticonquenett river, which runs between the Land of Arthur Fenner and the said Land and Eastwardly by the Land of the heires of Hugh Buett,.....sixth day of January.....one Thousand six hundred seventy three.

Wit.   Joseph Wise Senr
   Rhoda Remington
   Jno. Gore.

Acknowledged by Joseph Wise.....18th day of the 9 month 1674   Thomas Harris Assistant

[105] John Vaughan—Land Recorded.
.....John Vaughan junr.....of Newport, beinge.....in.....posession of a percell of Land Lyinge.....at the place.....called Greene End within the Towne-shipp of Newport.....Containeinge Twelve Acres.....bounded North by the Land of mr Francis Brimley East, and West by the Comon, and South by the Land of mr Peleg Sanford..... with all dwellinge houses, Barnes,.....Gardings, Orchards,.....according to a Law made the 22th of May 1662.....All Land.....declared Ratefyed.....Recorded Fifteenth day of June 1675.

                                              John Sanford

   William Haviland to Robert Malins.
.....William Havaland of Cornhill Bay of Flushing in the North Rideinge.....of New Yorke have for.....Thirty pounds.....paid by Robert Malins of Rhode-Island in.....

Rhode-Island.....have sold.....Land lyinge neere to a place called Pettacomscutt bounded as on the North....by a hie way of forty rods wide.....between the Land of (J) Irith Bull and the said Land, on the East.....by a River.....called .....Saquatuckett River, on the south.....by land not yett dispossed off, on the West.....by land not yett dispossed off .....four-hundred Acres.....Twenty third day of Aprill one Thousand and Six hundred seventy and five.
Wit.   William Haviland
   Thom. Hicks
   Providence Williams
   Walter Wood
   Weston Clarke.
.....Hannah wife of William Haviland.....Release..... my Right of Dowry thirds.....twenty third of Aprill 1675
Wit.   Hannah **X** Haviland
   Thomas Hicks   her marke
   Weston Clarke
   Walter Wood.

[106]   John Champlin to Peleg Sanford.
.....one Thousand six hundred seventy and five,.....Ninth day of Aprill.....John Champlin late of fyall but now..... of Newport.....Merchant,.....Peleg Sanford of the same Towne.....Merchant,.....percell of Land.....twelve foott in bredth beinge the proper Land of John Champlin.....to begin at the west end of the out kitchin standing within..... John Champlins land, and soe upon a streight lyne to runn .....west southerly unto the street or hie-way that runs..... North and South.....12 foott in bredth by the street is bounded by land in the posession of John Champlin on the south and on the North side by the Land of Peleg Sanford .....John Champlin.....doth make over.....unto Peleg Sanford.....in Exchange.....of land containinge twelve foott in bredth lyinge.....in.....Newport.....abutts at the Eastern end twelve foott upon the West side of the aforesaid street and,.....on the south by land late in the posession of Willia Brenton Mercht deceassed and on the North by

Land now in the posession of Peleg Sanford and soe bearinge the bredth of 12 foott extendeth down to the Sea &c.....
Wit.   John Chimplyn
  Henry Palmer
  William Dyre
.....Henry Palmer aged 57 or thereabout & William Dyre aged 63 or thereabouts.....testify that they were witnesses.....of the above deed.....Walter Clarke Assistant.
  Thomas Gould to William Brenton.
.....Eight day of May one Thowsand six hundred seventy & five.....Thomas Gould of Aquednessett did in.....March.....in one Thowsand six hundred sixty and four.....sell to William Brenton Esqr. then of Newport.....the three hundreth part of Quononoqutt Island and Dutch Island for.....sixteen pound.....which percell.....was formerly purchassed of Thomas Fish of.....Portsmouth, and havinge not here to fore given.....William Brenton.....any deed of sale.....which Land.....William Brenton.....did.....give to his daughter Mary the then wife of Peleg Sanford of.....Newport.....by a writeinge.....bearing date the nin (torn) June one Thowsand six hundred sixty and six.....the three hundreth part of Quononaqutt Island and Dutch Island..... I.....doe.....disclaime.....all Right.....thereto,.....and .....make over.....to Peleg Sanford.....
Wit.   Thomas Gould.
  Jireh Bull
  Edw. Richmond.
[107]   James Barker Senr.—Land Recorded.
.....James Barker Senior of Newport.....beinge.... Owner By vertue of Deed of Sale.....of mr Nicholas Easton Senr.....of Newport.....bearinge date the one and Thirtith day of December.....1674.....of Land.....Scittuate within the.....Towne-shipp of Newport.....bounded North by Land now or late in the posession of Richard Tew.....on the East by Stony River, and on the West and South by the farme of.....Nicholas Easton beinge about Fourscore Rod in length, and Twenty Rodd in bredth,.....Containinge.....

Tenn Acres.....with all.....Housis out-housis.....Gardins Orchards,.....&c.....according to a law made the 22th of May 1662.....all.....promisses are.....Ratefyed.....Recorded 31t of August.....1675:

John Sanford Recorder.

Peleg Sanford to Caleb Carr.
.....Peleg Sanford of Newport.....for.....full satisfaction.....Received from mr. Caleb Carr of.....Newport senr. Doe.....make over.....one halfe part of Rose Island, ...Eleventh day of October.....1675

Wit. Peleg Sanford.

The **X** marke of
Philip Dodridge
Michall Coly.

[108] Thomas Cornell—Land Recorded.
.....Thomas Cornell Eldist son to the late.....Thomas Cornell Eldist son to mr Thomas Cornell.....of Portsmouth on Rhode-Island.....By Vertue of his Granfather and Gran Mothers wills beinge.....in.....posession of.....Land Contayneing one hundred acres.....Bounds.....Northward by the Land of Thomas Hazard &c Eastward by the Comon, Southward by the Land of mr Joshua Coggeshall, Westward by the Sea,.....with all.....dwellinge Houses, Barnes, buildings.....Gardins, Orchards,.....This.....Record according to Law made 22th May 1662.....all.....promises Ratefyed .....Recorded 25th day of January.....1675

John Sanford Recorder

Richard Tew to Seaborne Billing.
.....Richard Tew.....of Newport.....in the fourteenth yeare of.....Charles the second.....give unto my Eldist Daughter Seaborn Billing Widdow late wife of Samuell Billing deceased.....Land lyinge within.....Newport..... boundinge as followeth,.....on the west part by the Comon, on the South by the Land of David Akin, on the East by the hie waye, on the North by the land that was latly Samuells

now deceased,.....and then at her deseacease.....to be devided between her.....Daughters Amy and Mary.....
Wit. Richard Tew
William Rogers
William Shattock

[109] Seaborn Higgin—Land Recorded.
.....Seaborn the wife of Owin Higgin (late Widow to..... Samuell Billinge).....beinge.....in.....posession of Land lyinge.....within.....Newport.....Fifty Acres.....bounded north by the Comon Eighty Rod, East by the Comon and one hundred and twenty Rodds, south by the Land of Jeremiah Clarke one hundred and Twenty Rodds, and West by the Land of Thomas Rogers one hundred and twenty Rodds,..... with all.....dwelling, houses, barnes,.....Gardens, Orchards .....according to a Law made the 22 of May 1662.....all .....Land and promisses.....are Ratefied.....Recorded 16th day of February 1675:

John Sanford Recorder

Thomas Wood to Richard Tew.
.....first day of January.....one Thowsand six hundred Fifty seven; Thomas Wood of Portsmouth on Rhode-Island .....hath.....sold.....unto Richard Tew of Newport..... Forty Acres.....lyinge within.....Newport.....which Land was freely given.....by the Townsemen of Newport..... unto John Wood of Portsmouth.....lately deceassed, whoe dyinge intestate the.....land was given to.....Thomas Wood by the Towne Councell of Portsmouth.....Viztt. mr. William Baulston, mr John Roome, mr John Briggs, and mr Philip Shearman.....Land is.....bounded on the East, West, and North by the Comon on the South by William Weedens Farme beinge Eighty poles.....square.....
Wit. Thomas X Wood
John Sanford his marke.
John Anthony
Samuell Sanford

[110] Towne order.
The Towne.....in.....a former.....motion made the Gov-

ernor. Concerninge some monys disburced, by him and John Green Senr. to the Indians about goat Island and Coasters harbour.....have appointed mr John Coggeshall, mr Peter Easton and mr Thomas Ward,.....to treat with the Governor about the same. That soe he may not incuar damage by any kindness he intended to doe for this Towne.....January 31 1671

Weston Clarke
Town Clerke

Towne order.
.....There was appointed mr John Coggeshall mr Peter Easton and mr Thomas Ward, to agree with mr Benedict Arnold senior of Newport, about Coasters harbour and goate Island, and they did not agree.....whereupon the Towne thought fitt to ad unto them mr francis Breinly, mr Caleb Carr, and mr Jireh Bull.....30th of Aprill 1673.....

Weston Clarke
Town Clerke

Benedict Arnold to Towne of Newport.
Wee.....Francis Breinly John Coggeshall Caleb Carr Thomas Ward & Jiereh Bull,....freemen of.....Newport.....Beinge.....Nominated.....to treat with Benedict Arnold .....in the.....Townes behalfe to agree.....about two Islands volgerly knowne by the name of Goate Island and Coasters harbour, lyinge on the west of and neer.....to.....Newport.....by a (torn) writeinge signed by Cachanaquant a cheife sachim.....of Narragansett that the.....Islands were sold to.....Arnold.....neer upon fifteen yeares since by the.....sachim for six pounds ten shillings then paid.....and Benedict Arnold hath from the.....date hereof.....made over the said Islands to.....Newport.....for.....tenn pounds in cuntry pay or six pounds tenn shillings in New England mony.....first day of May.....sixteen hundred seventy three
Wit.

Richard Baily	Francis Breinly.
Josiah Arnold	John Coggeshall Senr.

                        Caleb Carr
                        Thomas Ward
                        Jiereh Bull

[111]   Acquittance of John Coggeshall by Generall Assembly.
.....We.....are.....by the Generall Assembly for this
Collony.....held.....att Newport on the 30th day of October 1672 to Auditt the Accounts of Mr. John Coggeshall late Treasurer of the sayd Collony.....give.....A full Acquittance.....it apeares the Collony is.....indebted unto.....John Coggeshall in the.....sum of Two Pounds, Eleven shillings and Seven pence half-penny the full Balance of Accounts betweene hime and Collony the forth Day of May .....Eleventh Day of July one Thousand sixe hundred Seventy and Three.

                        Walter Clarke
                        John Easton
                        Francis Brinley
                        Peter Easton
                        Peleg Sanford
                        Richard Bailey
                        Weston Clarke

        Recorded Augt. ye 4th 1676
                        John Coggeshall Recorder.

[112]   Walter Clarke to John Coggeshall.
.....Walter Clarke of Newpt.....for.....Threescore pounds sterling.....paid.....by John Coggeshall of Newport.....doe.....sell.....two parcells.....of Land.....in .....Newport.....the one.....containeing in Length Tenn rodd and a halfe and Nine inches, and in breadth att the East and foure Rodd and a halfe and two Foott & Six Inches, an in breadth att the West end, Foure rodd & a halfe and Fourteene inches,.....bounded on the North by Land now, or late in the Possession of William Richardson.....on the East and South by Land now.....in the Possession of Peleg Sanford.....on the West by the High-way; and the other .....Land.....is bounded on the East by the High-way afore:sayd, on the South by Land now.....in the Possession

of Peleg Sanford.....on the west by the Sea, or Harbour of the.....Towne of Newpt, and on the North by Land now .....in the Possession of William Richardson, the breadth .....being.....layd out According as the sayd lines of the Parcell abovementioned.....first day of June.....1674

Wit.   Walter Clarke

   Daniell Gould

   Joseph Bryer

   Richard Bailey.

   Hannah Clarke Releases Rights.

.....Hannah Clarke wife of.....Walter Clarke, doe..... Relinquish,.....any right..... which I now have..... to the two Parcells of Land above mentioned.....

Wit.   Hannah Clarke

   Daniell Gould

   Joseph Bryer

   Richard Baily

   Agreement between William Coddington and John Coggeshall.

.....William Coddington of Newpt senr.....is to.....mainetaine......A......fence......against......John Coggeshalls farme.....to begin att the Lower end of the Neck comonly called Jefferys Neck (being Land which.....William..... bought of Robert Jefferys,.....) att the mouth of the Creeke which runeth into.....Johns Marshes, from the salt sea, being the Southwesterly corner of the sayd Johns farme, and soe to run as the fence now stands untill it comes to A peice of ditch which runs about five or sixe rodds from the Upland Easterly into ye sayd marshes.

Likewise it is.....agreed.....that.....John Coggeshall is to.....mainetaine......A.....fence.....as the fence now stands, beginning at the corner of the abovesayd Ditch which runs into the sd Marsh, & soe untill it meets with the sayd Williams outside Westerly line next the Comon.....William doe grant.....John free Egress.....to draw out stones off

his.....Ground.....to make the.....line of fence betweext them.....25th of Augt. 1668.
Wit. William Coddington.
   Francis Brinley
   Elizabeth Burden

[114] Grounds for Divource between John Coggeshall and wife
.....for as much as you Elizabeth Baulston whome I epoused,.....soe fare failed, neglected, and utterly refused to Performe the Marriage Covent., and by your.....urgiant Oppertunity to be Divourced, and to be sett free;.....am I forced to give you this Dismission.....3d of Oct. 1654.

[115] Agreement to Divource by Elizabeth Baulston.
.....This sheweth, that.....ye Divource which my Late Husband, John Coggeshall gave me,.....is.....by me desired 3d of Oct. 1654
Wit.   her
   Thomas Cornell senior.   Elizabeth X Baulston
   Henry X Bulls marke   marke

Court frees John Coggeshall from his wife.
Providence, 25th 3d (55)
.....Mr John Coggeshall Exhibited his Petition to ye Collony Court of Comissiones for A legal discharge from his Late Wife Elizabeth Baulston,.....hee is Absolutely free.....to Contract Another Marriage.
                        Roger Williams President

[116] John Coggeshall—Land Recorded.
.....Mr John Coggeshall of Newpt.....beinge.....this Thirteenth Day of Septr.....one Thowsand sixe hundred sixty and five, in.....Possession of.....Lands in.....Newpt ....bounded.....on ye East & South by ye sea, on ye west and South-west by Land in the Possession of Mr William Coddington on ye North-west and North by A High-way, & Land by hime formerly sould to Isaac Page now in the Possession of William Reape, on the north and Northerly by Land in the Possession of Hugh Mossier, William and Francis Vahan and Mr Wm Brenton; which Land some of it layd

out to Mr John Coggeshall Senior deceaced; which part amounts to.....Three Hundred Akers.....alsoe one percell bought of Mr Robert Jefferys, formerly of Newport..... amounting to.....Ninety Akers.....Ajoyneinge to the first some layd out,.....lyes on the West and Southwest against the land of.....Coddington.....Alsoe one part.....bought of Capt Jerimy Clarke and William Vahan and Frances his Wife that was formerly the Wife of.....Jeremiah Clarke, to the number of one Hundred and Twenty Akers.....all which Land.....Amounting to.....Five Hundred and Ten Ackers.....is now in.....Posession of.....John Coggeshall.....Thirtenth Day of September.....one Thowsand Sixe-Hundred sixty and Five.....

Joseph Torrey Generall Recorder

[117] John Smith to Stephen Sabeere.
.....John Smith of Providence Junior Brother and heire unto Leonard Smith late Resident of Newport.....deceased,..... for.....Seventeen Pounds currant Silver Money of New-England.....Payd.....by Stephen Sabeere of Newport..... doe.....sell.....A certaine house Lott being in.....Newport.....being fourty foott Square, bounded.....on the North-East by A high-way, on the South East by Lott not yett Granted, the south west by a Lott now.....in the Possession of Edward Watterson, and on the north west by the Brooke, or Comon, together with A frame for A Dwelling House on the.....Lott Erected, and all the worke thereunto done, and all Materialls.....now brought.....Twentieth day of Octr.....1676.

[118] Wit.   John X Smith
  John Hulme   his marke
  James Browne
  Richard Baily

John Sanford to James Rogers
.....John Sanford of Portsmouth.....doe.....sell unto James Rogers of Newport.....A forth part of Cononicatt Island.....and Dutch Island.....being one Hundred and Twenty Akers.....Bounded.....south upon the Towne shipp

west upon the Sea, North upon the Land which is Peleg Sanfords, East upon the high way,.....Nineteenth Day of November.....one Thousand sixe Hundred fifety and nine.
Wit.   John Sanford
  Richard Pearce
  Richard Bulgere.

James Rogers to William Brenton.
.....James Rogers of Newpt.....doe.....make over this Present Deed unto Mr William Brenton of Newport.....one and Twentieth of March 1659.

60

Wit.   The **X** marke of
  William Baulston   James Rogers
  Will Dyre

[119] Jahleel Brenton to Joseph Browne.
.....Jahleel Brenton of Newport.....Gentleman.....doe.....release,.....unto Joseph Browne of Charles Towne Minister of the Gospell.....all such.....Lands.....Granted unto hime by my Honoed Father William Brenton lat of Newport.....deceased.....Eighteenth Day of November.....One Thousand, Six Hundred, Seventy and Sixe.
Wit.   Jahleel Brenton
  Benja Browne
  Richard Baily.

[120] Edward Rainebrow to William Browne.
.....Edward Rainebrow of Knights bridge in the County of Middx.....England Esqr.....for.....five hundred Seaventy and five Pounds of.....mony of New-England to me .....by William Browne senr of Salem in.....Essex in.....Massathusets.....Marcht.....Doe.....sell.....one Moitie .....of Prudence Island.....lyeing.....in the Bay of Narraganset neare unto Rhod-Island.....Twenty first day of February.....one Thousand six hundred Seaventy and two .....
Wit.   Edward Rainbrow
  Thomas Deane
  John Paine
  John Hayward senr

[121]   Prudence Island Deed certified.
Boston in the Mattachusetts Colony.....
.....certifie.....that the.....Deed herewith annexed.....
of Edward Rainbrow.....unto William Browne senior for
the Moity of Prudence Island is.....Legall.....according to
Law.....before Edward Tyng Esqr an Assistant in the Government of this Colony.....first day of September..........
1676.   John Leverett Govr.

[123]   James Barker and Elisha Smith.
16 day 8 mo. 75.
.....between us James Barker senior and Elisha Smith.....
both of Rhod-Island.....have Agreed.....that the Bounds
betweene our two Farmes is......First that the old bound
marked Brooke neare ould mr Smiths House where.....
Barkers fence comes downe on the South side to the old bound
by the brooke side,.....from that bound to that end of the
farme the fence that old Mr. Smith made and mainetained for
many yeares mentioned, shall Perpetually for ever betweene
us, and to end att James Mans corner of his fences of the
Land had of Mr Smith by Agreement......
Wit.   James Barker
   Obadiah Holme   Elisha Smith
   The marke of John **X** Pepodey
   The marke of Georg **X** Keech

   Jeffery Champlin to Walter Clarke.
.....Eight Day of May.....Sixteene Hundred sixty and
nine.....Jeffery Champlin senr. Inhabitant now in Squamacutt, (Alis Kings Province Shoemaker, hath.....sold unto
Walter Clarke of Newport.....Land and Houseing, lyeing
in Newport.....Bounded on the East by the Land of Walter
Conigrave, on the north by ye Land of Robert Burdick and
Andrew Langworthy, and on the South and west to the Highways, Containeing Fourty Akers.....
Wit.   The marke of
   James Barker   Jeffery **X** Champlin
   Joseph Bryer
   Nicholas Easton Junr.

[124] Walter Clarke—Land Recorded.

.....Walter Clarke (son of Capt. Jeremiah Clarke Deceased) of Newport.....beinge.....this.....fourth Day of October .....one Thowsand Sixe Hundred sixety and five, in..... Possession.....of Land in.....Newport.....Bounded..... one Parcell being Fifty Ackers.....bounded on the north by Land.....of Mr Nicholas Easton formerly by hime bought of John Smith Deceased, on the East, and part on the South by other Lands of.....Nicholas Easton, and further on the Southerly Line by a swampe haveing there A Turneing before it comes to the Swampe, that the sayd Eastons Land border againe upon it on the East, which Swampe aforesayd is comonly called Bracys swampe, as alsoe bordering on..... Land.....of Thomas Clifton, and Westerly by Land.....of Benedict Arnold, or high-way; alsoe one Parcell Lyeing neare and fronting against are Towne, bounded North.....by the Common, and A high or Drift way goeing out of the Streete or Comon up Easterly betwext the Land of the sayd Walter Clarke And the Land.....of Thomas Waterman, that was formerly the land of Robert Griffon, on the East or South-East by Land sold by.....Clarke to Mr William Brenton, and on the south by Land of ye William Brenton bought of Walter Clarke and Jeffery Champlin, and on the West by Land of Peleg Sanford, Mr John Gard, and the sayd Brenton, which Percell amounts to.....Twenty Ackers.....Alsoe one Orchard bounded East by the Land of Peleg Sanford, South by Land of Mr John Coggeshall, West by the Highway, North by the Comon, with A smal Percell betweext the Last mentioned High way and the sea, south by John Coggeshall North by the High-way; all.....Parcells.....Amount to seventy Ackers.....with all.....belonging As one Dweling house, one Barne, with all housing, fruit Trees.....this Deed, ...is to Ratifie.....the same.....unto the sayd Walter Clarke;.....

      Joseph Torrey Generall Recorder.

[125] Mathew West to Nathaniell West.

.....mathew West of.....Newport.....Tayler,.....unto

my Grand-Child Nathaniell West, sonn of my Eldest Son Nathaniell West who did depart this life many yeares agoe; And for as much my.....Grand-child.....doth, live with mee,.....I.....have freely Given,.....my.....Grand-Child .....my Dwelling Howse I now live in, with all Land there unto.....belonging.....Fowrty Akers.....lyeing.....within.....Newport,.....bounded, Northerly by the Land of John Crandall, Southerly by the Land of John Thornton, Eastwardly, and Westerly by the Common which.....Formerly belonged unto John Roe, and Edward Brouse.....with All dwellings, or mansion Howse,.....Fenceings, Gardens, Orchards.....belonging,.....Sixteenth day of January..... one Thowsand Sixe Hundred Seventy and Sixe.....77.
Wit.   Mathew West

  The marke of
John X Parker
    The marke of
Dorathy X Haward
Edmond Colverly

[126]   William Richardson to Walter Newbery.
New Yorke the 9 - day of.....July 1674.
.....William Richardson - marrinar, master of the Catch May-Flower, now in the Road of New-Yorke and late Inhabitant of Rhod-Island.....for.....valliable Satisfaction..... payd;.....Have.....sold.....unto Walter Newbery of London Mchant - now residing in Rhod-Island - One Dwelling House,.....standing in.....Newport Towne.....now in the Possession of one Amey Paine Widdow, Tenant,.....unto the aforesayd William Richardson.....with all.....Lands, Orchards, Gardens, woods, underwoods, Timbers,.....Commons, Pastures, ways, Waters,.....Ware-Houses, Wharfreige, Cellers,.....Nineth day of.....Fifth month,.....1674.
Wit.   William Richardson

  Walter Clarke
  Robt Ford
  The marke of
Tho: X Winterton.

[127] John Porter to William Gardiner.
.....John Porter of Petiqomscut in Narrogansett.....
have.....Granted unto William Gardiner, son to Georg Gardiner at Newport,.....Land, bounded Westerly on Henry Gardiners Land, Northerly on A High-way lyeing next Benony Gardiners Land, Southerly on Samuell Wilbors Land, and Easterly on John Porters Land.....containeing two Hundred Acers of Land.....first of January one Thowsand sixe hundred seventy and one,.....

Wit.   John Porter
  Henry Gardiner his **X** marke   Horad Porter
  Benany Gardiner his **X** marke   her **X** marke

[128] Protest of John Herbert.
Newport on Rhod-Island February 26th 1676.
.....be it knowne.....That.....did Personally apeare before me John Coggeshall.....John Herbert Commander of the Sloope Swan; and did Alleage.....by the Testimonies of these Wittnesses.....Israell Spencer and John Harcer, marriners aboard the - sloope.....on the 13th.....being on A voyage.....bound for New-York, they were by Tempestuous wind and seas, and.....Darkness of the Wether Concurring, forced A shore upon the Sandy point of Monnainoy.....on behalfe of himselfe and Company, and alsoe for the owners of the - Sloope,....:.doth - Publickly.....Protest against the sea, winde, and bad wether, for all Losses.....

Mathew Boomer—Land Recorded.
.....Mathew Boomer of.....Newport.....beinge.....in Posession of.....Land, lyeing.....in.....Newport,.....Ten Acres.....Purchased of Henry Stevens of Peter Easton..... beinge.....bounded.....on the North side and East and upon the Land of Henry Tew, formerly belonging to Richard Tew Deceased on the south upon the Land of Peter Easton, being Twenty Pole wide from.....Richard Tews Land, now.....of his son Henry.....on the West end on the Hye-way.....with all.....Dwelling, or Mansion Houses, Barnes,.....Orchards, Gardens,.....according to a Law made.....the 22th of May 1662.....All.....Promisses, are hereby Ratified.....Recorded 26th of February 1676.
                                          John Coggeshall.

[129] John Parker—Land Recorded.

.....John Parker of Newport.....being.....in.....Possession of.....Land, lyeing in.....Newport.....Thirty one Acers - bounded Southerly upon the Land of Edward Robinson - Easterly upon the Land of John Allin, and upon the Common, Northerly and Westerly upon the Comon, Twentone Acres was Purchased of John Allin, Ten Acres was Purchased of Robert Tayler Husbandman,.....with all Dwelling, or Mantion Howses, Barnes,.....Orchards, Gardens,.....belonging.....according to a Law made.....the 22th of May 1662.....All.....are hereby Ratified,..... Recorded.....26th of February 1676.

John Coggeshall.

[130] Henry Stevens to Mathew Boomer.

.....Henry Stevens of Newport.....Blacksmith, did about Eighteene yeares since,.....make over unto Mathew Boomer of Newport.....Land, lyeing.....in Newport.....tenn Akers bounded on the North and East with Land formerly in the Possession of Richard Tew deceased, on the South by Land.....of Peter Easton, and on the West by A High way, ...being Twenty Pole wide.....the.....Deed.....was lost when his House was Burned by the Indians during these late Warrs. These are.....to confirme unto.....Mathew Boomer.....the.....Tenn Acres.....six and Twenteth Day of February, one Thowsand, six hundred seventy and six.
Wit. Henry Stevens.

   John Coggeshall
   Richard Baily

   Mathew Boomer to Georg Browne.

.....Mathew Boomer of Newport.....for.....one and Thirty pounds currant Silver money of New England..... paid.....by Georg Browne of Newport.....Planter,..... have Granted.....Land, Lyeing.....in.....newport.....Ten Acres......bounded.....on the North and East by Land lately in the Possession of Richard Tew deceased, on the South by Land.....of Peter Easton, and on the West by A

High way, the.....Land.....Granted.....in bredth Twenty Rod.....six and Twentieth day of February.....1676.
Wit. Mathew Boomer
  Thomas Ward
  Richard Barnes
  Richard Baily

[131] David Greenman—Land Recorded.
.....one Thowsand six hundred and fourty Eight.....Land Containeing Thirety Acres.....lyeing on the Easterne end of David Greenmans, Edward Greenmans, and John Greens Lands.....bounded on the Southern side by.....Land which .....David, Edward and John bought.....of Mr Easton, and bounded on the East by the Hie-way to the Land of Mr Brenton comonly called the Pinnfold, and boundeth upon the border of the.....Land by markes at the Brooke side downe to Jeremy Goulds fence, and then by the corner of.....Jeremiah Goulds farme down to the Eastern end of John Wests Lands, and soe by the afore-sayd line,.....of.....David, and Edward.....Thirty Acres of Land.....is fully Impropriated.....first of Aprill.....1648.
                        William Dyre Genr Recordr.

[132] Nicholas Easton to David and Edward Greenman.
.....Land Containeing Twenty Acres.....lyeing at the Eastern end of David and Edward Greenmans Land, bounded on the south by John Greens Land on the East by the hie way to the Pinfold, on the North by the Land of David and Edward Greenman, which.....Land being the.....Possessions of Nicholas Easton of Newport.....doth.....sell unto David and Edward Greenman.....with another Percell..... containeing seven Acres.....lyeing at the west end of..... David and Edwards Lands, and bounded all else by the Comon,.....First Day of Aprill.....1648
Wit. Nick: Easton
  William Dyre
  Jeremiah Willis
  John Horndells **X** marke.

Edward Greenman from Towne of Newport.

.....28th of July.....sixteene hundred fifety and eight,..... Edward Greenman Wheelright on the Thirteenth of Aprill .....1656 made.....Complaint unto the Towne of Newport for want of Land. The Towne then ordered that Georg Bliss, Mr Edward Smith, Obediah Holmes should near his Dwelling House out of the Comon lay out to hime what he wanted, not infringing any hyeway, which.....they did.....bearing date the tenth of July 1656.....Bounded, the breadth..... aboute Ten Rod long at one side, which is Northerly, and some Twenty two Rod long at the other side,.....southerly, the west and East side is as long as the Land bought of Jeremiah Clarke is broad, bounded at the Northwest and Southwest corners by two smal white oakes, Containeing four Acres and halfe.....on the Twenty seventh of January 1657 .....the Towne Clerke Marke Luker should.....make A deed.....unto.....Edward.....

Wit.
   John Gould
   Samuell Hubbard

Marke Lucar
Towne Clerke

[133] Robert Carr to Samuell Davis.

.....Robert Carr of Newport.....senior.....for.....one Hundred pounds currant silver money of New-England part .....was payd.....by Nicholas Davis late of Newport..... deceased.....and the Remainer, by his son Samuell Davis .....have.....sould.....Samuell Davis.....two pieces..... of Land, lyeing.....in.....Newport.....bounded.....on the north by Land.....of mee.....on the East by Land..... late.....of William Brenton Deceased, on the South by Land .....of Caleb Carr, and on the West by the streete, or highway,.....being in bredth at the East end Seven Rodd, and at the west end six rodd & two fott, out of which I.....have reserved to myselfe,.....A smal piece of Land for a Burieing place to contain Eight foott of Ground each way from A Rock there being; The.....other.....Land.....is bounded on the North by Land in ye Possession of mee,.....on the East by the streete or Highway - on the south by Land.....

late.....of.....Caleb Carr, and on the west by the sea or Harbour of.....Newport.....sixteenth day of March..... 1676.
Wit.   Robert Carr

  John Cranston
  John Greene ser
  Richard Baily

[134] John Porter to Nicholas Gardiner.

.....John Porter December 27 - 1671 - have.....made over.....my whole Intrest.....of A sixt part of the Thowsand Acres..... Layd out to us the six Purchassers of the Narragansett Land. Viz - John Porter, Samuell Wilbore, John Hull, Thomas Mumford, Samuell Wilson, and William Brenton; which.....Land lyes neare the Land Layd out to Henry Knowles, which sixt part.....I have made over.....unto Nicholas Gardiner haveing received full Satisfaction.....

Wit.   John Porter
  Lodowick Updicke   Horad Porter
  Georg Gardiner   her X marke
    his X marke.

[135] Georg Gardiner to Nicholas Gardiner.

November the 7 - 1673

.....Georg Gardiner have made over.....unto Nicholas Gardiner Threescore Akers of Land, bounded.....on the south side on Benony Gardiners Land, the 1000 Acres lyeing on the north side of it, and the sayd Land is to be layd out at the Eastward end of the sayd Georges Land.....

Wit.   Georg Gardiner
  John Watson   Tabiatha Gardiner
  Dorcus Watson   her X marke.
    her X marke

John Porter to Nicholas Gardiner.

November - 22th 1673.

.....John Porter & Horad Porter my wife doe.....give unto Nicholas Gardiner one Hundred Akers of Land bounded..... northerly, on the Thowsand Acres formerly layd out to Benedict Arnold.....and Easterly on John Watsons Land,

and Westerly on Benony Gardiners Land, and sotherly on John Watsons Land.....

Wit.
  John Watson
  Georg Hikes
  his X marke

John Porter
Horad Porter
her X marke

[136] Protest of John Goose.

Newport.....March 28th 1677.

.....on the.....Date hereof did.....appear before mee.....John Coggeshall.....John Goose Comander of the Ketch Society, with his Company.....and doth.....enter their Protest against the said Ketch for her Insufficiency to indure the sea.....in ordinary wether her seames would open.....and when they carryed sayle,.....she would - take in soe much water to Lee-ward,.....that we were forced to keepe the pumps goeing.....

      John Goose
        signed
      Thomas X Banfield
      Edward X Barton
        his marke
      John Cheritrie
      Passongers
        Ralfe Blackhall
        Frances Ellis

[137] John Hickes to Stephen Sabeere.

.....John Hickes of Newport.....shipcarpenter.....for.....Twenty and five shillings.....payd.....by Stephen Sabeere of Newport.....have remised.....a.....House Lott lyeing.....in.....Newport.....which was granted January.....Twenty eight one Thowsand six hundred seventy six being forty foott square, and bounded.....on the north east by A High way; on the south east by Lott not yett Granted; on the south west by a Lott.....late.....of Edward Waterson, and on the north west by the Brooke or Comon.....first day of Aprill.....1677.

Wit.   John Hickes
   Peleg Santora
   Edmund Colverley
   Samuell Andrews Protests.
Newport.....Aprill 11th 1677.
   .....on the.....Date hereof, did......Samuell Andrews, Comander of the Ketch Providence, and did.....Prove by .....these Wittnesses.....John Weeden, John Coe, Thomas Rapere, Marriners aboard the sayd Ketch, that.....Samuell Andrews being on a Voyage with the sayd Ketch,.....bound for New-York, they were by Tempestuous wind and Seas, ...and very firce Raigne Concurring, forced A shore Upon A sandy Beach, on Rhod-Island.....being open to the Otion, and very great Brakers,.....on behalfe of himselfe and Company.....doth.....Protest.....
                                              John Coggeshall
[138]   Walter Todd to Thomas Greene.
   .....Walter Todd.....of Warwick.....for.....full satisfaction.....payd by Thomas Greene of the sayd Towne..... have.....Granted.....one Lott lying in Shawomett Neck neere.....Warwick, Containeing Eighteene Acres.....being amongst the second Devision of Lotts (there).....the Sixteenth Lott, Bounded upon the Southerly side by A Twelve Acre Lott.....of Captaine John Greene, Northerly by A Lott.....of Benjamine Barton of the same Tenner knowne upon Record.....to be the Seventeenth Lott, there being at the Northerne corner of this Sixteenth Lott A Pine Tree blowne downe, and A stone pitcht at the roote thereof by the highway, from thence Easterly upon A straight line to A Saxefrex stumpe upon the brinke of the banke by the sea, also at the North east side of Captaine John Greenes Twelve Acre Lott, is A great stone pitcht, And from thence upon A straite line Northerly to A yong Walnutt Tree with stones pitcht at the roote thereof, and from thence upon A straight Line Easterly downe to the sea, A stone being there pitcht by the sea, Alsoe.....one smal Lott, sett.....in..... Shawomett Neck, five Acres,.....Numbered.....the Eleventh

Lott, And lyeth amongst the Third Devision of Lotts in the
.....Neck, Bounded by Captaine Randall Houldens Lott of
the same Tennure, Numbered.....the Tenth Lott, and on
the Northerly side by A Lott of the same Tenure.....in the
Tenure.....of John Warner, Numbered.....the Twelfth
Lott, westerly by A High way that leads through.....Shawo-
mett Neck, and - Easterly by the Meadows that lye by the
Sea,.....Ninth Day of March.....one Thowsand six Hundred Seventy and Three, 74.

Wit.   Walter Todd
   Edmund Colverley   Margrett Todd
   Richard Codner

[139]   Leiftenant Eliza Collins to Thomas Greene.
.....Leiftenant Eliza Collins.....of the Towne of Warwick
.....have Indented,.....unto Mr Thomas Green.....of
Warwick my dwelling house and house-Lott.....the - House
Lott being bounded, Northeasterly by Mr Edmund Calverly
his house Lott, Southerly by the streete; Southwesterly by
the house Lott of Thomas Greene aforesayd, and at the North
end - by A sixe Aker Lott.....being likewise Bounded on
each side by the Land of Thomas Greene, and Edmund Calverly, as alsoe Three shares of Meddow, one of them lyeing
att Toskeunke, Alias Papiassit being.....the Sixteenth share,
another share lyeing at Potaomet, being - the Nineteenth
share, as alsoe the other share lyeing neare the sea side on
the Southwest side of Nausaucut Neck of Land.....23d day
of June.....1664.....

Wit.   Eliza Collins
   John Green   Sarah Collins
   Edmund Calverley
   John Potter

[140]   John Greene to James and Thomas Greene.
.....John Greene.....in.....1662 the sixteenth Day of
June bought A percell of Land fronting on my Neck of land
att Occuppessuatuxet westerly being Bounded, Southerly by
Warwick North line, and Northerly by A due West line from
the head of Patiunco Cove, and soe downe to Petuxet River,

as by an Instrument beareing date ye Sixteenth of June aforesayd under Mossups hand.....may Apeare, Therefore I.....doe give,.....unto my two Brothers Mr James Greene and Mr Thomas Greene.....A certaine percell of the sayd Land, bounded.....begining at A white Oake Tree marked in Warwick North line, being about one Hundred fifty six Pole westward from the front fence of my Neck aforesayd, as alsoe beginning at A bounder the same depth from the front fence on the south side, and is to range the whole breadth Westward soe farr as the Boggie Meddows by the spruse swampe it being A bounder thereof, and soe ranging by the North end of the spruce swampe to A black-Oake, and thence to A smale Oake, and further to A Great white Oake neare Warwick north line, and from those two last Bounders being about halfe the breadth of the Purchase unto too marked trees at the west end thereof being about 272 Rodd deepe further about halfe the breadth as aforesayd, reserveing six Rodd for the High way to Petuxott at the Valley, as alsoe a Highway six rodd wide from my share of Land fronting on my Neck aforesayd to the sayd Valley, neare where the Cartway now is, and from the Valley due West neare the middest of this Land before specified leading towards Potaconksitt.....30th of March 1675.

Wit.   John Greene senr.
  Jaremiah Wastcott
  Phillip Greene

[141] Will of William Almy.

William Almy doe.....bequeath.....my Body to be Buryed by my son John if I dye here upon my farme, and. my Wordly goods if my Wife out Live mee shee shall have.....and after her Death Christopher shall have halfe my farme,..... which is next to the Land which gave to my son John Almy; and for my Mault-House, whose share it falls into they shall have equall shares of it, not to devide it but to keepe it for A mault-House for every season, And the other halfe of my farme, I give it to my Son Job Almy, with my Dwelling House, & too Orchards;.....and for my Catle, and the move-

able,.....remaining at our Deathes, I give to my Daughter Anna and my Daughter Kathren each of them two parts, And to my son Christopher Almy. And my son Job Almy each of them one part, and to my Grand Child Bartholmew West, ...Twenty Pounds silver money to be payd hime when he comes to Age Last of February 1676.
Wit.   William Almy.
  Robert Hodgson
  James Barker seanr.

[142] Atestation of Robert Hodgson and James Barker.
.....Robert Hodgson and James Barker on the 23 - of - Aprill 1677 did Apeare before.....the Councell of the Towne of Portsmouth and did afirme that the above written was the Will of the Deceased William Almy.
  John Heath
  Francis X Braiton
     his marke

                                Joshua Coggeshall Assist.
                                Wm. Cadman Assist.
                                John Sanford
                                Samuell Wilbor

  Orders of Councell.
.....Genll. Councell.....of Rhod-Island.....21th of 2d mo called Aprill 1677.
.....ordered that the Powder & Amonition, & Bread, in the Custody of John Coggeshall Treasurer & William Brinley Comissary belonging to the Island......be. Delivered unto Walter Clarke Governr. by him to be keept for security, in part,.....
  William Cadman   Assistt.   Walter Clarke   Govr.
  Randele Houlden Assistt.   Jon Cranston   Dept. Govr.
  Samll Gorton   Assistt.   James Barker   Assistt.
  John Coggeshall   Assistt.   John Easton   Assistt.
                                    Joshua Coggeshall Assistt.

[143] William Coddington to David and Edward Greeneman.
.....William Coddington Esqr. doe Assigne.....Sixty two Akers.....lyeing on the Easterly side of the mil brooke,

bounded on the south by the High-way that goes to Portsmouth, or the great Comon, and on the North, by John Smiths Land,.....to David Greeneman, and Edward Greeneman of the sayd Towne.....which Percell of Land was Purchased by mee of Robert Carr of the sayd Towne.....tenth of Aprill one Thowsand six Hundred fourty and two.

William Coddington Gor.

[144] Benedict Arnold to Penelope and Roger Gouldinge.
.....Benedict Arnold of Newport.....senr.....unto my .....Daughter Penelope Gouldinge wife of Roger Goulding, as.....part of her dowrey;.....Have, Given,.....two peeces of land, lyinge.....in.....Newport.....whose bounds..... are.....on the west by the sea or harbour of the. Towne, on the North by a Comon hie-way, on the East by a certaine hie-way of two Rod wide, which I have laid forth of my owne land for the use of my selfe.....To Extend to certaine land by me Given.....to my Sonn Benedict Arnold junr., and on the south by land in posession of mee.....The.....land..... beinge in bredth at the East and Seven rod and a foot, and at the west and six Rodd the North side beinge.....as the fence now stands, and the south side on a straight line from one of the ends unto the other., The other.....Land.....is bounded on the west by the hie-way, and on the East and South by land in the posession of me.....beinge in bredth, at the west end seven Rodd and a foot, and at the East end Six Rodd, the North side beinge in length Seven Rodd and three foot and the south side six Rodd,.....four and twentith day of June.....1676.
Wit.   Benedict Arnold Senr.
   Aron Davis
   Benedict Arnold junr.
   Richard Bayly.

[145] Peleg Tripp to George Sisson.
.....Peleg Tripp of.....Dartmoth in.....New-plymoth .....yeoman.....for.....the.....Mutuall Exchange of thirty two acres of Land in.....Portsmouth.....made between my selfe and George Sisson.....of Portsmouth.....

doe alien unto.....George Sisson.....three eight parts of a whole share.....in.....the Towne-shipp of Dartmoth..... The devided part - beinge.....bounded.....Thirty acres .....North by the way to the fishinge place, Easterly by the great river, southerly by the land of Joseph Tripp, and westerly by the Comon, Thirty acres.....lyinge at the fresh pond, lyinge westward, from the afore-named thirty acres;..... bounded North with the land of Richard Sisson, west with the said fresh pond, south, and East by the Comon, and fifteene acres of land.....bounded south by the land of William Cadman East by the River North and west by the Comon All .....land.....amounting.....to.....seventy five acres..... with all houses Orchards.....To bee Holden of his Majtie .....as of his manner of East Greenwich.....seventh day of Aprill.....one Thowsand six hundred seventy seven.

Wit.   Peleg Tripp.
  John Sanford.
  Benj. **X** Congdon.
    his marke

[146]   Thomas Burge to Thomas Ward

Thomas Burge of Newport.....for.....six and Twenty pounds and tenn shillings currant Silver mony of New-England,.....paid.....by Thomas Ward of Newport..... Merchant.....have.....sold.....one quarter.....of a..... share of Land both upland and medow. beinge at Achushena in the Towne-shipp of Dartmoth in.....Plymoth.....and alsoe one third part.....of a halfe.....share of Land, both upland and medow.....beinge at.....Pescomancusk in the Towne-ship of Dartmoth.....both.....percells.....I purchassed together with other land of Robert Bartlett of Plymoth.....nine - and Twentith day of July.....1671.

Wit.   Thomas Burge
  John Read   Lillia Burge
  Richard Baily   her **X** marke

[147]   William Mirick to Thomas Ward.

.....William Mirick senr. of Eastham in.....New-Plymoth .....husbandman.....for.....nine pounds.....paid by

Thomas Ward of Rhode-Island Merchant.....doe.....sell .....one halfe of all my share of Land at Seconnett..... which.....Land was granted by the Court of New-plymoth .....to the old servants whereof.....William Mirick is one.....31 of January.....one Thowsand six hundred seventy and three.

Wit.   William Meyrik.
  Samuell Treate.
  Stephen Peaige.

                   .....William Mirick and Rebeckah
                   his wife made apeareance.....
                                John Freeman Asistant

[148] Thomas Burge to Thomas Ward.
Thomas Burge of Newport.....for.....twinty pounds currant Silver money of New England.....paid.....by Thomas Ward of Newport.....Merchant.....have.....sould..... one quarter.....of a part.....of land.....beinge at Acushena in the Towneship of Dartmouth in.....New Plimoth .....five and twentieth day of January.....1674.

Wit.   Thomas Burge
  Richard Barnes.
  Richard . Baily

Thomas Burg of Newport and Liddia his wife.....acknowledged the above.....June 27th 1677
                                 Joseph Clarke Asistant

[149] John Almy to Thomas Ward.
.....John Almy of portsmouth.....Merchant.....for..... seven pounds sterll.....paid by Thomas Ward of Newport .....Merchant.....doe.....sell.....one halfe share..... of Land on the Neck called Seconnet and parts adjacent..... Twenty seventh day of January.....one Thowsand six hundred and seventy five.

Wit.   John Almy
  William Hiscox   .....Mary Almy the wife of.....
  John Read.   John Almy doe.....give my
                       consent.....
                                     Mary Almy

[150] Mathew Mayhew to Peleg Sanford, etc.

.....Mathew Mayhew of Martins Vinyard in America son and heire of Thomas Mayhew Junr. deceassed.....my Grand father Thomas Mayhew, and my Father Thomas Mayhew .....did.....receive.....of the Honod the Lord Sterling a grant of.....certaine Islands neere to Martins Vinyard afore-said called.....Elszabeth Islands.....under certaine Conditions.....I.....for.....twelve pounds currant mony of New-England.....paid by Peleg Sanford, Phillip Smith and Thomas Ward, all of Newport.....doe.....make over ....the two westermost of the.....Elsabeth Islands..... seven and Twentith day of October 1674.

Wit.   Mathew Mayhew
   Tristram Coffin
   Richard Barnes
   Richard Baily

Newport.....September 16th 1681 Richard Barnes..... Testefieth that the above.....was signed.....by Mathew Mayhew   Before mee Caleb Carr Asistant

[151] freemen of Newport to Thomas Fry.

.....the freemen.....of Newport.....29th of January 1672 .....granted unto Thomas Fry.....of Newport.....a hause lott of forty square.....beinge among the small lotts, latly .....layd out in the Towne, the lott bounded.....on the East by a hie-way of two Rods wide on the South by the broad Street, on the west by a lott granted unto Nicholas Easton now in - posessition of William Edwards, on the North by a lott granted unto Walter Wood.

.....Order of - free-men.....30th day of July 1673..... to confirme.....said Lott of forty foot square,.....third day of February 1676

                         Weston Clarke, Towne Clerke.

freemen of Newport to Michall Kaley.

.....freemen of Newport.....Asembled January Twenty eight 1673.....granted unto Michall Kaley a house lott of forty foot square.....beinge among the small lott.....layd forth in the Towne.....the Lott bounded.....on the west by a lott laid out, but not yet granted on the South by a Lott granted unto William Weeden, on the East by a hie way of two rod wide, on the North by a lott granted Robert Taylor Ropemakr.....Order of freemen.....Thirtith day of July 1673 to confirme.....the said Lott,.....25th of| October 1676.

Weston Clarke Towne Clerke

[152]   Joan Reape to Zacheriah Rhodes.
.....Joan Reape.....to the performance of ye will of my .....Husband Deceassed.....Zacheriah Rhodes of Pawtuxett.....who.....dispossed of his lands on the South side of the Pawtuxett river.....among three of his Sonns.....I Doe.....appoint my sonn Malachi Rhodes to take.....that Land lying next to Pawtuxett Falls.....which Land is bounded on the North side by Pawtuxett river, on the South by a fence....., on the East by the cove or harbour by a small brooke that runs a Cross the end of it into the great river.....28th day of February 1676/77

Wit.   Jean **X** Reape
   Samuell Gorton junr.   her marke
   Thomas **X** Eldrich
       his marke.

Testimony of posession by John Albro and George Lawton August the 4th 1677.
.....Wee John Albro and George Lawton, both of Portsmouth.....doe by Vertue of the power.....given to us..... of Captn Thomas Clarke Iron Munger, and Ann Clarke his wife.....have taken posession of the Northermost halfe of Prudence Island with all buildings.....belonginge together with all the Lands that did ever belong to Mr Parker father to.....Ann Clarke,.....Viz. the houses, which stands upon the Northermost part of the Island towards Providence Neck.....
Wit.
   The **X** marke of
       John Snooke.
       Henry Mattesson

[153] Claim of Robert Hassard on his father.
.....my sonn Robert Hassard of.....Portsmouth.....doth claime.....intrest unto my lands in.....Portsmouth by vertue of some.....writeinge..... I Thomas Hassard..... of Portsmouth.....doe.....protest.....I never made any writeinge to my.....sonn Robert.....Only in a will drawne by mr John Porter at George Lawtons about Thirty yeares past.....my said sonn was to have had my lands and my other children my Moveables,.....Since which time I..... make Voyd and Null.....the wills.....And doe.....abolish .....heire-ship.....to my son Robert Hassard.....sixt day of August.....1677.....my. wife Martha Hassard.....Sole Executrix.....of my Estate.....

Wit.
   Francis Gisborne
   David Lake
                    The marke **X** of
                    Thomas Hassard

Delivered before me Samuell Wilbore Asistant 6 day of August 1677

[154] Will of Thomas Hassard.
Thomas Hassard of Portsmouth.....doe hereby will..... my land in.....Portsmouth.....Containeinge.....Thirty acres.....accordinge to.....a.....deed of Bargaine..... made by me unto Thomas Shriefe of Portsmouth.....date the tenth day of December.....1666.....by which deed..... Land is declared to be Mine.....and after.....unto.....my beloved Yoakfellow Martha Hassard.....unto my daughter Hannah Wilcocks one shillinge to be paid in Silver quoyne .....unto my daughter Martha Potter wife of Icobod Potter of Portsmouth.....one shillinge.....all former wills..... made voyde.....Thirteenth day of November.....one Thowsand Six hundred seventy and six.

Wit.
   Thomas Gould.
   John Coggeshall
   John Heath.
                    Thomas **X** Hassard.
                    his marke

[155] John Paine to Samuell Apleton.
.....John Paine of Boston.....Merchant.....for.....Sev-

erall legicies amounting to the sum Fifteen hundred pounds, payable accordinge to the Will.....of my.....Father William Paine Late of Boston.....unto the three children of Samuell Apleton of Ipswich in the County of Essix.....Gent..... Have.....sold.....unto.....Samuell Apleton.....All my Right.....in the Island called.....Prudence.....as houses lands fences wood Timber Waters.....Mineralls.....Provided.....If.....John Paine.....shall pay.....at Boston .....the sum of fifteen hundred pounds.....answerable to the said Will,.....Then this.....Deed of Mortgage.....be .....of None Efect,.....Twentith day of January.....one Thowsand Six hundred sixty and three.....

Wit.   Jno. Paine
 Thomas Danforth
 Joell X acoomis
 Caleb Cheeshahte au nuk
 John Evins

     John Paine.....before me this 21th day of January 1663.....made acknowlidgment of this Deed
                 Danill Gookin
.....1676.....Entred.....in.....Records.....of Suffolk p.....Edward Rawson Secretary June 6t 1677..... I doe certefie that Captn Daniell Gookin was Majestrate.....Edward Rawson was Secretary 63 at the same time.....
         Samuell Symonas Dept. Govr.

[156] William Brenton &c. to William Clarke.
.....five and Twentith day of Aprill.....1674, Between William Brenton, John Hull, Benedict Arnold, John Porter, Samuell Wilbore, Samuell Wilson & Thomas Mumford of the one part and William Clarke Weaver of the other part .....for.....five pounds Currant pay.....paid.....by William Clarke.....Have Sold.....a.....Neck of Land Containeinge.....one hundred Acres.....beinge part..... of Land in the Narragansett Cuntry.....beinge about six Miles Westerly of Petacomscutt Rock, and bounded.....on the East partly by a hie way and partly by a pond, on the

south by a small river as it runns under the North side of the great swamp, on the North partly by a hie way and partly by a great river, called Chipsuck River, and on the west by the Chipsuck river,.....if.....any minneralls shall be discovered.....shall be devided into Eight Equall shares, seven shall.....remaine unto us.....and one Eight part.....to the use of him.....
Wit.

 Freeborn Harte   John Hull
 Richard Baily   Benedict Arnold
 Joseph Morry   John Porter
 Samuell X Helmes   Samuell Wilson
    his marke   Samuell Wilbur
 William Cadman.   Thomas Mumford

 Asignement of Land to John Peirce from William Clarke By.....Letter of Aturny from.....William Clarke I Jireh Bull of Pettacomscutt, doe asigne.....the Land therein Mentioned unto John Peirce of Portsmouth Mason.....6t day of September 1675
Wit.   Jireh Bull

 Henry Beere
 Rowse Helme
 Richard Baily

[157] Jireh Bull for William Clarke to John Pearce.
.....Jireh Bull of Pettacomscutt.....am.....Authorized, by William Clarke late of Pettacomscutt.....to.....sell.....Land, granted unto him neere Pettacomscutt.....for.....Fifteen pounds.....payd.....by John Pearce of Portsmouth.....Masson,.....Land which is a Neck.....lyinge.....about six miles Westerly from Pettacomscutt Rock & Containeth.....one hundred acres,.....bounded.....on the East partly by a hie way, and partly by a pond, and on the South by a small river as it runs under the North Side of a great Swamp, on the North partly by a hie way and partly by a great River called Chipsuck river, and on the West by the.....Chipsuck river.....any Minnerralls shall be discouvered.....shall be devided into eight Equall parts, Seven

.....unto the purchassers.....And one Eight part.....unto
.....John Peirce.....sixth day of August.....one Thowsand
six hundred seventy & five
Wit.   Jireh Bull
   Henry Beere
   Rowse Helme
   Richard Baily.

[158] Myantonomey to Randall Houldon, &c.
.....Myaptanamy Chefe sachim of the Nanheygansett have sold unto the persons heare Named one percell of Lands..... Lyinge upon the West side of.....the sea Called Sohomes Bay from Copassuetuxet over against A Litle Iland in the sayd Bay beinge the north Bounds, and the outmost point of that Neck.....called Shawhomett, beinge the South bounds from the sea shore of Each Boundery, Upon a straite line Westward Twenty Miles,.....the proportion.....accordinge to the mapp under written.....beinge the forme of it, unto Randall Houldon, John Greene, John Weicks, Francis Weston, Samuell Gorton, Richard Waterman, John Warner, Richard Carder, Samson Shotton, Robert Potter, William Wuddall For one hundred and forty 4 fathom of Wampum peage..... Twelfth day of January 1642.
Wit.   Myanto X nomey
   Totanomans
      X marke
   Sachim of
   Showhomett Pumham
   Jano X his marke
   John Greene .

[159] Roger Williams to mr Parker of Boston
Providence 13. May 1678 (so called)
.....Roger Williams of Providence.....about thirty yeares since out of the.....love I bare to.....honnor. Gentlen. mr John Winthrop Senr. (.....the first Governr at Boston) .....to be my halfe in the purchass of the Island called Prudence Island (Chibbssueasickk) in English.....lyinge in (the soe Caled) Cowessett and Nanhygonsett Bay.....The.....

Honoed. man, and I did Joyntly.....purchass the said Island of the 2 great sachims.....Cunnounicus and Miantunnomu whose favor it pleassed God to give me.....That.....Gentlm. and myselfe injoyed the.....Island in peace untill I was forced (beinge in want) to sell my halfe to mr Parker (my .....freind of Boston) and I have.....heard that.....mr Winthrop Gave his halfe to his sonn mr Stephen Winthrop since which.....Transfer mr Winthrops Right and mine, unto divers others.....to mr Paine of Boston Deceassed. and mr William Browne of Salem unto whom.....I humbly beg of God a blessing.....in this Barbarous wilderness.....
Wit.   Roger Williams
   Thomas Olny snior
   Joseph Williams
   Samuell Comstock
                    May the 13th 1678.....before me.
                          Thomas Olny Asistant
   Testemony of Nathaniell Colson and Stephen Cooke.
Nathaniell Coalson aged thirty yeares.....and stephen Cooke aged twenty three yeares.....they beinge at Prudence Island, heard Benjamin Browne speake to the Inhabitants of the south end.....to remove to the North side of the devission line of the Island that he might take posession of the South Moyety of the Island in the behalfe of his father William Browne senr. of Salem,.....and wee did see sd. Benjamin Browne take posession.....William Allin.....beinge present..... the Twenty seventh day of Aprill one Thowsand six hundred seventy and Eight
William Allin of Prudence Island aged (44 yeares) doth Testefy to the truth of.....above.....by Nathaniell Colson and Stephen Cooke.....
                2e. of May 1678 Samuell Gorton Asista.
   Devision of Prudence Island.
Nathaniell Coltson.....Testefyeth, that.....eighteen months since, I beinge appointed by Joshua Coggeshall Coll. Crowne and William Alline of the one side and Benjamin Browne of the other.....to survay Prudence Island, and now.....

desired to devide the sd Island in Equall halfs between them, have begun the line at a Rock neer halfe a rodd on the south side a dwelling house on the west side of sd Island in which John Davis now dwelleth, and from thence East twenty three degrees South to the waeter on the East side of said Island.....da. 27 da. Aprill 1678:
2d. of May 1678 Samuell Gorton Asistant.

[160]   William Browne—Land Recorded.
.....William Browne of.....Salem.....beinge.....in..... posession of.....that southermost end and halfe of Prudence Island lyinge in Coweessett and Nanhygonsett Bay..... bounded Northerly by a line began at a rock on the West side of.....Island, neer halfe a rodd on the south side a dwellinge house in which John Davis now dwelleth, and from thence East twenty three degrees south to the water on the East side of the.....Island, and is on all other parts bounded by the sea or salt water.....with all uplands, meddows, woods..... dwelling.....houses,.....Barnes, Orchards, Gardens, according to a law made the 22th of May 1662.....All..... premises.....Ratefyed Recorded.....One and twenty day of May.....One Thowsand six hundred Seventy and Eight.
John Sanford, Recorder.

[161]   John Crandall to Jeremiah and Heber Crandell.
.....John Crandall of Newport.....sonn and heire of John Crandall of Newport.....Deceassed.....unto my..... brothers Jeremiah Crandall and Heber Crandall now residents in Newport,.....and in the tuition of their mother Hannah Crandall.....have given,.....a certaine house (formerly the Mantion house of my Father John Crandall) .....with two hundred acres.....belonginge both upland and Meddow,..... lyeinge.....in.....Westerly alias Squomacutt,.....bounded.....On the West by land of Nicholas Cotterills, on the East by the fresh meddows, on the North by Pawcatuck river, on the south by land formerly belonginge to Edward Smith late of Newport deceassed.....with all .....Edieffices, Gardens, Orchards,.....thirteenth day of May.....one Thousand six hundred seventy Eight.

Wit.   John **X** Crandall
   William Turpin.   his marke
   Thomas Ward.

[162]   Land of Richard Bulger to Joseph Anthony.

.....William Hall.....have layd out of the Land of Richard Bulgar.....to Joseph Anthony two Acres.....in two percells.....one acre upon the Rocky hill, bounded North with the Land of.....Joseph, East by Pocassett river, South by .....land.....of.....Richard West partly by a hie-way and partly by.....Land of.....Richard—the other acre bounded North with.....Land of.....Joseph East with a hie-way, South by.....Land of.....Richard, bounded with foure Stakes two rod from the fence of.....Richard as now it stands West upon the great Cove.....layd out.....29th of July 1674

                         Witnes: William Hall.
                                     John Anthony Junr.

Wee.....are.....satisfyed with the.....premisses.....
Wit.   Richard Bulger
   John Anthony Junir.   Joseph Anthony.
   William Hall.

   William Brenton to Francis Brayton.

.....William Brenton of Boston have.....sold unto Francis Brayton of Rhode Island.....one house and twelve acres of Land,.....belonginge.....in the Towne of Portsmouth..... bounded on the south with the Land of mr Richard Smith, and on the North side with the Land of William Baulston, ...for.....forty nine pound.....Twenty fift day of September sixteen hundred and Fifty.

Wit.   William Brenton
   William Sanford   Martha Brenton
   Peleg Sanford.

[163]   Wrastlin Brewster to Thomas Durphey.

.....Wrastling Brewster & John Rogers.....of Duxbury in.....New-Plymoth.....for.....sixty five pounds..... mony of New-England.....paid by Thomas Durphey of Portsmouth.....have.....sold.....one Moyety.....of a share.....of a freemans Lott of Land.....beinge at Tanton River in.....New-Plymoth.....in Number the 10. lott..... buttith westward upon the sd. River and Extendeth Eastward four mile from the said River, Southward with the land of Major James Cudworth and Northward, with the Land of mr Richard More, bounded and Marked on the sd Northerly side with a Chesnutt tree near the water side below the path, and a Red oake tree above the path Marked & Numbered 10 on the Southerly side & -11- on the Northerly side, which..... halfe Lott is to begin at the.....trees & to extend southward to the Midle of the sd. 10 Lott, and there to be devided from the other halfe of.....Lott, And alsoe.....one halfe part of a freemans share of.....Meddow, at a place called Scipican, which sd Land and meddow was formerly of Mr Love Brewster one of the old freemen off.....New-Plymoth..... deceassed:.....twenty ninth day of May: 1678:

Wit.   Wrestlin Bruster
 John Cushing   John Rogers
 Nathll. Thomas.....acknowlidged by Wrestlin Brustor and John Rogers.....Before Josiah Winslow Govr.

[164] Cachanaquant to Randall Houldon & Samuell Gorton.

.....Cachanaquant alias Tassaconohutt.....kindnesses Received from Captn. Randall Houldon and Samuell Gorton senior. both of Warwick.....have.....given.....one percell of Land by the Name of Nannaquoksett being a Neck of land.....beinge upon.....Nanhygansett Bay over against the Midle of Quononoqutt Island.....and over against a small Iland in the Bay lying about betwixt Quononoqutt Island the above-said Neck of land called Arokquanessett; .....with free leave to feed their Cattell upon my land lying about the same neck provided they wrong not the Indians corne in the sumer time from.....planting.....till it be gathered in.....And I am greatly provoaked to my free act .....with respect unto that great sachim of old England..... of the.....fame I heare of him, to whom.....these my

friends are.....servants.....May.....27th day.....according to the English account 1659
Wit.

   Newcom **X** his mark   Caganaquanak **X** his marke.
                   Indian   Alequaoomett **X** Eldist son of
the marke of   the abovsd.
Awashause **X** Indian   sachim
Walter Todd
Amos Westcott—:

.....little Island.....being in the River or Bay which Island is called.....Arockquonosett.....is not spescefied in the .....Deed wherein.....is mentioned.....a percell of Land lying between.....River or Bay and that comon path or hieway in the cuntry of the Nanhygansett, which gift had a being before.....of a promise made by my Ansesters.....yeares ago.....to the.....men Randall Houldon and Samuell Gorton.....the said small Island.....was.....given.....with the.....Neck.....lyeth.....in a.....map drawne out with pen and inke.....

Witnes English   Cachanaquaneck **X** his marke
   Samuell Gorton junir.   alias Tasseconohutt
Witnes Indian
   X Mautotanamitt

[165]   Massup consents to Deed of Cachananquant.

.....Pessicus alias Mawsupp of the Nanhygansett though .....not present at the writing of this Deed.....penned on both sides.....this paper.....did.....give my.....consent .....19th day of Septemr. 1667:

Testes: John Green   Massup alias
        Phillip Green   Sucquans his **X** marke
Quoanock **X** his marke

   Deed of Cachanaquant confirmed.

Cojanaquont.....declares.....he was not in drink but sober .....and.....when he sold the land to Major Atherton and .....the Baymen in presence of Richard Smith he..... excepted the Neck of Land herein.....given to Captn Randall Houldon and mr Samuell Gorton senr. and.....never made any lease.....to Richard Smith for more then three yeares.

.....John Green Asistant

Warwick 18th of May 1668.

Samuell Gorton and John Gorton.

.....Samuell Gorton senr. Professor the Misterys of Christ. and purchasser of Shaomett Inhabitant of.....Warwick..... unto my.....sonn) John Gorton.....doe.....give.....one third part of my.....Lands.....beyond the.....Towne of Warwick Westward the other two thirds being betwixt my sonn Samll. Gorton junr. and my sonn Benjamin Gorton..... to be devided as the Major part of my three sonns.....shall agree.....unto my sonn John Gorton.....my share of Meddow at Taskeunck.....Twenty seventh of November 1677: Wit.   Samuell Gorton Senr.

John Greene Asistant
Randall Howldon

[166] .Will of Nicholas Easton.

.....my son Nicholas.....my houses and Lands and my daughter Elizabeth.....the Corner house and Land that I had of Adam Wooly and alsoe that Land that by my Gran father was given to my sister Mary which I bought of hir Husband Weston Clarke My plate.....my son.....one halfe and my daughter the other halfe; Christopher Holder to have my best hatt my Uncle Daniell halfe a peece of Worsted Chamlett, my uncle John Easton my old horse my mother to have my gray paceing horse, my Brother John to have all my wearing apparrill Except handkercher and Neckercloths..... these I give to my sonn Nicholas; my small Lott and house at Towne, I give to Christopher Holder and my Uncle John Easton, or to whome they shall asigne it to for to be improved to give in yearly to the publick stock of.....my friends called Quakers, and I give.....to my brother John, Thirty pounds.....to help build a Towne house,.....to my sister Mary a barrill of porke, and a barrill of porke to my sister Patience.....my son I leave to the Tuition of my brother

John untill my Son be Twenty one yeare old.....my Daughter,.....to the Tuition of Amy Borden untill she be Marriead or twenty yeare old.....my brother John to be.....Executor .....My Overseers are Christopher Holder, Daniell Gould and John Easton,.....

Newport:15 d. 11 m. 1676. Nicholas Easton.
Wit.

   John Easton senior
   John Easton Junir.

.....to my brother Peter.....Twenty shillings and Twenty shillings to my brother Joshua, and ten Shillings to my Sister Elizabeth, and my sister waite shall have a silver spoone of ten shillings price—my Indian Squa to be free.....my Indian childe to be free at twenty five yeares of age.....to Joseph Bryer my best sadle.....

15 d. 11 m. 1676
John Easton senior John Easton Junior.
.....

John Easton senr. and John Easton junr.....5th of 1 mo called March 1676-7.....did affirme the afore.....written Will.....of Nicholas Easton (deceassed) late of Newport.
                    Robert Malins Dept. Clerke of
                                     Councell.

[167] Ralph Earll to Thomas Butts.
.....Ralph Earll of.....Dartmouth in.....New-Plymoth .....Thomas Butts of.....Portsmouth.....have.....sold .....one fourth part of medow belonging to a purchassers share within.....Dartmoth, and.....one Eight part of Upland belonging to a whole purchassers share, and alsoe tenn acres of Upland within.....said Towne, the which percells of Upland is......at..Cocksett, at the Eastermost side of.....Ralphs Land,.....To be Holden of his Majtie..... as the manner of East Greenwich.....Twentith day of November.....One Thowsand six hundred sixty and Eight.
Wit.   Ralph X Earll.
   William Earll.   his marke
   William Hall.

[168]   John Brigs to Thomas Brigs.
.....John Brigs of.....Portsmouth.....Yeoman.....unto my second sonn Thomas Brigs.....Doe.....give.....Thomas Brigs and Mary his wife.....one fourth share.....of Land lying.....in Dartmoth.....part whereof is.....layd out at .....Ponagansett.....Thirty five Acres.....bounded North by the Land by me given to my Sonn John Brigs East by the Cove or Creek, South by the Land of me..... and West by Land lying in Comon.....Eleventh day of March.....one Thowsand six hundred seventy Eight.....

Wit.   John **X** Brigs senr.
   John Sanford   his marke.
   Richard Tarr

[169]   John Simmons—Will.
.....John Simmons Resident neer Tanton.....unto my Children Mary—my Eldist Daughter, and John Simmons my Eldist sonn, and Rememberance Simmons my second sonn and Edward Simmons my third sonn.....doe.....give..... all my Estate.....Either.....Lands Goods household stuff mony Cattell.....to be Equally devided.....doe.....appoint my.....wife Martha Simmons.....sole Overseer.....first day of February.....One Thowsand six hundred seventy Eight or nine.

Wit.   John Simmons
   Mathew **X** Grinell
      his marke
   John Heath
   Elizabeth Holderbee

Henry Brightman to Mathew Boomer.
.....Henry Brightman of Portsmouth.....for.....five and Forty pounds of currant silver mony of New-England..... paid.....by Mathew Boomer of Newport.....Have.....sold .....one halfe of a Lott.....lying.....on the East side of Tanton River in the Collony of New-Plymoth being the fourth in Number and the Moiety.....sold is the Northmost halfe .....bounded.....on the north by land.....late.....of Samuell House.....on the South by Land.....late.....of

Robert Hassard.....with all.....Medows.....belonging, the medows at Scipecan only Excepted.....sixt day of March.....1676-7.

Wit.   Henry Brightman
  Thomas Ward.   X
  Richard Baily.   his marke

[170] Joan Brightman consents to Deed.

.....Joan Brightman wife of.....Henry Brightman doe..... give my consent unto the Deed.....sixt day of March 1676-7

Wit.   Joane X Brightman
  Thomas Ward   her marke
  Richard Baily.

Owned by Henry Brightman.....thirtith day of May one thousand six hundred seventy & Eight.

                                             John Albro Asistant

[171] Mathew Boomer to John Reade

.....Mathew Boomer of Newport.....for.....two and twenty pounds and tenn shillings currant silver mony of New-England.....paid.....by John Reade of Newport..... Corwainer,.....have.....sold.....one quarter part.....of Land lying.....on the East side of Tanton River.....and is the Moiety of a halfe share.....which I.....purchased of Henry Brightman,.....with all.....Medows.....the Medows at Scipecan only Excepted.....Twentith day of June..... 1677.

Wit.   Mathew Boomer
  John Drury
  Josias Lyndon
  William Hiscox
  Richard Baily

This deed was owned this thirty day of May one Thousand six hundred seventy and Eight by Mathew Boomer before mee   John Albro Asistant

[172] Inventory of mr. John Alcock Deced.

.....Inventory of.....Estate of mr. John Alcock Deced. .....amongst his Children.....August.....8th 1677.

	£	s	d
House & house Lott...5 Acres	160	00	00
Land upon....Meeting house hills at Roxbury	80	00	00
20 Acres more upon ditto hill	60	00	00
25 acres of Land at Mudy River	40	00	00
Land & medows at Boston Gate	240	00	00
Stony river Lott wch. Jno. Graunt Occupies	80	00	00
17 acres at Stony river in mr Clarkes hand	85	00	00
2/3 of Land at Ainsworth hill	80	00	00
Land at Maulbery with.....stock.....	218	02	00
Land at Assabeth with stock	167	15	00
Charges upon bringing up Georg Alcock	204	15	00
Sum is ———————————	1415	12	00

Besides Land at Block Island & land at long Island, and land at Merimack not yett apprised and a great part of the moveables not yett devided. It being agreed upon that John Williams shall have one 3d part of Assabeth which comes to £55-18s-4d and the remainder of his share at Block Island according to apprisement wch. sd. £55-18s-4d being deducted, out of the whole there will Remaine 1359-13-8- to be devided into 8-Equall Shares.

	£	S.	d.
Each parte being — — — — — —	169	19	2¼
To George Alcock-2 shares			
Expences upon Education and payment of Debts & mr Greens sallery — — —	204	15	00
House & house lott about 5 Acres — —	160	00	00
	364	15	00
To John Alcock one share			
17 Acres of Land at Stony river in mr Clarks hand	085	00	00
1/2 of .. Land at Ainsworth Hill	040	00	00
1/6 of .. Land & stock at Maulburry	036	07	00
	161	07	00

To Paussgrave Alcock 1 share	£ s d
.. lot at stony river in Graunts hands	080 : 00 : 00
1/2 .. Land at Ainsworth hill ————	040 : 00 : 00
1/6 .. Land & stock at Maulburry ————	036 : 07 : 00
	156 : 07 : 00

To Elizabeth Alcock one share.

1/3 of .. Land & stock at Maulbery ———	072 : 14 : 00
1/2 .. Land at Mudy river ————————	020 : 00 : 00
1/2 the 2 parts on the Meeting house hill.	070 : 00 : 00
	162 : 14 : 00

To Joanna Alcock.

1/3 of the land and stock at Maulbery ———	072 : 14 : 00
1/2 the land at Muddy river ————————	020 : 00 : 00
1/2 the 2 parsells on the meeting house hill—	070 : 00 : 00
	162 : 14 : 00

To Joshua Lamb one share.

halfe the land & medow at Boston gate	120 : 00 : 00
1/3 of the land at Assabath ———————	055 : 18 : 04
	175 : 18 : 04

To Zacheriah Whitman one share.

..1/2 the land & medow at Boston gate——	120 : 00 : 00
1/3 of the land at Assabath ———————	055 : 18 : 04
	175 : 18 : 04

The above devission the children & Guardians of the children of the sd John Alcock deceased…consent…to…8th of August 1677……….

                    John Hull Gaurdian
                    John Williams.
                    Zacher Witman for himselfe
                        & as Gaurdian.
                    John Alcock Joshua Lamb

The partys...appearing in Court August 9 : 1677...
Jsa. Addington Cler.
...taken out of the Records of the County Court of Suffolke.
pr Jsa. Addington Cler.

Boston...

[173] Inventory of John Alcock.
Inventory...of...John Alcock (of Roxbury deceassed) At Block Island alias New-Shorrum.

	£	s.	d
...Eight part of said Island	085	00	00
8 Cowes and 8 oxen & 10 sheep	035	00	00
	120	00	00

April 7. 1679.
Robert Guthrig
his
Turmutt **X** Rose
marke.

...Book of Records for Block Island and the Towne of New-Shorrum.

Robert Guthreg Towne Clerk.

John Williams—Land Recorded.

...mr John Williams of New-Shorrum alias Block Island ...being...in...posesion...of land lying...in...Newport ...lately purchassed of Nathaniell Dickins...of Newport ...containinge...Twenty acres...bounded...on the East by land...of Mary Timberlake on the South by land...of mr John Easton senr. on the Southwest by land that was Robert Griffins, and the head there of lying Westerly against the land...of Henry Bull, and alsoe on the Southwesterly side lyes against the land...of Jireh Bull and Northerly on the great street...with all...Dwellinge or Mansion houses out houses, Barnes, Orchards...Gardens...according to law made...the 22th of May 1662, every part of the...premises is hereby Ratefyed...Recorded 10th of May...1679:

[174] Thomas Hicke to Lawrence Springer.
...Thomas Hicke of Portsm-...Carpenter...twenty two pounds tenn shillings Currant Silver mony of New-England, ...paid by Lawrence Springer of the Collony of New-Plymoth...planter...Have...sold...one Quarter share...of Land,...being at Seconett and places Adjacent...being formerly the land of Thomas Pinchin of Scittuate and sonn to Thomas Pinchin senir, one lott...is the three and Twentith lott...with all...other allotments purchased and unpurchased from the Indians...Except some tracts of land, that the Company have seen cause to dispose off...Eight day of May One Thousand six hundred seventy Nine.
Wit.   Thomas Hix.
   Henry Lilly.
   Thomas Ward.

   Lawrance Springer to Robert Gibs.
...Lawrance Springer late of Portsmouth...now sideinge neer a Neck of Land called Puncatas-in the Collony of New-Plymoth planter...for...twelve pounds Sterling of New England,...paid by Robert Gibs of the same place planter,...Have...sold...One Eight part of a share...lyinge...at Saconett and places Adjacent...being Formerly the land of Thomas Pinchin of Scittuate and sonn of Thomas Pinchin senr...lott...is the three and twentith lott...Twenty third day of June...One Thousand Six hundred seventy Nine.
Wit.   Lawrance **X** Springer
   Richard Barnes   his marke.
   Thomas Ward.

[176] Francis Brinley—Land Recorded.
...mr Francis Brinley of...Newport...Merchant, being...in...posesion, of...Land...in...Newport...one percell of ...Land is lying...at Green End, containing thirty Acres...by him purchased of Daniell Hinchman...bounded, on the Southward by John Vaughan Junr. and a Comon leading to the old mill of James Rogers, on the Eastward by a hie way leading to the said Comon, on the Northward by the great

hie way, and on the westward by the Comon leading to...
Newport, And one percell of Land Containinge four
Acres...by him purchased of Stephen Mumford...bounded,
Southward by the land of John Horndall, on the Eastward
by Land of John Easton, senior. on the Northward by land
of John Maxon, and on the Westward by the Comon : And
one percell...Containing Thirteen Acres, by him purchassed
of William Dyre and Samuell Dyre...bounded, on the southward by land lately of John Clarke, on the Eastward by land
of Roger Goulding and Peleg Sanford, on the Northward
and Westward by land lately of Samuell Dyre,...three
percell...Containge the Number of forty Seven Acres...
with all...Dwelling or Mansion houses, Barnes, Out houses,
Orchards, Gardens...according to a law made...the 22th
of May 1662 All ...premisses, are hereby Ratefyed...Ninth
day of August...1679.

John Sanford Recorder.

[177] Carew Clarke to Thomas Ward.

...Carew Clarke of Newport...Edward Larkin of Newport...planter did...yeares part, purchass...Land herein
after Mentioned of My Brother John Clarke of Newport...phisitian Deceased...I...release...unto Thomas
Ward of Newport...(the...asigne of...the...Edward Larkin)...land lyinge...in...Newport...Eighteen Acres...
now in the posession of Thomas Peckham,...bounded...on
the East by a hie way belonginge to the said Towne on the
South by land...of Peter Easton, on the west by land...of
the Asignes of the asignes of my Brother John Clarke deceassed, on the North by the hie way leading to the said land
late the farme of my...Brother John Clarke..., which said
hie way partith the said Land, hereby...Released...from
the land...of Henry Tew...thirteenth day of June...One
Thowsand six hundred seventy Nine.

Wit.   Carew Clarke.

William Hiscox
John Paine.

Newpor...July 9th 1679
...Carew Clarke...Owned...Deed
      Before mee John Cranston Gover.

[178] Peter George to his wife Mary.
...Peter George of New Shorrum (alias Block Island) Yeoman...for...a Joynture granted to his...wife Mary George, ...for her...maintanence...and for the settlinge...of all...lands and tennements together with halfe the stock he hath, upon the said Land, and one Negro man called Langoe (all which Estate...being on New-Shorrum-(alias Block-Island)...unto...Mary George, and Simon Ray, Turmutt Rosse and John Williams as Feofees in Trust for my...wife ...all...my manner Mesuage and farme Called a sixteenth part of Block-Island together with the Medows I bought of Thomas Terry...during her natural life...to my sonn Samuell after her and my decease but if he die without Isue...to goe to my daughters Mary, Hannah, and Sarah...Twenty Ninth day of July Sixteen hundred Seventy Nine,...
Wit.   Peter X George
                                                his marke.
Trustram Dodge.
Margrett X Guthrig
  her marke.

[179] Land of John Paine to William Clarke.
...Thomas Fry Gen. Serjat of...Collony of Rhode Island ...by Vertue of an Execution...date...22th of November 1677. ...by Authorety of...the Genll. court of Tryalls held at Newport the 24th of October 1677 on...action...by William Clarke plantiff against the Estate of the deceassed mr John Paine of Prudence Island defendt, I have...given posession of...Land formerly belonginge to the said John Paine,...three hundred and fifty acres...unto...William Clarke...the...land...lyinge...in...Land Called Boston Neck in the Narragansett Cuntry and...between the land of the late...captn Thomas Willitt on the South, and the Land of mr John Browne on the North,...

Wit.   Thomas Fry Genll. Serjat.
   Enoch Place Senr.
   Enoch Place junr.
   John Kinion.
      Valluation of Land of William Clarke...an action...by William Clarke of...Portsmouth...against the Estate of John Paine late of Prudence Island Deceassed...date the 29th of August 1677: and...Obtaining...a percell of Land...being in the Narragansett Cuntry on a place called Boston Neck beinge the halfe of a share...between Captn John Browne of Swansy and the fore-said John Paine, and the said John Painee part was to be the south side thereof...Wee...being desired to Vallue...the...land...Wee doe...aprise the...land...to be worth Ninty five pounds   according to New England mony Rhode Island September 23: 1679.
                                       Peter Talman
                                       John Greene
   William Clark-Land Recorded.
   ...William Clarke of...Portsmouth...Ship-Carpenter being ...in...possession...of Land,...in the Neck...called Boston Neck...Containinge three hundred and fifty Acres ...bounded by the Land of Captn Willitt on the south side, and the Land of Captn John Browne on the North side,...being halfe a share, and was formerly the land of mr John Paine late deceassed of the Island Prudance;...and by the Genll. Serjant delivered into the posession of...William Clarke...with all...houses, Orchards, Gardens,...according to a Law made the 22th of May 1662 All...premises, are hereby Ratefyed...26th day of September One Thowsand Six hundred seventy Nine...
                             John Sanford Recorder.
[180]   Indenture between Peter George & Samuell George ...twenty third day of December...One Thowsand six hundred seventy and eight, between Peter George of Block-Island alias New-Shorrum...and Samuell Georg sonn to... Peter George...doth...give...unto...Samuell my sonn all ...my farme where now I dwell containinge two hundred and

tenn acres...with all my land in the Corne Neck and Else where on Block-Island...with all...houseing fences...
Wit.   Peter George.
   Benjamin X Miles
     his marke
   Nathanill Miles.

[181]   William Clarke to Edward Lay.

...William Clarke of...Portsmouth...Ship-Carpenter... for...full...Satisfaction...Received...from Edward Lay of Portsmouth...yeoman...Have...sold...One halfe...percell of land by me Recovered...by Vertue...of the Genll. Court of Tryalls...against the Estate of...John Paine of Prudence Island, the whole...being three hundred and fifty acres, soe that halfe...sold is one hundred seventy five acres...is the Northermost halfe...lying...in...Boston Neck...Bounded ...on the North side by the land of Captn John Browne, and on the south side by that other...moiety to me belonging. ...twenty seventh day of February...One Thowsand Six hundred seventy nine:...

Wit.   William Clarke
   John X Brigs senr. his marke
   John Sanford
   Joseph Remington

    Joseph Devell to Thomas Ward.

...Joseph Devell of Newport...for...Nine pounds...mony of New-England...paid by Thomas Ward of Newport... have...sold...one share...both Upland and Medow, lying... at...Puncatess...Eighteenth day of February...One Thowsand six hundred Seventy Nine:
Wit.   Willia Coggeshall.
   John Paine
   William X Devell
    his marke.
      Joseph Devell
Newport...February the 18th 1679
  ...Joseph Devell...acknowlidged above...
      Caleb Carr: Asistant

[183] John & William Coggeshall to John Manchester.
...John Coggeshall and William Coggeshall heirs to the deceassed William Boulston of...Portsmouth...for...seven pounds tenn shillings in Currant Mony...Received of John Manchester of...Portsmouth...Have...sold...one Eight part of a share...in...Dartmouth...New Plymouth...with all...Uplands, Medows, walters, woods,...belonginge... Excepting One percell...sold by...William Baulston (Our grandfather) unto Richard Sisson...To be Holden of his Majtie...as of his manner of East Greenwich...first day of June...One Thowsand Six hundred Seventy Eight:

	John Coggeshall
Wit.	Joseph Devell
John Sanford	Elizabeth X Gould
Thomas X Brigs	
his marke	

...Elizabeth Gould their mother doth give her consent...
March 1678-79
Wit.
Robert Brownell Thomas Gould

[184] John Manchester to Vallintine Hudlestone.
...John Manchester of Portsmouth...twelve pounds of... mony of New-England...by Vallintine Hudlestone of Newport...Have...sold...all Land purchassed by me...twenty Eight day of 12mo called February...One Thowsand six hundred seventy nine...
Wit.

John Hulme	The marke
Hannah Clarke.	John X Manchester

John Manchester Acknowlidged...before me the twenty Eight day of...february 1679 As Attest Walter Clarke De Govr.

[184] Henry Chamberlin to Vallintine Hudlestone.
...Henry Chamberlin of Sandwich in...New plymoth,... Eldist Sone of John chamberlin of Rhode-Island deceassed ...Satisfaction...Received...of...Vallintine Hudleston of Newport...Have...sold...all the Right...unto...my...

fathers Estate now on Rhode-Island...20th of the first month called March One thowsand six hundred & 79 Eighty:
Wit.   Henary Chamberlin.
   William Chamberlin
   Walter Newbery:
The Eighteenth day of may...one Thousand six hundred and Eighty Henry chamberlin...acknowlidged...above...
                         Walter Clarke Dept. Govr.

[185]   Mathew Allen to Vallintine Hudlestun.
...Mathew Allen of Dartmoth...New-Plymoth...for...six pounds...mony of New-England...paid...by Vallintine Hudlestun of Newport...Have...sold...Land lying...at Acocksett in...Towne-ship of Dartmoth...neer the Land of Samuell Cornell,...Twenty five acres...bounded...On the West by a line drawne from a black oake tree at the south end thereof unto a white oake being the Northerly end of the said line, on the North, by a line drawne from the said white Oake unto a Maple standing in a Swamp being the east end of the said line   on the East by the said swamp to a Black Oake being the South end of the East bounds, on the South by a line drawne from the last mentioned black-Oake to the first mentioned black Oake being the west end of the said South line,...(which said land is a part of the halfe share of Land, on which I...now live...to be Holden of his Majtie...as of his manner of East Greenwich...16th day of February... One Thowsand six hundred seventy nine...
                                 his marke
Wit.   Mathew **X** Allen
   his marke
   Richd **X** Kirby
   Hannah Clarke
   Mathew Allen before me acknowlidged the above-written...
                              Walter Clarke Dt Govr.

[186]   Henry Tibbitts to Thomas Ward.
...Henry Tibbitts of Narragansett...for...tenn pounds Sterling...paid...by Thomas Ward of Newport...have... sold...a whole share of Land,...at...Sandy Pointe and soe

runing along the Bay West Northwest, till come to the mouth of the Raritans River, from thence goeing along the said River to a certain point of Marsh land, which devides the River into two parts, and from that point to run in a direct south-west line into the woods twelve miles and then to turne away Southeast and by South, till it falls into the maine Ocean, which are the bounds,...according as they are Expressed in the Charter or pattent...Granted by Richard Nicolls Esquire,...fourteenth day of June...1672.

Wit.   Henry X Tibbitt
   Richard Bailey   his marke.
                                       John Read

Newport...the 13th of May 1680 Henry Tippits...acknowlidged the above-written...
                John Green Asistant

[187] Daniell Wilcocke to Joseph Devell.
...Daniell Wilcocke of Dartmoth...New-Plymoth...for... five pounds Currant pay...paid, by Joseph Devell of Newport ...have...sold...a Purchassers Share, both upland and medow...at...Punckatest...Twentith day of January... 1672:

Wit.   Daniell X Wilcoke
   Thomas Ward   his marke
   Richard Baily:

...Daniell Wilcock...acknowlidged...above...27th day of July 1680
              As Atests Walter Clarke Dpt Govr.

[188] John Simmons to Thomas Ward.
...John Simmons Inhabitting on the southeast side of Tanton River on...land called the freemens land...planter...for... fifteen pounds...mony of New England,...paid...by Thomas Ward of Newport...Merchant...have...sold... land lying,...on the Southeast side of Tanton River, containing one hundred Acres...in bredth fifty Rods,...in length three hundred and twenty Rods being part of the fifteenth share of Land, and lying between the fall River and Tanton bounds, in...Collony of Plymoth...bounded...on

the Northwest by land...of William Mackepeace, and on the Northeast by land of Job Winslow, on the Southeast by the land of...William Mackepeace, on the Southwest, by land... of William Mackepeace,...with all...hie ways, Comons,... tenth day of December...One Thowsand Six hundred Seventy Nine:

Wit.   John Simmons
  William Hiscox
  John Read

The 6th of Sept 1680 Newport...John Simmons...acknowlidged...Caleb Carr Asistant

...Martha Symmons, the wife of John...give asent unto...Sale...

Wit.   Martha X Symmonds
  Marke Athy   her marke
  Samuell Rowland

[189]   John Cooke to Thomas Ward.

...John Cooke of portsmouth...for...Eighteen pounds five Shillings Currant Silver mony of New-England...paid...by Thomas Ward of Newport...doe...sell...one sixt in deale of a part...both upland and medow...being in the Towneship of Dartmoth...which...land I...bought of Thomas Burge of Newport...Thirtith day of Aprill...one Thowsand six hundred Eighty.

Wit.   John X Cooke
  Henry Tew   his marke
  Richard Barnes
  Jabess X Cotterell
    his marke

...John Cooke...acknowlidged the above-written...May 29th 1680

  Before mee William Coddington Asist.

[190]   Samuell Gorton to Daniell Coles-etc.

...Samuel Gorton senr. proffessor of the Mistries of Christ ...of the Towne of Warwicke...doe...give...my Right...

in that Neck of Land which was given unto mr Randall Howldon and my selfe lying Southward from mr Richard Smiths place where his house stood, and bounded Southerly by a Brook Running downe betwixt the said Neck and a place where Captain Hudsons house stood, at Narragansett, the bounds thereof, being more largly Expressed in the deed bearing date May 27th 1659...unto my Sonn Daniell Coles, and his wife Mahor Coles one sixth part of...the said Neck ...unto my sonn John Sanford and my Daughter Mary Sanford One Sixth part,...unto my sonn William Maze and my Daughter Sarah Maze, one sixth part...unto my sonn John Warner, and my Daughter Anna Warner one sixth part,... unto my sonn John Crandall and my Daughter Elizabeth Crandell one sixth part,...unto my sonn Benjamin Barton and to my daughter Susanah Barton one sixth part,...provided that each of them shall...help defend the title against the intrusions of Richard Smith...in case all doe Refuse... I...give it to my Sonn Samuell Gorton to performe the same ...27th of November 1677 in Warwicke

Wit.   Samuell Gorton Senr.
  John Greene Assistant.
  Randall Howldon

[191] Elisha and Hannah Hutchinson to Willian Brenton. ...Elisha Hutchinson of Boston...and Hannah his wife,... for...a house and a percell of Land lying...in the Towneship of Boston...belonging unto William Brenton Esq. of Newport...made over to...Elisha and Hannah Hutchinson ...hath...sold...unto...William Brenton Esgr....that... land or farme which lately did belong unto my Uncle mr Samuell Hutchinson of Boston...deaceassed, and by him... given unto me...in which farme then John Acres dwelt,... lying in the Towneship of Portsmouth...bounded on the Northerly side...with the land of Elisha Sanford, and on the Easterly side...with the Comon shore next the sea, and on the Southerly Side...with the Land of Obadiah Holmes, and on the Westerly side...with the Comon land of the towne,... two hundred acres,...with all houses, Ediffices, buildings,

fences, Gardins, Yards, trees, fruits, ways dreanes,...belonging...twenty seventh day of September...One Thowsand Six hundred Seventy

Wit.   Elisha Hutchinson—
  Stephen Burton   Hannah Hutchinson—
  John Winchcombe

Newport...the 8th day of May 1674...John Winchcombe...did see Elisha and Hannah Hutchinson signe...deed...

William Coddington Gor.

[194] William Brenton to Peleg Sanford.

...William Brenton now Resident in Newport...Marriner ...for...one hundred and five pounds...Mony of Boston ...paid by Peleg Sanford of Newport...Have...sold... land in the Township of Newport...and is part of my Farme Comonly Knowne by the Name of Breases or Cases farme ...forty two Acres...bounded...on the North...on the land of John Easton senr. begining at a Ditch on the banck neer unto the Beach, and soe to Extend by the said ditch and fence on a Straight line West...Eighty two Rods or poles, Eighty two Rods South Eighty two Rods on...Brentons land...East unto the salt water banck and Soe to Extend North...on the said Sea Banck upon a straight line Eighty two Rods or poles unto the ditch first above-mentioned,...with all...wood ...stones Quarries...if...William Brenton...shall...pay... unto...Peleg Sanford...one hundred and five pounds of... monys of Boston...in the Towne of Newport...then...Deed ...Shall be voyd and of None Efect...sixt day of March... One Thowsand six hundred seventy nine or Eighty:

Wit.   William Brenton
  Nathaniell Coddington
  Josiah Arnold

Newport March 10th 1679-80...Josiah Arnold and Nathaniell Coddington...saw William Brenton signe...above-said Mortgage and acknowlidged it

John Albro Asistant

[195] James Badcocke—Will.

...James Badcocke senr...Verbelly...before us...unto his

sonn Job Badcocke all his Smith tooles...
...one Cow...unto his daughter Mary Champlin...a Cow Calfe to William Champlins Eldist daughter...
...unto his sonn Joseph all his housing and lands...
...all...Remaining...Estate...unto his wife Elizabeth Badcocke...
          John Badcocke
          Job Badcocke.
This Testator dyed the 12th of June 1679.
John...and Job Badcocke...appeared...at a Court Held at Westerly the 17th of September 1679...
        John Sanford Secretary:
[196] Inventory...James Badcocke Senr.
...Inventory of...James Badcocke Senr. Deceassed in June last in Stoning Towne...Leaving a Widow with three Children the Eldist a Sonn about Nine Yeare Old.

	£	s.	d.
house & Land about twenty Acres	30	00	00
Bellows: Anvil Vice and other Smiths tooles	05	00	00
2 Cowes 2 Yearlings & 2 Calves	11	00	00
7 small swine £2 : 1 bed & bedstead with bedding £5	07	00	00
one small bed & beding £ 1:5s: 2 chests 10s.	01	15	00
Churn pailes & tubbs...	01	10	00
Iron pott scilitt pan. tramills...Iron spitt & slice	02	00	00
3 Spining wheels 12s. axes Spade...10s.	01	02	00
hand saw drawing knife Reaphooke 2 botle one hamer	00	05	00
puter and tin, one brass skillit 2 sives	00	14	00
one paire of Cards with some wools & flax & yarne	01	05	00
Chaines Cradle with other lumber	00	10	00
Sum Tottall..	61	01	00

...Inventory...Taken...5th of July 1679 by us
 James Pendleton Thomas Wells Ephraim Minor
[196] Richard Carder to Samuell Gorton.
...Richard Carder of Warwick...mony...Received have...

sold...unto Samuell Gorton of...Warwick...land...being upon that Neck of land Called Shaomet by the...Towne of Warwick,...about twenty acres...bounders...Northeast end of it butteth upon the hie way goeing from the said towne unto the Neck...called Shaomett, and the southwest end Butteth upon a certaine Swamp Runnet or Small passage of water Issuing into a cove or inlet of water from the sea, upon the Northwest side it is bounded upon a percell of land belonging to mr John Wickes an other percell of land of mr Randall Houldons coming from the said cove or inlet of water, an other percell of land of mr Robert Potters, an other of mr Walter Todds, and a small peace of Medow or Marsh ground belonging to John More all of Warwick, and the southeast side bounded by a percell of Land of Richard Watermans of...Providence:...seventeenth day of January ...one thousand six hundred fifty—:

Wit.   Richard Carder.
   Randall Houldon
   Walter Todd
   John Wickes
   John Hadon

[197]   William Manchester to John Cooke.

...William Manchester of Punkatest in New Plymouth... Yeoman... for...sixty pounds...mony of New-England... paid...from John Cooke senr. of...Portsmouth yeoman... Have...sold...one halfe of Thirteen shares of land by me purchassed of Thomas Lawton, then of...Portsmouth...as by Deed...bearing date the twentith day of Aprill...one thowsand six hundred Seventy Seven doth appeare to be by him purchassed off...Alice Bradford, Gersham Cobb, William Nelson, William Crowe, John Brigs, senr., John Richard, Samuell Dunson, Andrew King, Thomas Southworth, Thomas Morton, John Jourdane and Joseph Ramsdon—...land... lying...in the...Punckatest Neck...to Bee Holdon of his Majtie. ...as of his manner of East Greenwich...twenty four day of November...One Thousand Six hundred Eighty:

Wit.   William Manchester
   James Card   X
   John Sanford.   his marke
                                Mary X Manchester
                                her marke

William Manchester...sixteenth day of February one Thousand six hundred and Eighty...owne above...
                                John Albro Asistant

[198] William Manchester to John Cooke.
...William Manchester of Punckatest...Yeoman...for...seventy three pound six shillings and Eight pence...mony of New-England...paid by John Cooke senr. of Portsmouth...Yeoman...have...sold...two shares...belonging unto a late purchass of the lands of Pocassett and...adjacent; as will...appeare by a Deed from...New Plymoth Collony...fifth day of March 1679. Unto Edward Grey Nathaniell Thomas Benjamin Church my selfe and some other our friends...therein being Thirty Shares...in the whole,...bounded Northward & westward by the freemens lotts neer the fall River Westward by the Bay or Sound that Runnith between the said land and Rhode Island, Southward partly by Saconnett Bounds and partly by Dartmoth Bounds, Northward up unto the woods till it meet with land formerly granded by the Authorety of Plymoth to other men...Exprest in said Deed, as alsoe...former Grants therein Excepted as to Captn Goulding. David and Thomas Lake, and Captn Morris:...Twenty fourth day of November...1680.
Wit.   William X Manchester
   James Card   his marke
   John Sanford   Mary X Manchester
                                her marke:

William Manchester...sixteenth day of February One Thousand six hundred & Eighty...owned this...
                                John Albro Asistant

[199] Caleb Carr to Susanah Relict of William Hieffernan ...Caleb Carr of Newport...Administrator to...Estate of William Hieffernan deceassed have sold unto Susanah the

Relict of said William Hieffernan, a percell...of Goods, which belonged to...William Hieffernan...28th day of February 1680-81.
Wit.   Caleb Carr
  Ephraim Turnor
  John Odlin

[200]   Robert Bartlett to Thomas Burge.

...Robert Bartlett of...Plymoth...for...fifty pounds...Currant Silver mony of New England...Recived...of Thomas Burge junr. of...Newport...Have...sold,...one Moiety...of land both upland & Medowland,...at Acushnett in...Towneship of Dartmoth...alsoe one Moiety...in deale ...of land both upland and medowland...being at a place...Knowne by the Indian Name of Poscomansett in...Towneship of Dartmoth...Reserveing unto my Selfe one third part or one part of three of the halfe share last named...Excepting the one third of the latter (which is alredy Excepted)...To be houlden...to his Majtie. his manner of East Greenwich ...Seventeenth day of February...1670...

Wit: the marke
  William Clarke   of Robert X Bartlett
  James Clarke

                    ...acknowledged...
                    Before me Thomas prence Gor.

[201]   John Brigs to John Brigs.

...John Brigs Senr. of...Portsmouth...Yeoman...unto my ...Eldist Sonn John Brigs of...Portsmouth,...doe...Give ...one halfe...of a whole purchassers Share...both uplands and Medows...in...Towneship of Dartmoth...Next adjoyning to the land of the widow Fancy at the place formerly called Ponagansett...if my Sonn John shall decease...before his wife Hannah...Lands...shall be to the...use of...Hannah provided she remaine a Widdow...Then...shall...decend unto my Grandson John Second Sonn to my...sonn John...then...is to decend to my next, youngist Grandson ...Then...shall decend unto Edward Eldist Sonn to my...sonn John Brigs...fourteenth day of October One Thowsand

six hundred Seventy Nine,...
Wit.   John Brigs
  Edward X Lay   his X marke
    his marke
  John Sanford.
[202] William Manchester to John Pearce.
...William Manchester of Punkatest in New Plymouth...
Yeoman,...for...Sixteen pounds of sterling mony of New-
England...paid...by John Pearce of...Portsmouth...Have
...sold...One fourth part of a...Thirtith part...of land at
Pocassett...bounded...Northward and Westward by the
freemens lotts neer the fall river, and westward by the Bay or
sound that runnith between the said Land and Rhode Island
Southward partly by a line that is Sett at a great Rock on
which is a Seader bush marked neer the way that leadith to
Punkatest Eastward to a pond at Dartmoth Towne bounds,
and westward to Suppowett Creeks mouth and partly by Dartmoth bounds, and Northward up into the woods to Midlebury
Towne bounds and quitquissitt pond (alwaies Excepted of
this...Sale Suppowett neck of land, and the Medows belonging to Punkatest proprietors, and the land formerly granted by
the Court of Plymoth to Captn. Richard Morris, and soe much
...as shall be alloted...for the use of the ministry) All...
I with others lately purchassed of...Agents of...Collony of
Plymoth...by...Deed of feofment...date March 5th 1679
1680...seventh day of October...One Thowsand six hundred
Eighty one.
Wit.   William X Manchester
  John Sanford   his marke
  William Coggeshall   Mary X Manchester
  Joseph Tripp: her marke
Wit. to...Mary Manchesters hand this 17th January 1683
  Thomas Butts
  Elizabeth X Butts
      her marke.
...William Manchester...acknowlidged the above written
...Decembr. 13th 1681 Peleg Sanford Governor.

William Manchester to Mathew Greenell.
...William Manchester of Punkatest...for...thirteen pounds of Sterling mony of New England...paid...by Mathew Greenell of...Portsmouth...Maulster...Have... sold...one full fourth part of a Thirtith part...of land at Pocassett...bounded...Northward and Westward by the freemens lotts neer the fall river, and Westward by the Bay or Sound that runneth between the said land and Rhode-Island Southward partly by a line that is Sett at a great Rock on which is a seader bush marked neer the way that leadith to Punkatest Eastward to a pond at Dartmoth Towne Bounds Westward to Suppowett Creeks mouth, and partly by Dartmoth bounds, and Northward up into the woods to Middlbury Towne bounds and quitquissitt pond:—(alwaies Excepted out of this...Sale Suppowett Neck of land and the Medow belonging to Punkatest proprietors, and the land... granted by...Plymoth to Captn. Richard Morris, and Soe much...as Shall be alloted...for the use of the Ministry)... which...Land, I...with...others latly purchassed of...the Collony of Plymoth...Deed...bearing date March 5th 1679 1680...seventh day of October...one Thowsand Six hundred Eighy one.

Wit.   William X Manchester
  John Sanford   his marke
  William Coggeshall
  Joseph Tripp

...William Manchester...acknowlidged the above-written...
                     Peleg Sanford Govr.

[205] Agreement between John Brigs senr. and John Brigs. Memorandum:
...agreed that...the medows to the within mentioned halfe share of land Given me by my...father John Brigs, is to be the medow adjoining to that land herein given the medow Called boggy Medow and the Medow at a place called bare need, and the Medow adjoining to a percell of land, by my father sold to Ralph Earll;...being tenn acres...reserved

against the land of Ralph Earll;...to continue till the decease of my father...14th of Octobr 1679:
...I...John Brigs Senr. doe...Give...my son John Brigs ...halfe of my...land...the bounds...shall...take in all the land...John hath broken up and Cleered...14th October 1679:...

Wit.   John X Brigs Senr.
  Edward Lay   his marke
    his marke
  John Sanford: John X Brigs junr.
                                        his marke

William Manchester to Thomas Dorfie.

...William Manchester of Punkatest in New-Plymoth... Yeoman...for...thirty four pounds of Sterling mony of New-England...paid...by Thomas Dorfie of...Portsmouth ...yeoman,...have...Sold...one...halfe of a thirtith part ...of land at Pocasset...bounded...Northward and Westward by the freemans lotts Neer the fall river, and Westward by the bay or sound that runneth between the said land and Rhode Island Southward partly by a line that is Sett at a great Rock on which is a Seader bush Marked neer the way that leadith to Punkatest Eastward to a pond at Dartmoth Towne bounds and westward to Suppowett Creeks mouth and partly by Dartmoth bounds and Northward up into the woods to Midlebury Towne bounds and quitquissitt pond, (alwaies Excepted out of this...Sale, Suppowett neck...and the Medows belonging to Punkatest proprietors, and the land formerly granted by:...plymoth to Captn Richard Morris, and soe much...as shall be allotted...for the use of the ministry)...which...land I...with...others...purchassed of ...the Collony of Plymoth...Deed bearing date March 5th 1679-1680...thirteenth...of December...One Thowsand Six hundred Eighty one.

Wit.   William X Manchester
  John Sanford   his marke
  George Sisson

...Wil Manchester...acknowlidged the above...December 13th 1681

Peleg Sanford Governor

[207] Thomas Manchester to John Pearce.
...Thomas Manchester junr. of...Portsmouth...Black Smith...For...fifteen pounds Sterling mony of New-England...paid...by John Pearce of...Portsmouth...Yeoman,...Have...sold...one...fourth part of a Thirtith part...of land at Pocassett...bounded...Northward and westward by the freemens lotts neer the fall river and westward by the bay or sound that runneth between the saide land and Rhode Island, Southward, partly by a line that is sett at a great rock on which is a seader bush marked neer the way that leadith to Punkatest Eastward to a pond at Dartmoth Towne bounds, and westward to Suppowett Creeks mouth, and partly by Dartmoth bounds and quitquisset pond (alwaies Excepted out of this...sale, Suppowet Neck...and...Medows belonging to Punkatest proprietors and...land...granted by ...Plymoth to Captn Richard Morris, and soe much...as shall be allotted for the use of ministry) which...I bought ...of William Manchester, who with others latly purchassed ...of Plymoth,...Deed...bearing date March 5th 1679-1680 ...one and thirtith day of December...one Thowsand six hundred Eighty one

Wit.   Thomas **X** Manchester
  John Sanford.   his marke
  Mary Sanford—.

[208] John Warner to Thomas Brownell.
...John Warner of...Warwick...for...Valluable sum by ...Thomas Brownell of Portsmouth...doe...sell...one...quarter...share of Land lying...to the westward of the bounds of the Towneship of Warwick Comonly Called Coweesitt...Twenty fift day of October...1677:

Wit.   John Warner
  Caleb Arnold
  William Coggeshall

[209] John Tripp received of Rose Weeden.

...John Tripp and Mary my wife have recieved of Rose Weeden (Executrix to Anthony Paine deceast)...what... was due us...18th day of March (1650)
 James Weeden
 Richard Harte   John Tripp
       the marke of Mary X Tripp

  John Tripp to Mathew Grenell.
...John Tripp of Portsmouth...with the consent of Mary my wife have sold unto Mathew Grenell of the same Towne ...Twenty seven Acres of land lying within...Portsmouth ...bounded Eastward partly with land sold William Havens and partly with land...of Rose Paine, Southward with the hie way to the sea Westward with land of Rose. Paine and Northward with the mill river,...beinge Twenty seven Rod broad upright through the whole lott...being that...Land that I...had in part of the Legusie given to my wife... Twenty Seventh of Aprill...one Thowsand Six hundred fifty and one —

Wit.   John Tripp
 the marke of   the X marke of
 Henry X Lake   Mary Tripp
 William Hall

[210] Ursamequen, etc to James Cudworth, etc.
...Ursamequen Wamsetta Tatapanum. Natives...of New-Plymoth...have sold...unto Captn James Cudworth, Josiah Winslow senr. Constant Southworth John Barnes, John Tisdale, Humphry Turnor, Walter Hatch, Samuell House, Samuell Jackson, John Damon; mr Timethy Hatherly, Timethy Foster Thomas Southworth, George Watson, Nathaniell Morton, Richard Moore, Edmond Chanler, Samuell Nash, Henry Howland, mr Ralph Partridge, Love Bruster, William Paybody, Christopher Wadsworth, Keanelme Winslow Thomas Bourne John Waterman the son of Robert Waterman...all the...upland and medow, lying on the Easterly Side of Tanton River,...bounded towards the South, with the river Called the Falls or Queqateand, and soe Extending

it selfe Northerly untill it come to a litle brooke Called by the English...Staseys Creek, which Brook Isues out of the woods into the Marshes, and Bay of Asonett close by the Narrowing of Asonett neck, and from a Marked tree neer to the said brook to the head of the marsh to Extend it selfe into the woods on a North nor East point four miles; and from the head of the said four miles on a Straite lyne southerly untill it meet with the head of the four mile line at quequeteand or the falls...Including all Medows Necks or Islands lying... betwixt Asonett Neck and the falls...(Except the land that Tabatacoson hath in present use) and all the medow upon Asonett Neck upon the south side of the said Neck, and all the Medow upon the westerly side of Tanton River from Tantons upland bounds round untill it come to the head of Wepoissett river, in all Creeks Coves rivers and inland medow not lying above four miles from the flowing of the tide:... for...twenty Coates two Rugs to Iron potts to Ketels and one litle Ketle 8 paire of shooes, six paire of stockins one dozen of hows 1 dozen of hatchets two yards of broadcloth, and a debt satisfied to John Barnes, which was due from Wamsitta ...before the 24th of December 1657...wee Ursamequen, Wamsitta, Tattapanum sett our hands...second day of Aprill 1659

Wit.   Wamsatta **X** his marke
  Thomas Cooke   Tatapanum **X** her marke
  Jonathan Brige
  John Sasomon —.
...Before us Jos. Winslow
        Will. Bradford
Ju th 1659 Wamsitta did acknowlidge...
      Before us - Jos. Winslow
         Wilt. Bradford
        June the 9th 1659...Tattapanum did acknowlidge...
        Jos. Winslow Wilt. Bradford

[211]   Samuell Nash to Benjamin Bartlett.
...Lieutent Samuell Nash of...Duxbury in...Plymoth... for...28 pounds Sterling...paid by Benjamin Bartlett of...

Towne afore-said...Cooper,...have...sold...all...my...
land...about Tanton River belonging to me as one of those
twenty six Antient freemen or old Comers (comonly soe
Called)...granted...bearing date the third day of July...
1656 which...containes all...land...from Tanton Bounds
on the west side of the River to Wepoissett river and on the
East side of the River...from Asowett Neck to Quequee-
haent, or the place called...the falls, and soe to Extend into
the woods four miles on each side of Tetucutt River, as alsoe
the Twenty Sixt part of all the grant of Medow, lying between Plymoth grant at Sepecan and the purchassers grant
which Extendeth three miles to the Eastward of Acushnett...
my lott of the afore-said land...being...the one and
Twentith lott lyinge Next unto the land of mr Thomas Bourne
on the South Side, Begining at the range, betwixt the said
lotts, and Extending...towards the North...untill it come
Neer to Asonett river and meets with the range that Crosseth
the path, to a read Oake below the path, and a white Oake
above the path, it being Marked and Numbered towards the
South with twenty one, and towards the North with twenty
two...To Bee Houldon as of his Majtie. his Manner of East
Greenwich...29 of May...1666
Wit.   Samuell Nash

      his
Francis   West
      X
      marke
Jonathan Alden.

[213] Raph Powell to John Simmons.
...Raph Powell of...Marshfield in...Newplymoth &
Martha his wife...for...forty & seven pounds tenn shillings
...paid by John Simmons Inhabitant on the freemens lotts
at Tanton River...doe...sell...one...halfe part of the one
and twentith lott on the Easterly side of...Tanton River,
It being...one hundred Rods wide, and four Miles long from
the said river Eastward and to be devided Soe...John Simmons Shall have the South Side of...lott, and alsoe...one

halfe...the Land belonging...on Swansey Side being the westerly side of the river...which is...two sixteen acre lots ...and one halfe of all the medow belonging...on both Sids the said river Excepting only...that Medow belonging... that is at or neer...to a place...called Scipican...sixteenth day of February...1679:

Wit.   Ralph Powell
 Samuell Spruge   Martha **X** Powell
 Samuell Litle.   her marke

  16th Ralph Powell and Martha his wife...February 1674...acknowlidged this...
    Josiah Winslow Govr N. P.

[214]   John Simmons to Thomas Ward.

...John Simmons Inhabitant on the freemens Lotts aboutting on the South Eastward Side of Tanton River in the Collony of New Plymoth...for...fifty two pounds of Currant mony of New England...paid...by Thomas Ward of Newport... Have...Sold...one...halfe part of the one and twentith lott on the Easterly Side of the said Tanton river, being in bredth ...one hundred Rods wide, and four Miles long from the... river Eastwardly...to be soe devided,...that...Thomas Ward shall have the South Side...and alsoe the one halfe of the land belonging to the...share on Swansey Side, being the Westerly Side of the...River which is...two sixteen Acre lotts...and the one halfe of all the Medow belonging to the... share on both sides the...river...(Excepting only...that Medow belonging to the said share...that is at...Scipican) ...Sixteenth day of September...1680:

Wit.   John Simmons
 John **X** Jerson his marke
 Gilbert Magick.
 Richard Barnes

...John Simmons...in Newport acknowlidged the above-written...17th day of Septemr 1680

     Before peleg Sanford Governor

...Martha Symmons the wife of...John Simmons, doe... give...asent,...to sale...18th...of Aprill 1681.

Wit.　　　　　　　　　　　Martha **X** Simmons—
　Marke Athy　　　　　　　　her marke
　Samuell Rowland

[216] William Makepeace to Thomas Ward.
...William Makepeace Inhabittant on the freemens land... abutting on the Southeastward Side of Tanton River in... Collony of New-Plymoth...Ann his wife for...fifty pounds ...Currant mony of New England...paid by Thomas Ward of Newport...Have...sold...one Moiety...of a freemans Lott...the one & Twentith Lott on the Easterly Side of the ...Tanton River being in bredth...One hundred Rods. and four miles long from the...River Easterly, and being the Northeastly Side thereof, and alsoe...one halfe...the land belonging to the...Share on Swansey Side being the Westerly Side of the...River which is...two Sixteen acre lotts ...and...one halfe of all the medow belonging to the... share on both sides the...River (Except only...that Medow belonging to the...Share that is...neer to...Scipican)... Twenty seventh Day of October One Thowsand six hundred and Eighty...

Wit.　　　　　　　　　　William **X** Makepeace
　James Man　　　　　　　　his marke
　John Peckum jur.　　　　Ann **X** Mackepeace
　Gilbert Magick　　　　　　her marke
　John **X** Jerson
　　his marke.

...William Mackepeace and Ann his wife...in Newport... acknowlidged the above...
　　　　　　　　　　　Peleg Sanford Governor.

[217] Thomas Waite to Thomas Ward.
...Thomas Waite of Portsmouth...Taylor...for...twelve pounds tenn shillinge...paid...by Thomas Ward of Newport ...Have...sold...one fourth part of a share in Deale of land...upland and Medow...Scittuated in the Collony of New Plymoth...bounded...on the South...partly by the North line of the Towne of Dartmoth and partly by the north line of the lands belonging to the purchassers of...Punc-

katess in which...line....is A seader tree marked and is standing on or Neer Supowet Rocke and partly by a Creek Called Supowett Creeke and partly by Sepowett neck which ...is belonging to the said lands of Punckatess On the west partly by the...Creek & Neck called Supowett and partly by the Salt water or bay, and partly by the Neck of land called Nunnaquaqutt On the North or Northwerstwardly by the salt water Called Tanton River up to the River called the fall river, and partly by the head or Eastwardly and of the... freemens lands...and on the East or NorthEastwardly...by the...freemens Lands...as the...lands Extends...into the Cuntry from the Salt water called Tanton River neer...the place Called the fall River, and partly by the Southwestward bounds of the lands of Midleburough, and partly by the westward Line of...Dartmoth...Twenty Eight day of August... One Thousand Six hundred and Eighty.

Wit. Thomas Waite:

  John **X** Manchester
    his marke
  Richard Barnes
  Mary Billinge—

...Sarah Waite the wife of...Thomas Waite doe...Asente unto...Sale,...6th day of June 1681

                      Sarah **X** Waite
                          her marke

...Thomas Waite and Sarah his wife...acknowledged... 6th day of June 1681

          Before peleg Sanford Govr.

[218] William Makepeace to Thomas Ward.

...William Makepeace Inhabitant upon the Lands called the freemens Lands...abutting on the Eastward Side of Tanton River...and Ann his wife...for...fifty pounds Currant silver mony of New England...paid by Thomas Ward of Newport...have...sold...one Moiety...of a Freemans Lott ...the one and Twentith lott on the Eastwardly Side of the ...Tanton River,...in Bredth...one hundred Rods four miles long from the said River Eastwardly, and being the

Northwardly side thereof, and alsoe...one halfe...the land belonging...on Swansey side,...the westerly side of the...River, which is...two Sixteen Acre lotts...and one halfe of all the Medows belonging...on both sids the...river (Excepting only,...the Medow...at...Scippican)...with all...belonging...as by a Deed...bearing date the twenty seventh day of October...One Thowsand six hundred and Eighty...if wee...at any time...mollest...Thomas Ward...then...it shall be lawfull...for...Thomas Ward...to...take...one Moiety...of a freemans Lott,...the fifteenth lott on the Eastwardly side of the...Tanton River...in breadth,...One hundred Rods being four miles in length from the...River Eastwardly, and being the Southward side of the...Lott, and Adjoining to the land where...William Makepeace now, Inhabiteth,...twenty one day of June...one Thowsand Six hundred Eighty and one

Wit.
  John **X** Jerson
    his marke
  Richard Barnes
  Stephen Arnold

William **X** Makepeace
  his marke:
Ann **X** Makepeace
  her marke

[220] Samuell Hickes to Thomas Ward.

...Samuell Hixe of...Dartmoth...Yeoman...for...thirty pounds...paid...By Thomas Ward of Newport Merchant ...Have sold...full share of a purchass Right,...uplands and Medows...being in Dartmoth in the Village...of Acushnett on the west side of the...River,...butting upon the River ...To be Houldon of his Majtie. as of his Manner of East Greenwich...Ninteenth day of October One Thowsand six hundred seventy-two:

Wit.
  James Shaw
  Daniell **X** Wilcock Marke:

Samuell Hickes
Lidia Hicks

...acknowlidged by Samuell Hicks...29 of October 1672.
                      Will. Bradford Asistant.

[221] Purchassers of Pawtuxett to Stukely Wastcote. Pawtuxett Novemr. the first 1648:

Wee the purchassers of Pawtuxett have layd out to Stukely Wastcote Two hundred and fifty acres of upland to his spectickle meddow joyninge...bounded on the Northwest side with the Share layd out to Ezekill Hollyman, and on the Southwest, with his owne medow and Pawtuxett River,...tow hundred pole...Square,...Witnes our hands:

Richard **X** Waterman   Ezekill Hollyman
William Harris.   John Green junr.
William Field in the behalfe of Richard Parker
Richard Harker.

     Stukely Westcott to Robert Weskot.

...Stukely Westcott of Warwick...being one of the thirteen and a free purchasser of Pawtuxett...doe...give...unto my son Robert Weskot,...my...lands and medow...
11th of December 1656:

Wit.   pr mee Stukly Weskot.
   Henry Reddocke
   John Wislake:

     Samuell Shivereck to John Reckes.

...Samuell Shivereck...of Tanton, doe Oblige my Self to John Rekes to cleer...from all debts...that...may be betwixt each other in their Copartnership Samuell...doe likewise Engage to deliver two hundred of Iron and...one great Vice,...his working tooles unto...John Reckes. July the 8...1680

Joseph Hall   Samuell Shivereck.
Samll. Hall.

[222]   Robert Westcot to Andrew Harris.

Providence 13d. 11mth 1656

...Robert Westcot of Warwick have sold unto Andrew Harris of Providence all my Right in Pawtuxett, and in pertickular my Spectickle medow, and two hundred and fifty Acres by the Eighteen foot pole thereto, adjoyning and one share of six acres in the last devision at Pawtuxett neck, with all my Right...according to the Grant of Antenomeah, and Roger Williams for one horse and two Coults paid...Received by me Robert Westcoate...

Received by me Robert Westcoate...
Wit. Robert Wesscot
  Nicholas Ide pr mee Stukly Westkott.
  Thomas Harris
  Mathew Greenell to Thomas Manchester.
...Mathew Greenell of...Portsmouth...Maulster...for... six pounds Currant mony of New-England...paid by Thomas Manchester Junior of...Portsmouth Blacksmith,...Have...sold...thre fourth parts of an Acre...being at the Northeastward Corner of my lands in...Portsmouth...bounded, on the Northwestward side by the land lately belonging to the deceassed Nathaniell Browninge, to extend from the Corner tree at the brook and Comon westward twenty Rods, on the Eastward is bounded, by the brooke and Comon extending from the said Corner tree southward six Rods and a halfe to a Rocke, and southward bounded by my lands, twenty Rods from the Brook and Comon to a damson tree, and westward by my lands Extending from the said damson tree five Rods and a halfe Northward to the lands lately belonging to... Nathaniell Browning:...Twentith day of February One Thowsand six hundred Eighty one:...
Wit. Mathew **X** Greenell
  John Sanford his marke
  Caleb Arnold
  William Corey.

[224] William Coggeshall to Roger Goulding.
...William Coggeshall of...Portsmouth...Yeoman...for... one hundred pounds Currant mony of New-England...paid by Roger Goulding of...Newport...Marrinor...Have...sold...my...percell of land...being in the place called the Comon fence in the Towneshipp of Portsmouth...fifty Acres ...bounded Southwardly the land of John Pearce...and partly by the Comon, Southwesterly is bounded by the land of Thomas Hicks. (by him purchassed of John Coggeshall) and on all other parts is bounded by the Bay or Salt water... the said land formerly belonginge to the deceassed my Grandfather William Baulston, and by him to mee bequeathed...

fourth day of March...One Thowsand six hundred Eighty one:

Wit.
  John Coggeshall
  John Sanford
  David Lake

William Coggeshall
Rachell Coggeshall.

[225] Robert Brookes—Land Recorded.

...Robert Brookes of...Newport...being in...posession...of land scittuate...within...Newport...Twenty five acres...bounded Northward by land belonging to Edward Greenman-Eastward by the Comon, Southward by the Comon and hieway, Westward part by land belonging to Aron Davis, and by land belonginge to Edward Greenman,...with all Dwelling or Mansion houses, outhouses, Barnes,...Orchards, Gardens,...premisses are...Ratefyed...11th day of Aprill 1682. According to a law made the 22th of May 1662

                                John Sanford Recorder

[226] Job Almy to Thomas Ward.

...Job Almy of Portsmouth...for...twenty six pounds of Currant Silver mony of New England,...paid...By Thomas Ward of Newport...Have...sold...one fourth part of a Share...upland and Medow,...being...in the Collony of New-Plymoth...bounded...On the west by the Bay or Salt watter neer Rhode Island on the South...by the Sea, on the East...by the salt walter, and the west line of the Towneship of Dartmoth, and Northerly by the South line of Punckatest land, which...lands...were granted to the old Servants,...and formerly belonged unto my Brother John Almy of Portsmouth...Twenty Ninth Day of Jully...One Thowsand Six hundred Eighty & one.

Wit.   Job Almy
  John X Jerson
    his marke.
  Gilbert Magick.
  Richard Barnes.

...march the twenty first one Thowsand Six hundred & Eighty and one,...Mary Almy the wife of...Job Almy...

consent to...sale...
Wit.   Mary Almy
   Phillip Shearman.
...Job Almy...in Newport...acknowledged the above...
may the tenth 1682
                           Peleg Sanford Gover.
[228]   Christopher Almy to Thomas Ward.
...Christopher Almy of Portsmouth...for...thirty pounds Currant Silver mony of New England...paid...by Thomas Ward of Newport...Have...Sold,...one fourth part of a share...both upland and Medow,...lyinge...in the Collony of New-Plymoth...bounded...on the west by the Bay or Salt walter neer Rhode Island, on the South...by the sea, on the East...by the Salt walter and the west line of the Towneship of Dartmoth and Northerly by the South line of Punkatest lands, which...were granted to the old Servants,...and formerly belonged to my Brother John Almy of Portsmouth... Ninth day of February...one Thowsand six hundred Eighty and one.
Wit.   Christopher Almy.
   William Hiscox
   Richard Baines
   Mary Billing
...Elizabeth Almy the wife of Christopher Almy doth...consent to sale...9th day of February 1681
Wit.   Elizabeth Almy.
   William Hiscox
   Richard Barnes
...Christopher Almy...acknowlidged the above written...
Before mee   Walter Clarke Dt Gove.
[229]   William Earll to William Correy.
...William Earll of Portsmouth...Yeoman...for...full... satisfaction...paid by William Correy of...Portsmouth house Carpenter...Have...Sold...One third part of a... lott...belonging to the lands formerly called by the Names of Acushnett Ponagasett Acockesett &c. since...Called...the Towne of Dartmoth.... The first Devition of the said lands

to the...date hereof...Scittuate on the Westermost part of my lands...Called the Westermost Arme within...Dartmoth, ...with all...Medows belonging...To be holden of his Maj'tie...as of his Manner of East Greenwich...fourth day of December...1669.

Wit. William Earll.
    Thomas Fish - sen.
    Joseph Holderbe

...William Earle...2nd of June 1674...acknowlidged...
                          Before me Tho Hinkly Assista.

[230] William Manchester to Captn. William Correy...William Manchester of Punckatest...Yeoman...for...forty six pounds thirteen shillings & Eight pence of sterling mony of New-England...paid...by Captn. William Correy of Portsmouth...house Carpenter...Have...Sold...one thirtith part of all that...land, at Pocassett...bounded...Northward and Westward by the freemens lotts neer the fall River, and westward by the Bay or Sound that runeth between the Said land and Rhode Island, Southward partly by a line that is sett at a great Rock on which is a seader bush marked neer the way that leadith to Punckatest, Eastward to a pond at Dartmoth Towne Bounds, and westward to Suppowett Creeks mouth, and partly by Dartmoth bounds, and Northward up into the woods to Midleburrough Towne bounds and Quit-quissitt Pond (alwaies Exceptinge out of this...Sale Suppouitt Neck of land, and the medows to Punkatest proprietors, and the land...granted by...Plymoth to Captn Richard Morris, and soe much...as shall be allotted for the use of the ministry)...which...land...I...with others lately purchassed of...Collony of Plymoth,...bearing date March 5th 1679-1680...Eleventh day of October...1681:

Wit.   William X Manchester
    John Sanford   his marke.
    James Green   ...Mary Manchester...doe...
    Thomas X Manchester   consent to...Deed...by my
      his marke: husband...
    Mathew X Greenell   Mary X Manchester
      his marke: her marke:

William Manchester...29 day of Aprill 1682...acknowlidged this....
                                            John Albro Asistant

Edward Fisher to Hannah Briggs.
...Edward Fisher senior of Portsmouth...have given...unto my daughter Hannah Briggs wife to John Briggs of...Rhode-Island...Thirty Acres of land lyinge Neer the Circuitt...being the...land which John Briggs hath in possession... bounded...upon francis Brighten lands, at the wester end, lyinge at the south Side of Thomas Waytes lands, the East and south side butting upon the Comon,...To be holden as of his Majtie his Manner of East Greenwich...24th day of May ...1677:

Wit.   Edward Fisher:
Benjamin Cheacs.
Elias Williams:

[232] Thomas Manchester to John Pearce.
...Thomas Manchester Junior of...Portsmouth...Blacksmith...for...fifteen pounds sterling mony of New-England ...paid...by John Pearce of...Portsmouth...Yeoman,... Have...sold,...one...fourth part of one thirtith part...of all that tract of land at Pocasset...bounded...Northward and Westward by the freemens lotts neer the fall River and Westward by the Bay or Sound that Runneth between the said land and Rhode-Island, Southward partly by a line that is sett at a great Rock on which is a Seader bush marked neer the way that leadith to Punkatest, Eastward to a pond at Dartmoth Towne Bounds and Westward to Suppowett Creeks mouth and partly by Dartmoth bounds: and Northward up into the woods to Midlebury Towne bound and Quitquissitt pond (...Excepted out of this...Sale Suppowett Neck,...and the Medows to Punkatest proprietors, and the land...granted...by...Plymoth to Captn Richard Morris, and soe much...for...the use of the ministry) which...I... purchassed of William Manchester who with others...purchassed all...tract of...Plymoth...by...Deed...bearinge

date March 5th 1679-1680...one and thirtith day of December...one Thowsand Six hundred Eighty one

Wit.
 John Sanford
 Mary Sanford:

Thomas **X** Manchester
 his marke.

Mary **X** Manchester
 her marke

Thomas Manchester acknowlidged March 6, 1681-2

Wit.   John Albro Asistant
 Benjamin Hall
   X his marke
 Francis Hall

John Warner to John Warner.

...John Warner...of Warwick...to my son John Warner Have Given...land...in the Township of Warwick...that ...butteth over against my now dwelling house on the Easterly side of the Street being Six Acres...with the Orchard planted thereon, also two Six acre lotts adjoyning together and Scittuate in Warwick Neck and bordering upon a hie way that leads to the Northerly end of the long medow one of which Lotts was formerly my Gran father mr Ezeckiell Hollymans the other belonged to John More also I give unto my sd son my Medow share being Neer the South end of the afore-sd long medow...but if my son...decease...without ...heir...the whole grant shall be to my daughter Precilla... fourth of May One Thowsand six hundred Eighty and three:

Wit.   John Warner.
 Benjamin Gorton
 Benjamin Barton

[234] William Coggeshall to John Pearce

...William Coggeshall of...Portsmouth...Yeoman...for ...one pounds ten shillings Currant mony of New England... paid by John Pearce of...Portsmouth...Yeoman...have... sold...land...being in the place Called the Comon fence in the Towneship of Portsmouth,...one Acre...bounded Northward partly by the land of me...and partly by Sanfords Cove

Eastward by the Salt water or sound, southward by the land of...John Pearce sold to him by my deceassed Gran father Baulston, and westward by the Comon...Twenty three day of February...One Thowsand six hundred Eighty one

Wit.
 John Sanford
 Mary Sanford
 Stephen Brayton
 Anne X Brayton
  her marke:

      William Coggeshall
      Rachell Coggeshall

[235] William Costin—Will.

...27th day of...March 1679.

...William Costin Carpenter in the Narragansett Cuntry and sixty years or upwards, the father of Phebe White...and... of Lidia Dolliver...Not to hinder...my aged wife.....of my ...Estate...one halfe...to the Children of my daughter Phebe White and the other halfe...to the Children of my daughter Lidia Dolliver after my decease & my wife's decease ...lett it be in housing Orchard...

Wit.   William Costin
 John Brigs senr.
 Francis X Brigs
  her marke

John Brigs of Kings Towne aged forty Yeares...and francis his wife...Taken in King's Towne...10th day of July 1682

      Walter Clarke Dept Gor
      Caleb Carr Assista.
      William Cadman Assista.
      William Coddington Asista.

[236] William Browne to George Sisson.

...William Browne junr. of Salem in the County of Essix... Merchant and Hannah his wife; Benjamin Brown of Salem ...Merchant and Peter Sergeant of Boston...Merchant as Atturney unto Thomas Deane of...London...Merchant, Executors of...Joseph Browne late of Charles Towne in New England...Clerke decd...for...five hundred pounds of...

Currant mony of New England...paid...by George Sisson of Portsmouth in...Rhode Island...Yeoman...Have sold... All...Land or farme...being within the Towneship of Portsmouth...Comonly Called...Midleford farme late belonging to the sd Joseph Browne deed...two hundred and forty Acres ...bounded Northerly by the land of Mathew Borden, Easterly by the sea or sound Southerly by the land late in the Teanure...of Thomas Cooke senr. decd. and Westerly partly by the hie way and Comon and partly by the land latly in... Teanure...of John Cooke senr. and partly by the land of the late Widow Cooke, and partly by the land late in...Teanure ...of Anthony Shaw...with all...houses,...yards gardens Orchards, trees woods...Swamps Marshes Medows waters ...Eleventh day of February...1681-82.
Wit.

John Hayward Senr. Wm Browne
Eliezer Moody Servt. Hannah Browne
                                     Benj. Browne
                                     Peter Sergeant:
                                          atturney of Tho Deane

...acknowlidged by...William Browne and Benja Browne and peter sergeant...11th of February 1681-2
                Before me Symon Bradstreet Governor

[238] John Cooke of...Portsmouth...aged fifty one yeares ...and John Cooke junr of...Portsmouth aged twenty six yeares...in...March last...saw Major Peleg Sanford... deliver the premisses...unto...George Sisson,: 17th of July 1682...
                                     Wm. Cadman Assistant.

Daniell Wilcots to Joseph Mory.
...Daniell Wilcots of Namquid neer Punkatest neck...for ...thirty pounds sterling mony of New England...by Joseph Mory of James Towne in...Rhode Island...paid...Have... sold...halfe of one share of land or sixteenth part of all... land at Pocassett...bounded...Northward and Westward by the freemens lotts neer the fall River and westward by the

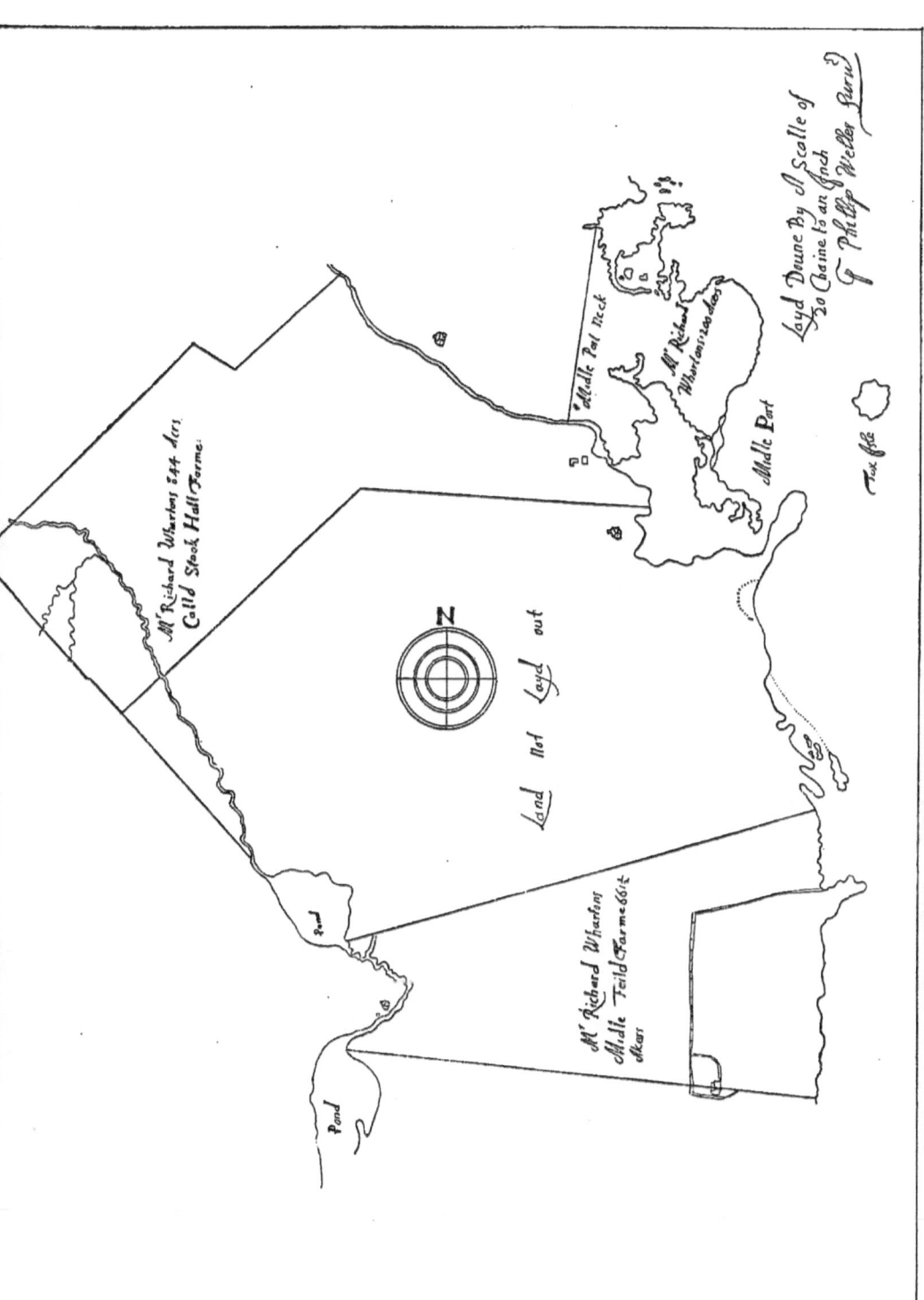

bay or sound that runneth between the...land and Rhode Island, Southward partly by a line that is sett at a great Rock on which is a seader bush marked neer the way that leadith to Punkatest, Eastward neer to a pond at Dartmoth Towne bounds, and Westward to Supowitt Creeks mouth, and Northward up into the woods to Midlebury Towne bounds and Quitquissitt pond...Excepting out of this...Sale Suppowitt neck of land and medow...and the land formerly granted by the Court of Plymouth to Captn Richard Morris, and soe much...for the use of the ministry...I...with...others purchassed of the Collony of Plymouth...Deed...bearing date March 5th 1679-80...nine and twentith of May...1682:

Wit.   Daniell **X** Wilcots
  Caleb Arnold   his marke
  George Brownell:

[240]   Thomas Terry to William Calhoane.

...13 of January...1662 or 63 : block Island. ...Thomas Terrey...of Block Island planter,...Have sold ...unto William Cahoane...40 acres...lying...upon block Island...30 acres...being on the south side of...the... Island being the Easterly end of Thomas Terrys great lott... bounded upon the hie way which makes the devission in the Island and goes from mr Dearings house to the sea, Eight acres in the planting Field at won end or side of...Thomas Terreys land as...William Cahoan shall see good alsoe two acres by the salt pond side ond that side where mr Dearings does live...according to...deed...by mr John Alcocke unto Thomas Terrey...

Wit.   Thomas Terrey:
  William Shepard.
  Peter Taelman

  William Cahoone to Samuell Hagbourne.

...William Cahoone...for Valluable Consideration...recieved of Samuell Hagbourne of block Island...make over ...two percell...latly procured...of Thomas Terrey, That is...the thirty acres in the great lott, and the eight acres in the Neck or planting field...13th of November 1670:...Block Island.

Wit.   William Cohoun.
   Abigall X Putney
     her hand
   Isaac Negus:

[241] Thomas Terry to John Klarck.
...20 Aprill...1663 on Block Island
...Thomas Terrey...of block Island have sold...unto John Klarck...of block Island fifty acres...upon block-Island, thirty eight acres of land lyinge...on the South Side of mr Terrys great lott next unto William Cahouns the same bredth of Cahoons land eight acres in the planting field in mr Terrys great lott, alsoe next unto William Cahouns Sixteen rod wide and Eighty Rod long, two Acres and a halfe of land for a house lott between Samuell Staples and Robert Gutridge, alsoe one acre of Medow land in some Convenient place...
Wit.   Thomas Terrey.
   Pieter Taelman.
   The marke X of William Rieves
   The marke X of North Joans.
   Nathaniell Johnson to John Rathbon.
Novemb...2, 1671
...Assigne over...title...in this Deed...to John Rathbon...
Wit.   Nathaniell Johnson
   Michall Caly
   The marke X David Mathews
       of

[242] Miantunomu to Roger Williams.
The 10th of the 9th month & the first yeare the Pequts were subdued.
Memorand:...John Winthrop of Boston Ge. at present Governor of the Massachusetts) & Roger Williams of New Providence in the Naniggansick bay, have bought of the 2 chiefe Sachams of Naniggansuck Miantunomu & Cannonicus, the Island Called Chibachuwese...in...Naniggansick bay for... 20 fathem of wampam and 2 Coats,...promiss...that if cattell put thereon...be hurt by natives they will see satisfaction...

Wit.   the marke of **X** Cannunicus
  Jo Throckmorton.   the marke of **X** Miantunomu
  Roger Williams to John Throckmorton.
22th of 2d month in the 14th yeare of...Soverreigne Lord King Charles.
...Roger Williams of New-Providence...for...monys...paid...by John Throckmorton of New-Providence...doe...sell...all my...title...of the Island Called Chibachusse now Called Prudence...purchassed by mr John Winthrop of Boston and me Roger Williams...from Canonicus, and Miantunomu Chiefe Sachims of the Narrigansets...
Wit.   Roger Williams
  Richard Scott
  Thomas Olney

[243] John Throckmorton to Richard Parker.
...John Throckmorton of Providence gent...to...mr Richard Parker of Boston...Merchant...Have...sold...one halfe, of the Island Chabuchuesse now called Prudence formerly purchassed of mr John Winthrop and mr Roger Williams, and by them purchassed of Connonicus & Miantunomu...twenty sixt day of June...One thowsand six hundred fifty and four...
Wit.   John Throckmorton.
  William Hill.
  Peter Duncan.
  Hugh Drury
  Nathaniell Souther Not Publcus
     1654
           Hugh Drury...12th of May 1682...made Oath...
                                    John Hull Assist.
           Peter Duncan made oath:...30th of May 1682.
                                    Barth. Gidney Assist.

[244] Wm Gerrish to Asaph Eliott.
...Captn William Gerrish of Boston...and Anne his wife the only surviveinge Childe...of Richard Parker late of...Boston Gentn decest...have given...unto Asaph Eliott of

...Boston Taylor, and Hannah his present wife, and Anne Paine spinster (two of the Grand Children of...mr Richard Parker), in equall halves the...moiety of the Island Called Prudance...that halfe...next unto Warwick and all Tennements houses Barnes...fences...second day of October...1682:

Wit.   Wm Gerrish
  Charles Buckner   Ann Gerrish.
  Isa. Addington

Captn. Wm. Gerrish and Anne his wife acknowledged this ...Boston 2d Octo. 1682 Before me   John Hull Assistant

[245] John Tulie to Daniell Vaughan.

...John Tulie now of Newport...have...sold...to Daniell Vaughan of the above-said Towne...all my Right of Land in the Towneship of East Greenwich...one tenn acre lott lying in this Towne of East Greenwich and one...great devission Containinge Ninty acres lying on the East side of Thomas Nicolls his land,...fifteenth of September One Thowsand six hundred and Eight two:

Wit.   John Tulie:
  John Heath
  Charles X Macarte
    his marke
  John Spencer

Daniell Vaughan to Phillip Longe—agreement.

...15th of September 1682...wee daniell Vaughan of Newport...and Phillip Longe of...East Greenwich...have...agreed...to chainge Our farmes...in the Towne of East Greenwich each with other...the twenty fifth farme in the first devission which...Daniell Vaughan did posess now is Phillip Longs and the farme that...Phillip Long did posess ...the third farme in the first devission, is Daniell Vaughans, and...Danill Vaughan doe give...to Phillip Long a tenn acre lott that was John Tulies...

Wit.   Daniell Vaughan
  John Heath   Phillip X Long
  Charles X Mecarte his marke   his marke
  John Spencer:

[246] Bounds of Phillip Longes farme.

...wee have layd out to Phillip Long a farme or great devission lying in the bounds of East Greenwich...Ninty acres... bounded...at the North East Corner being a white Oake tree it being the northwest Corner of Clement Weaver his land and...ninty poles west unto a stake this being the North bounds which north end is bounded on a hie way of twenty pole that lyeth between Warwich and east Greenwich and from the said stake which is the West bounds Eight score pole south by leading trees to two oake trees standing together and one of them is marked on two sides this west side is bounded on a hie way of Eight pole wide, and from that said two trees East by leading trees Ninty pole to the stake that is the above-said Weavers southwest Corner, and from the stake Eight score pole on a straight line to the first mentioned white Oake being the East line, and the west line of the afore-said Weaver his land...layd out by us Chose... to Survay...the farmes

East Greenwich
March 19th, 1680-81

Samuell Bennett
John Spencer
John Spencer Towne Clerke.

John Tift—Will.

...Thirtith day of November...one Thowsand six hundred seventy & four...unto my sonn in law, Samuell Wilson my now dwelling house in Pettacomscutt...with my house lott ...of Twenty Acres...with all yards gardens Clossures... that my wife Mary Tift shall have all my Cattell or Chattells ...two Oxen two Cowes, two yearling Steers, Eight of swine kind, and one Ewe & a lamb...with all moveables of household Stuff,...my Sonn Samuell Tift shall have two shillings and my Sonn Joshua Tift...one shilling, and my daughter Tabiatha Tift one Shilling, as alsoe one Iron pott...

Wit.
   William Hiffernan
   Allexander X King his marke.

John X Tift
his marke

...Satisfyed...Octo. 19th 1679:

                    Mary **X** Tift
                    her marke
                    Tabiathy **X** Gardner her
                                         marke
                    James Donallsone his
                                    marke **X**

[247] George Sissons land bounded.

Wee...are...appointed...by the freemen of...Portsmouth ...to...straighten the lines of mens lands...and alsoe of former lines lost,...being desired by George Sisson of said Towne, to run the head line of his farme, by him lately purchassed of mr William Browne, mr Benjamin Browne &c which...formerly belonginge to the late...mr William Brenton (& called Midleford)...lyinge in...Towneship of Portsmouth...at the North-west Corner by a white oak-tree standing in Mathew Bordens Stone wall,...and from the white oake on a streite line Southerly to a great black oak standing neer the old raile fence, and...on a streite line Southerly to a Stake by us sett by Anthony Shaws stone wall, and standeth about thirteen foot to the westward of an old hollow wind shaken ash stump that hath some liveing branches; and from that stake southerly wee have...sett the Remaininge part... by stakes pitcht and marked trees the whole length...Eight day of February 1682-3:

Francis **X** Brayton   George Lawton
    his marke   John Albro
John Sanford: John **X** Brigs senr.
                                  his marke

[248] John Warner to Gidion Freeborne.

...John Warner of...Warwick...for...forty and three pounds Sterling mony of New England...by Gidion Freeborne of Portsmouth Yeoman...paid...Have...Sold... Three...quarters...of a purchase share...lying...to the westward of the bounds of the Towneship of...Warwick,... called...Coweesitt (there being seventeen shares in the whole purchase)...two and twentith day of December...1682...

Only Excepting...seven hundred and fifty acres out of this ...sale...
Wit: John Warner.
 Caleb Arnold
 Henry Timberlake:
 Wm Manchester & Mathew Greenehill to Thomas Ward. ...William Manchester of Punkatest...planter, and Mathew Greenehill of Portsmouth...Maulster...for...Thirty pounds Currant Silver mony of New England...paid...By Thomas Ward of Newport...Merchant...Have...sold...one Moiety ...of a share or thirtith part of all...land at Pocassett... bounded...Northward and westward by the freemens lotts neer the fall river partly by Tanton River, Southwestward by the bay or sound that runnith between the said land and Rhode-Island, southward partly by a line that is sett at a great Rock on which is a ceder bush marked neer the way that leadith to Punckatest and partly by the North line of the Towne of Dartmouth, and North Eastward up into the woods to Midleburough Towne bounds and Quitquissitt pond, and the west line of the...Towne of Dartmoth, (always Excepted Out of this...Sale Suppowitt neck...and the medows belonging to Punkatest proprietors, and the land...granted by...Plymouth to Captn. Richard morris)...which...Land ...William Manchester with...others...purchassed of... Plymouth...Deed...bearinge date March 5th 1679-80:...sixt day of October...one Thowsand six hundred Eighty and two:

Wit.   William **X** Manchester
 Phillip Smith   his marke
 Thomas **X** Manchester   Mathew **X** Greenhill
  his marke   his marke
 Mary Billing

...William Manchester and Mathew Greenhill...acknowlidged...October 6th 1682: Before
          peleg Sanford Governor.

[249] Samuell Hickes to Thomas Ward.
...Samuell Hickes of Dartmouth...for...four pounds of

Currant Silver mony of New England...paid...by Thomas Ward of Newport...have...sold...percell of lands lyinge... in the...Towne of Dartmouth...twenty Acres and bounded ...on the North by the land of...Thomas Ward on the East by salt medows belonging to...Thomas Ward and salt water, on the south by a hie way, on the west by undevided lands as it is now layd out,...with all...buildings Orchards...fourteenth day of March...One Thowsand six hundred Eighty and two

Wit.   Samuell X Hickes
  Stephen Mumford   his marke
  Mary Arnold
  Mary Billing:
...Samuell Hickes...acknowlidged...
                         Walter Clarke Dept Governor.

[250] Samuell Wilson to Thomas Ward.

...Samuell Wilson of Pettacomscutt...Twenty pounds Currant Silver mony...paid...By Thomas Ward of Newport... Have...Sould...the forty and two part of all...lands both upland and Medow land...within...Petaquamscutt... bounded...by the sea from point Judith to Petticomscutt River, and soe to the head of the pond called Quaskakaonkanuck which pond lyeth about Northwest from the Mill, and from that pond on a Northwest line six miles alsoe on a west line drawne from the head of the Cove North of Point Judith Neck six miles and a halfe, and soe on a straight line from the head of the afore-said Northwest line unto the head of the said west line of six miles and a halfe, and thence on the same straight line to the sea or south shore, and on the south by the sea, (reserveing out of the...whole tract according to proportion Eight hundred acres to be layd out to the heires ...of Benedict Arnold and Samuell Wilbore by an Agreement of the Company of purchassers...) which said forty two part Containeth...seven hundred acres,...with all... woods waters,...fourteenth day of December...One Thowsand six hundred Eighty two:

Wit.   Samuell Wilson

John **X** Phillips
  his marke
William Hiscox
...Samuell Wilson...acknowledged the above...Before me Walter Clarke Dpt Govr.

[252] George Sisson to John Cooke.
...George Sisson of...Portsmouth...for...the makeing of forty seven Rods of good Suffitient Stone wall, By John Cooke son of the late deceassed Captn Thomas Cooke of...Portsmouth,...Have...sold...land lying...within the bounds of...Portsmouth Containeing one Acre and a halfe ...on the Northward by a Straight line runninge westward as the Northerly line of the lands latly belonging to the deceassed Thomas Cooke senr. Extends, and soe from the uper Corner of that line to the hie way, Eastward and Southward upon the afore-said lands latly belonging to...Thomas Cooke senr, and westward is bounded by the hie way...twelfth day of May...One Thowsand six hundred Eighty three—.
Wit.   George Sisson
  John Sanford
  James **X** Hall
    his marke:

Peter Talman to Thomas Durfee.
...Peter Talman junior late...of Portsmouth Now of the Towne of Gilford in the County of New Haven...Conecticutt...Cor-wainer...for...Twelve pounds of Currant mony of New England...paid by Thomas Durfee of...Portsmouth ...Yeoman...Have...sold...Land lyinge...in the place called the Comon fence in...Portsmouth...Eight Acres...bounded Northwardly by the land of Richard Bulger Eastwardly by Pocassett River, Southwardly by the humuck Comonly Called Samuell Hutchinsons humuck, Westwardly by the great Cove...alsoe the full Right of a hie way [purchassed of Richard Bular (as Exprest in writing)...Eight day of June...One Thowsand Six hundred Eighty three—:
Wit.   Peter Talman
  John Sanford
  Mary Sanford

[253]   Thomas Lynch to Captn Thomas Paine.
   (Jemeco Ss)
   Sr. Thomas Lynch Knight One of the Gentlemen of his Majties. Bed Chamber Capt. Genll. and Governor. in Chiefe of this his Majties. Island of Jameco and Territories...depending & Vice Admiral to his Royall Highness James Duke of Yorke in the American Seas.
   ...I am Informed there are severall Pyratte that have most barbarously Murthered divers of his Majties. Subjects: robed others & taken severall Vessalls...not...pretending...to have any Comission of Warr: These are...to Authoreize you Captn Thomas Paine Comander of the Frigatt Pearle. to Seize...kill and distroy the said Pyratts and their ships... I...Assure you and yor men...you shall have all the favour they cann Expect or I Render you and them...13th day of October 1682:
By his Excelency Comand—)   Thomas Lynch.
Henry Harrington Sery:)
I have by his Exelly's Order
affixed the seale of the Admiralty:
   [two Illegible signatures]
[254]   Thomas Manchester to Mathew Borden.
   ...Thomas Manchester of...Portsmouth...Black-smith... for...Thirty seven Pounds in Currant New-England mony ...paid by Mathew Borden of...Portsmouth Yeoman,... Hath...Sold,...one halfe...of one whole share or thireth part of all...land at Pocassett...bounded...Northward and Westward by the freemens Lotts neer the fall River and Westward by the Bay or sound tht Runneth between the said Land and Rhode Island. Southward partly by a line that is sett at a great Rock on which is a Seader Bush marked neer the way. that leadith to Punckatest, Eastward to a pond at a Dartmouth Towne Bounds and Westward to Sapowett Creeks mouth, and partly by Dartmouth bounds, and Northward up into the woods to Midlebury Towne bounds and Quitquissitt Pond (alwaies Exceptinge Out of this...Suppowett neck... and Medows belonginge to Punckatest proprietors and the

land formerly granted by...Plymouth to Capt. Richard Morris, and soe much...as shall be...for the use of the ministry)...which...Land William Manchester with... others...purchased of...Plymouth,...Deed...beareing date March 5th 1679-1680...twelfth day of February...1682
Wit. Thomas X Manchester junr.
his marke
John Sanford February 12th 1682-3...Mary the wife
John X Manchester of...Thomas Manchester...consent to
his marke. ...sale...
Wm. Cadman Assistant.

[255] John Pocoke to Captn John Browne.
...John Pocoke...of Newport...for...Ninty Pounds of Currant New-England Silver mony...paid by Captn John Browne of...Swansey in the Collony of Plymouth...Have ...sold...a Certaine house or Tennement with the Lott of Land it stands upon within the Towne of Newport... bounded...on the North by the street on the West by the Lott of...Thomas Rodman, on the East by...Land...of John Holmes on the South by a Lott...of Christopher Almy ...forty foot square...if...John Pocoke...pay...unto... Captn John Browne...before the last...of October...One Thowsand six hundred Eighty and Eight...Ninty pounds of Currant New England Silver mony with...interest...annually...this...Deed...shall be voyd and of none Efect... Twenty second day of June...One Thowsand Six hundred Eighty and three.
Wit. John Pocoke.
Andrew Willett.
Thomas Terrey.
John Pocoke...28th of July...acknowlidged the above...
Caleb Carr Assistant.

[256] Thomas Deane to George Sisson.
...Thomas Deane of London Merchant One of the Executors of the...Will...of Joseph Browne late of Charles Towne...in the Massachussets Collony...Clerke deced and Anne wife of...Thomas Deane...Doe...Surrender...unto

George Sisson of Portsmouth...Rhode Island...Yeoman... percell of Land or farme Comonly Called...Middleford Farme,...within...Portsmouth...lately belonging to... Joseph Browne deceasd....two hundred and Forty Acres... And...Doe...Ratefy...The...sale...from William Browne and Benjan. Browne the other Executors...and Peter Serjeant as Attorney...unto...George Sisson...Thirteenth day of August...1683...

Wit.   Tho: Deane
  Joseph Dudly   Ann Deane
  John Richards.

[257] Nathanill Sylvester to James Lloyd.
...my son in law James Lloyd of Boston Mercht. hath... sett over unto me. Nathaniell Silvester of Shelter Island all his Right...to Horse Necke lying in the bounds of...Oyster Bay with the Medows at the South...I doe...at the Request of James Lloyd...give him a Deed of sale for...Horse Necke and Premises,...Shelter Island Novemr. the 5th 1678:

Wit.   Nathaniell Sylvester
  G. Sylvester
  Nathll Sylvester.

...30th of August 1680: Gyles Silvester and Nathaniell Sylvester...above...was...act of Nathaniell Sylvester their father...

                                    Peleg Sanford Governor.

  George Sisson to Henry Brightman.
...George Sisson of...Dartmouth...for...one hundred and sixty two pounds Currant mony of New England...payd... by...Henry Brightman of...Portsmouth...Have...sold... Land...within...Towneship of Portsmouth...adjoyninge to the Hunting Swamp Containeing...Forty five acres...by me purchassed of William Wood Thirty Acres thereof now in the posession of me...the rest...being now in the posession of Hugh Parsons his wife and after her decease—Shall Returne to Henry Brightman;...the aforesaid forty five Acres of... Land...bounded—Easterly by the late deceassed Thomas Lawtons Hunting Swamp farme, Southerly by the Land of

William Correy, Westerly partly upon the land of the said Correy and part on the Comon, Northerly...by the hie way and Comon,...with all...Mansion or dwelling houses, barnes, Outhouses fruite trees Orchards...third day of March... One Thowsand six hundred Eighty one.

Wit.   George Sisson
   John Sanford
   Isaac Lawton.

                February 6t 1683...George Sisson...acknowlidged...

                                 George Lawton Assistant

February the 6t 1682-3...Sarah the wife of...George Sisson ...Consent...to...Deed...

                                 George Lawton Assistant

[259]   John Williams acquitts Thomas Terry.
...John Williams of Boston...Mercht. Doe acquitt... Thomas Terry of Block Island alias New-Shorrum of all debts...29 of August 1677:...doe alsoe discharge...Terry as Attorny to Captn Williams from the debt of William Harris

Wit.   Jno Williams.
     his
John X Rathbone
    marke
   George Halsall:

   John Green to James Greene.
...John Green of Aquidnesett...in the Narragansett Cuntry ...thirtie shillings in Currant mony of New England to be paid...Yearly...unto John Green...and after his decease to Joane Greene. his wife...By James Greene (the natural son of John and Joan Greene...)...Have Given...Land ...lying...at Aquednessett...now in the posession of... James Greene...sixty Acres...bounded...Northerly by the land...John Greene Easterly by quidnesett harbour. Southerly by a River or brook and land of Daniell Greene, and Westerly by a hie way,...with all...wood,...Quarries,...

water courses, buildings...at the decease of...John and Joane Greene...James Greene...shall have...the...Premises forever...Twenty fourth day of March...one Thowsand six hundred Eighty & one or two...
Wit.   John Greene
  Henry **X** Tibbitts
    his marke.
  Arthur Aylworth
  John Nutsn:
John Greene...24th of march 1681-82 acknowlidged this...
                                   John Foanes Wardn.

[261]   Job Almy to Jedidiah Allin.
...Job Almy of...Portsmouth...for...forty five pounds Currant mony of New England...paid by Jedidiah Allin of ...Sandwich in the Collony of New-Plymouth...doe...sell ...share of land...in the Towneship of Shrosebury in the Government of East Gersey (Excepting Only in this...sale a house lott...neer the Meeting house in...Shrosebury and a percell of medows formerly sold by John Chamnies) The great lott alredy devided...adjoyninge to the land belonging to the Children of the deceassed Bartholmew West...with all ...medows...Premisses...are cleer...from all...Incumberances...Especially from any thing acted Concerning the premisses by my brother Christopher Almy—...Eight day of November...One Thowsand six hundred Eighty three:
Wit.   Job Almy
  John Sanford   Mary Almy
  Mary Sanford
  Eliphall Sanford.
Job Almy...with his wife Mary...did acknowlidge this... 28th of January 1683
                               John Albro Assistant

[262]   Mamanuett to Daniell Wilcock.
...Mamanewot Chife Sachem & Proprietor of Saconett and the lands adjacent...for...many...Curtecies...in the time of my great distress...which...amount to the Vallue of... one hundred Pounds...Give...unto my...friend...one hun-

dred Acres of land...unto...mr Daniell Wilcock of Naumquid...bounded...Eastwardly with partly Dartmouth line and partly with the River, Southerly with a Swamp Called... Semsuett, Easterly from that spring to the Salt river, and westerly from the spring up the hill till we came to a small Indian field to a heap of stones, and from that stone heap Northerly till we come to a great white oake tree; which standith in the line between Aldermans land and the land mentioned in this Present Deed,...Northerly with Aldermans land till we come to a black oake neer the great River, ...Twenty third day of June...one Thowsand Six hundred Eighty three:—

Wit.   The marke of Sachem
  Thomas Gatchell   Mamanuett X
  Joshua Rawlins.
  The marke X of John
  Mamuetts son and heire
  to the said Sachem.
  Richard Bulgar
  Sachem Mamiett...owned this...26 of June 1683
                                    John Albro Assistant

[263]   Mamamutt to Alderman.

...Mamamutt Chiefe Sachem and Proprietor of Saconett... for...service done...in the late warr...doe...Give...an Indian Called...Alderman now liveing neer Punckatest pond ...one hundred Acres...bounded...the Northermust line devideth the two Townships of Pocassett and Saconett land East...with dartmouth line, Southeast with a Black oake, westerly till it coms to a white Oake marked on four-sides and from thence to a Red Oake more westerly Standing neer to the top of a hill,...Twenty two day of June...One Thowsand six hundred Eighty three—.

Wit.   The marke X of Sachem
  Thomas Gatchell   Mamamewot
  Joshua Rawlins
The marke X of John Mamanuett
son of...Sachim   the marke of
The marke of Isaac   Daniel X Wilcocke upon
Isacke an Indian   the Request of the Sachem.

[264]   Testamony of Elizabeth Gould.
...it hath been...reported...That William Coggeshall...of Portsmouth...was Only the Reputed son of mr John Coggeshall of...Newport...I Elisabeth Gould Now wife of Thomas Gould of Kings Town...the Only Naturall Mother of...William Coggeshall, And formerly wife unto...mr John Coggeshall: Doe. declare...That...mr John Coggeshall ...is the Only Naturall father of...William Coggeshall... begett...before I was Parted from him being then his wife:...

Upon Oath the 4th of Septembr....1684.
Before me Will. Coddington Govr

John Dunham to John Brigs.
...John Dunham Senr. of the Towne of Plymouth,...Yeoman... For...Forty and two pounds...paid by John Brigs Senr of...Portsmouth...Yeoman...have...Sold...all my Lott...in the places Comonly Called...by the Indian Names of Acushnett Coaksett...in the Jurisdiction of Plymouth... with all...woods waters Medows...to be Houlden as of his Majtie. his manner of East Greenwich...sixt day of October ...1662

Wit.   John Dunham.
   Nathaniell Morton
   The marke of
      X Jonathan Pratt.

[265]   Peter Bussecot grant confirmed to John Warner.
...Peter   Bussecot   of...Warwick...yeares   since...Did Grant...unto mr Ezekiell Hollyman deceased,...One parcell of Land or house lott scittuate...in...the Town of Warwick bounded on the North Side with a small brook or river, and Easterly by the street directly over aginst mr. Hollymans former dwelling and bounded southerly by the Comon, and also Westerly bounded by the Comon. And...as John Warner of the Town...above-said is the...heire unto mr Ezekiell Hollyman his Grand father by Parantage; I...Doe...Ratefy ...my...Bargain...tenth day of March...1681-2:

Wit.   Peter X Bussecot
   Moses Lippit.   his marke

Hugh **X** Stone
his marke.

Phillip Sweet to John Warner.

...Phillip Sweet Now Resident in Kings Town...by the Consent of my father James Sweet senr. of...Kings Town...for ...full satisfaction...Paid...by John Warner of...Warwick...doe...sell...a house Lott...twelve Acres...in... Warwick Town, butting Easterly upon the main street of the said Town and joyning Northerly upon sd John Warners land, which he the said Warner now dwellith upon, the brook being only between, And southerly by a hie way and Comon, And alsoe one Township Right in all undevided Lands belonging to the said Town, and also a share of boggy medow On the Easterly Side of the Spruce Swamp, And a share of boggie medow at Touskeounk on the southerly side of the River called Patuxet river the which two...shares of boggy medow ...are...Known...by the Names of James Sweets medow, with halfe the third Lott in Number layd out in Potowomett Neck lately by John Smith Surveyer...the above said twelve acre Lott and Township being first granted by sd Town unto Peter Bussecot...Excepting Only all my Right of Lands upon the Northerly side of Patuxett River within the Township of sd Warwick...I...by the consent of my father...and...of my mother Mary Sweet...Doe...absolutely...disclaim... tenth...of September...One Thowsand six hundred Eighty and four,...

Wit.
  John Potter
  James Green junr.
  Nathaniell Osband

the marke of
Phillip **X** Sweet
his marke
James **X** Sweet
her marke
Mary **X** Sweet

Received from Mordica Bouden.

...Peleg Sanford Esq. Recovered a Judgment against Mordica' Bouden of Rhode Isle of Thirty five pounds...due to mr John Winslow deceased...after said Bowdens long Imprisonment severall Charges did arise, and he was forced to take part of a small house and land...which...amounts to but Eighteen pound...December 16: 1684.

      Elisha Hutchinson Administrator
      to the Estate of Jos. Winslow

[267] Testemony of John Sanford and John Porter.
...the litle Island lying in the bay on the North side of the Wading River was given mr Dyre by the Purchassers 31 October 1650

      Jno Sanford

...above...were by my fathers Order...by me written my father then being very sick...4th of October 1669

      John Sanford.

...as wee put along by the afore-said Island the Purchassers gave the...Island to mr William Dyre
No. 1. 1650.   John Porter.

 Testemony of Roger Williams and Captn Randall Houldon. Newport...10 Novembr 1664 (ut vulg)
...Roger Williams being acquainted...with the first Conception Birth and Growth of Rhode Island (alias Aquednick) doe Asert...that by...the first Purchassers of Rhode Island ...the little Island Comonly Called Dyres Island was from the first and allways (Some times in Meriment) but always in Earnist granted...mr William Dyre of Newport...

      Roger Williams Asista:

Captn Randall Houldon of Warwick...aged 57 years...the Purchassers gave that litle Island Called Dyres Island to mr William Dyre senr that was then one of us...24th day of June 1669:

      by me John Cranston Assistant.

 Testemony of William Coddington and others.
...wee the Purchassers of Rhode Island (my selfe being the chief) William Dyre desireing a spot of land of us as we passed by it, after we had Purchassed the said Island, did grant him our Right in the said Island and Named it Dyres Island...October 18th 1669:

      William Coddington

...Richard Carder being a Purchassers doe own the above writeinge:

November 2th 1669   by me Richard Carder.
William Cooley aged 66 years...Testefieth that in the first year of the setling of this Plantation of Newport he being Master of a boat and Jeffery Champlin and Richard Serles being of his Company, and stopping at the Island Called Dyres Island mr William Dyre in Presence of them took posession of the said Dyres Island...6th of December 1669:
                               John Green Assistant.

[268]   William Dyre to William Dyre.
...William Dyre of Newport...Gent...Do...Give...my...Sonn William Dyre,...my Island...Called Dyres Island lying and being scittuated in Narrogansett Bay upon the Northern side of Rhode-Island over against Prudence Island...fifth day of August...One Thowsand six hundred and seventie
Wit.   William Dyre.
  Daniell King
    1670
  John   Pertens.

William Browning to Thomas Manchester.
...William Browning of...Portsmouth...husbandman...for ...a Bargain of Exchange of a percell of land lying...in Punkatest...made with Thomas Manchester junr. of...Portsmouth Black Smith...Doe...Grant,...two percells of Land lying...in the...Township of Portsmouth the One parcell Containing Twenty Acres...bounded Northward on the Swamp or Comon, Eastward upon the great Road or hie way goeing towards Newport, Southward on land latly belonging to William Cadman, and Westward on the land of Gidion Freeborne the other parcell...Containing five Acres...between me and my sisters is butted...between the land of Gidion Freeborn where he now dwellith and the land now...in the posession of Mathew Greenell...with all...Medows woods trees gardens Orchards,...ninteenth day of March...1684-5
Wit.   William Browning
  John Sanford   X
  Mary Sanford jur.   his marke.

...wee saw William Browning...
March one & twenty day 1684-5
    Joseph Timberlake
    William Cory.

 William Browning...21 of march 1684-5...did...acknowlidge the above written...

        John Albro Assistant

[269] John Clarke to Richard Tew.

...27th day of the 12th Month 1650...John Clarke of... Newport Phisician have...sold unto Richard Tew of the same Town One Parcell of Land lying on the East side of my Farme neer the mill and adjoyning to the said farme on the west side thereof and on the east side to the hie way that leads to Sachuet being in length...77 Poles, and abutting on the North end thereof upon a parcell of Land by me... granted unto James Rogers, & on the south upon a way 3 ples wide reserved to my selfe as an Inlet and Outlet properly belonging to my selfe...thirteen Acres and a halfe...

Wit.   John Clarke:

 Marke Lucar
 Samuell Billing
   X
  his marke

...agreed that when Richard Tew Chainged land with mr Clarke that Richard Tew was to have 16 acres...for the land ...he bought of Staford but they agreed to give William Vaughan 5 acres...between them which was the Reason that this Deed was made but for 13 acres an a halfe.

         Marke Lucar:
         Samuell X Billing
          his marke.

[270] William Vaughan do Testefy.

Newport Octo. the 4th 1671.

...William Vaughan do Testefy, when Richard Tew did Exchaing the Land with mr John Clarke: the land that the said Richard bought of Thomas Stafford,...ten acres Eastward of the mill and a percell of Marsh lying in the fresh

Pond neer mr Clarkes farme...mr John Clarke did agree to give mr. Richard Tew sixteen acres, the East side of his farme betwixt his farme and the hie way, at which time mr Tew made the motion to mr John Clarke to give William Vaughan two acres and a halfe of his farme adjoyning to this sixteen acres...mr Richard Tew agreed...to give William Vaughan, two acres and a halfe out of mr Tews sixteen Acres adjoying to that the which mr Clarke accepting of...made mr Tew a deed but of thirteen acres and a halfe leaveing the two acres and a halfe out, I William Vaughan not accepting of it: when mr Clarke was gon for England, I and Thomas Clarke being his agents...layd it out length ways betwixt the sixteen and mr Clarkes farme...

Wit.
    John Harris
    Frances Vaughan.

                                  marke
                         William X Vaughan
                                  his.

[271] John Warner to Thomas Stafford.
...John Warner...of Warwick...Have...sold...unto Thomas Stafford (of the Town...aforesaid)...two shares of Medow ground...within the Towship of Warwick, at or neer the place Called Taskeunke, the... shares did Origonally belong to Richard Townsend and Christopher Haukshurst, and since Purchassed by me upon Exchainge of Land with mr Anthony Low...28th of February 1684-85

Wit.   John Warner
    William Burton
    Benjamin Gorton
    Samuell Gorton.

Thomas Stafford to John Warner.
...Thomas Stafford...of Warwick...have...Sold...unto John Warner of the same Town...my house lott Scittuate... in...Warwick neer the dwelling of Leiutent. John Low bounded on the front by the street, and parted with a passage of water or Brook from the Land of John Low, and on the other side bounded with the land of Joseph Carder, and on the other bounded by a hie way devideing it from the ox pasture,...with Orchard fenceing building...as it was given

...unto me by the will of my deceassed Father Thomas Stafford senior...28th of February 1684-85.

Wit.
  William Burton
  Benjamin Gorton
  Samuell Gorton

Thomas **X** Stafford
his marke.

[272]   James Leonard to Icabod Sheffield.

...James Leonard senr of Tanton...for...twelve Pounds sterling...paid by Icabod Sheffield of the Township of Portsmouth...hath...sold,...Parsell of Land...being down Tanton great River So Called, On the westerly side of the... River...being one full share (Excepting Only the litle Lott so Called)...of the Land which belongeth to the Inhabitants of Tanton...was Purchassed by the Inhabitants of Tanton... of Phillip Sachim Alias pumetacombe and mr Constant Southworth Treasurer for the Collony...in...which Tract...the said James Leonard senr. hath a full share...lyeth southerly from the Town of Tanton The lott...was Called the great Lott is the second Lott lying Neer a Place Called broad Cove bounded by the medows of Samuell Hall senr on the Easterly end and by the Land of Increase Robinson on the southerly side, And by the Land that belongith to the Inhabitants of Swansey on the Westerly End and by the Land of Jonah Austin junr. On the North side, Containing...Thre score Acres...to be holden as of...the King...his manner of East Greenwich...James Leonard and Margitt his...wife...six and twenty day of September...One Thowsand six hundred Eighty and one...whereas is writt Margit it should been writt Margreet...

Wit.
  John Hall
    his marke
  John **X** Leonard junr.
  Sharach Wilbore

his marke
James **X** Leonard
her marke
Margrett **X** Leonard.

James Leonard senr and Margreet his wife...acknowlidged this...24th October 1681

                           Daniell Smith Assist.

[274] Thomas Terry to Administrators of John Hulls Estate.
...Thomas Terry of Tanton...for...sum of mony...paid by Samuell Seawell of Boston...to the Estate of John Hull Esqr. deceased...Have...Sold...unto the...Administrators all that Remainder of my Lott...of Land purchassed of mr John Alcock,...Sixty Acres...in two parcells at the Northeast end of Block-Island...bounded...the one percell to the North-west by the Land of Phillip Wharton, to the southeast by the Land of James Sands, to the south west by the Land of Thomas Mitchell to the Northeast by the Land of John Rathbone, the second Parcell butted to the Southwest by the Land of John Rathbone, to the Northeast by the sea to the Northwest by the Land of Phillip Wharton to the southeast by the Land of James Sands:...five and twenith day of January... One Thowsand Six hundred Eighty and three...

Wit.   Thomas Terry
  George Shove   her marke
  Bar. Tipping   Anna **X** Terry

  mr Thomas Terry...with the Consent of his wife Anna... acknowlidged...28th January 1683
                                                         Daniell Smith Asist.

[275] Jireth Bull to his brother
...fifth day of December...1685...between Jireth Bull of Newport...Eldist sonn of Jireth Bull of Kings-Town...deceassed and Henry Bull, Ephraim Bull, and Ezekell Bull, sonns of...deceassed Jireth Bull...
...I...Eldist brother to...Henry, Ephraim Bull and Ezekiel Bull, Doe...make over all my Right...unto my deceassed Fathers lands or houseing...the housing and lands whereon he lived Containing Ninty two Acres...and five hundred Acres of Land...lying westward from the afore-said houseing and Land about two miles,...Caled Jireth Bulls Farme... I do hereby bind my selfe...in the full...sum of One Thowsand Pounds sterling Unto my...three Brothers...Provided that I...Injoy my Grand Fathers, Henry Bull farme after his decease adjoyning to my farme in Newport, but if I...shall not injoy the said Farme...Then...I with my...Brothers,...

are Equally to devide...the Lands of our deceassed father...
Wit.   Jireh Bull
   Roger Goulding
   Weston Clarke.

[276]   Edward Robyson to Margrett Hall.
...Edward Robyson...of Newport...Husbandman...Margrett Hall the wife of James Hall in the said Island...Have given...the said Margrett,...(...after my decease) all my houses and Lands...within...the...said Town...on Consideration, that...Margrett shall...bring up...Edward Robyson and Francis Robyson my two sons...And after the decease of...Margrett I...do...give...to my sons...all...the afore-mentioned houses and Lands...Equaly to be devided... I do...give...Margrett...all my...household stuff Redy mony Leasses Chattells...at her decease to be my...sonns... tenth day of December...1684.   his
Wit.   Edward X Robyson.
   Edward Greenman   marke.
   Elias Williams
...if either of my...sons...shall decease...then that part of my houses and Lands...shall be the...Right...of the survivor...Eighteen day of December...one Thowsand six hundred Eighty five.
Wit.   Edward X Robyson
   John Sanford   his marke
   Stephen Brayton

[277]   David and Edward Greenman to John Green.
...twentith day of February...One Thowsand six hundred forty and seven...David Greenman and Edward Greenman of Newport...Wheelwrites...for...mony...have... sold unto John Green of Newport...Husbandman, one percell of Land...being within or neer the endship or village Called Greenend, and there adjoyneth on the hie way leading from Newport unto Portsmouth on the south west side thereof And abutting at the West end of it over the mill brook (ackording to the markes thereof) upon the Comon, and adjoyning to the Lands of David and Edward Greenman on

the North side of it Contayning...Two and twenty Acres...
Wit.   David Greenman
   Jeremy Gould   Edward Greenman
   Will. Jefferay.
   Henry Bassett.
Newport...Edward Greenman acknowlidged 4th day of February 1681-2   Peleg Sanford Governor.

[278]   Joshua Coggeshall to Walter Cunagrave.
...30th day of May...One Thousand six hundred and fifty One...Joshua Coggeshall of Newport...the son of John Coggeshall the deceassed have...sold unto Walter Cunagrave of the same Town a Parcell of Land lying within the Precincts thereof and upon the East side of the River upon which Newport mill now standeth, and not farr from the said mill ...Eight score Acres of Land be it more or less adjoyning unto the Land of Richard Knight on the south side, and on the North unto the Land granted by the Town to Mary Clarke some times the wife of John Peckham. And abutting upon the great Comon On the East end thereof, And on the West upon the hie way that leads from the Mill to green end. Village:...
Wit: Joshua Coggeshall.
   John Clarke.
   Elizabeth Clarke.
...Mary Coggeshall the mother of Joshua...Consenting unto the sale...30th of May 1651:
                                            Mary Coggeshall.

[279]   Walter Cunygrave to John Green.
...sixt day of June...one thousand six hundred fifty and one...Walter Cunygrave of Newport Merchant Tayler, and Elisabeth Cunygrave his wife have sold unto John Green of Newport...yeoman four score Acres of Land...in Newport ...neer unto or in the hamlett of Greenend and adjoyning on the North Side of...Walter Cunygraves other land and towards the North on the land granted by the Town of Newport unto Mary Clarke now deceassed some time the wife of John Peckham, and abutteth on the Comon hie way leading

from Greenend unto Newport mill towards the West, and towards the east on the great Comon,...

Wit.   Walter X Cunygrave
  Will. Jefferay
  Jer. Gould.

[290] John Walley to William Brenton.

...William Brenton late of Newport...Now of Bristoll...Marriner did By...Deed 23d January 1679 Make Over...to John Walley late of Boston Now of Bristoll Merchant...a Certain Farme and houseing...in the Township of Newport ...and then in Posession of Richard Allison for Certain uses ...Now...Wim Brenton seemed...unsatisfied with what he had done, And...Refussed to give Posession of the Same...I...Walley Could not be in any Capassety to Act...without a sute at law...Considering his Necessety Called for such supply as Could not be procured without disposing of a Considerable part of the farme, And...by selling the whole farme he might Satisfy his debts, putt himselfe in some way of Lively hood and secure something Considerable for his Children after him in some other Estate more suteable, Alsoe his wife desireing and Consenting to the same...I...John Walley Do by these Presence Renounce the said Trust that by the above-mentioned Instrument was made or Committed to me, And as I never have Acted or done any thing in the Premisses by Vertue thereof So I doe for my selfe my heires ...forever Renounce and Refuse said Trust...And that it may be lawfull for said Brenton Notwithstanding said Instrument to sell...or dispose the Same as may be most for his benefitt...fourteenth day of Septembr. One Thousand six hundred Eighty and five.

Wit.   John Walley.
  Watching Atherton
  Richard Smith
  John Walley...15th of Aprill...acknowlidged this...
                                           Caleb Carr Assistant

  Peleg Sanford to William Brenton.

...Peleg Sanford of Newport...for...two hundred & six

Pounds and six shillings Currant Silver mony of New England
...paid...By William Brenton of Bristoll...Have Given...
A Certain Parcell of Land...within...Newport...Seventy
and two Acres...butted...North...by Land of John Easton
senr. & land of Walter Clarke & the Comon West by land
formerly belonging to Thomas Clifton, deceassed, Southerly
by Land of...William Brenton and Henry Bull Esqr. with all
...trees...wayes,...twenty fourth day of October...One
Thousand six hundred Eighty & five.

Wit.   Peleg Sanford.
  Archebell Forest   Mary Sanford
  Ralph X Earll junr
    his marke:

Peleg Sanford and Mary his wife...did Acknowlidge this
...Newport 15th day February 1685-6

                        John Easton Assistant

[292]   William Brenton to John Walley.
...William Brenton of Bristall alias, Mount hope...Marriner
and Hannah his wife...for...six hundred and twenty
Pounds of Currant mony of New Engand...by John Walley
of Bristoll...Merchant...Paid...have Given...a Certain
farme...being in the Township of Newport...Comonly
called...Brace's farme...about two hundred and forty Acres
...now in the Posession of Richard Allisson, being the whole
of the said Farme houseing buildings and Lands whether uplands Medows and Swamps...which was Willed to William
Brenton by his Father William Brenton Esqr. deceassed,
which farme...is butted...Westerly by the Land of Henry
Bull Esqr. and Irah Bull Southerly by the Land of Major
John Coggeshall. Easterly by the Sea Northerly by the Land
of John Easton senr. and Partly by the Comon,...Eighteenth
day of November...One Thousand six hundred Eighty &
five...

Wit.   William Brenton
  Will. Hedge: Hannah Brenton
  Richard Smith.

William Brenton and Hannah his wife 15th of Aprill 1686 Acknowlidged...

          Caleb Carr Asistant

[293] John Walley to William Stoughton—(mortgage)
...John Walley of Bristoll...Merchant, and Sarah his wife ...for...Five hundred Pounds Currant mony of New-England...paid...by William Stoughton of Dorchester in the Colony of the Massathusetts Esqr...Have Given...A Certain Farme lying and being in the Township of Newport...Caled ...Braces Farme...Two hundred and forty Acres—now in the Posession of Richard Allisson being the whole of the sd farme houseing buildings and Lands whether uplands or medows and swamps...which was willed to William Brenton by his Father Wim Brenton Esqr. deceassed which farme ...is butted...Westerly by the Land of Henry Bull Esqr. & Irah Bull Southerly by Land of Majo John Coggeshall, Eastwardly by the sea, Northerly by the land of John Easton senr partly by the Comon...if...John Walley...shall...pay... unto Wim Stoughton...the...sum of five hundred & Thirty five pounds of Present mony of New England...before the first day of March...One Thousand six hundred Eighty six seven...then this...Deed...shall be...voyd...fiveteenth day of February...One Thousand six hundred & Eighty five...
Wit.   John Walley
 Nathal. Byfield   Sarah Walley.
 Thomas Walley:

John Walley and Sarah his wife...15th of Aprill 1686... Acknowlidged...

          Caleb Carr Assistant

[295] Wamsetta to Peter Talman.
...Wamsetta alias Sepaquit or by his English Name Alexander, the greatist and Chiefest Prince or Sachim hereabout... freely Give unto my well beloved Friend Peter Talman of Portsmouth...a Parcell of Land,...bounded...At the Northermost end with a River Comonly Called the Seven Mile River, and from the said River upon a streight line Eastward till it meet with the bounds of Cocksett., and then it is to Run

upon a streight line Southward till it come to the main sea, And then to run by the sea Westward to Saconett, and from Saconett up the Eastward side of the great River till the line meets at the Seven mile River again; with all...Land, Medows, hearbidge, timber, under-woods, Creeks Coves or Islands fresh Rivers or Springs...Only the Purchass which Captn Richard Morris bought is Excepted in this deed... And Punckatest Neck...formerly bought by some men of Plymouth...Twenty day of January...One Thowsand six hundred Sixty and one,...

Wit.   The marke of Alexander.
   Richard Bulgar   Or Wamsitta Else. X
   The marke of Edward Lay X..   Sepawquit
   John Sasoman the Interpreter Indian
   Thomas Durfi

[296]   Testemony of Richard Bulgar and others.

Richard Bulgar Aged Seventy years...and Thomas Durfi aged about thirty six years all of...Portsmouth...doe Testefy that the...Indian Sachim Caled Wamsetta Sepawquit or Alexander at the time of signeing...was in a very Sober Condition and not any way Over-come in or by drink,...it was his Free...Act...the said Subscriber was the Eldist Brother of Sachim Phillip (who first began the late Indian warr with the English.) and was the Chief Sachim of these Parts & deceassed before the warr:

Edward Lay of...Portsmouth aged about seventy one years ...doth Testefic to the Truth of all that is above...16th of August...1679 Before me

                      John Sanford Assistant.

   William Brenton to Thomas Ward.

...William Brenton of Bristoll...Marriner...for...Thirty Pounds Currant Silver mony of New-England...Paid...by Thomas Ward of Newport...Have Granted...one seventh part...of all...the devided lands in Pettacomscutt formerly belonging to my father William Brenton deceassed, And the forty ninth part of all...the Lands both upland and Medows now lying and being undevided within the said tract of Lands

Comonly Called Pettacomscutt in...Rhode-Island...bounded by the sea from Point Judith to Pettacomscutt River, and so to the head of the Pond Called Pausakaonkanuck which Pond lyeth about Northwest from the Mill, And from the Pond on a Norwest line six miles Also on a west line drawn from the head of the Cove North of Point Judith Neck six miles and a halfe and soe on a strait line from the head of the aforesaid northwest line unto the head of the said west line of six miles and a halfe thence on the same straite Line to the sea or South Shore, and on the South by the sea, which said forty Ninth Part Containeth...about seven hundred Acres...with all...woods water ways...if I...my heires or assignes... shall...Molest...Thomas Ward...it shall...be lawfull... for the said Thomas...to...take into his...Posession two Certain Peeces...of Lands...in the Township of Bristoll... one of which...is...in a Certain Place Called Papasquash neck Containing Twenty three Acres, And bounded East and west by the salt water North by Stephen Burtons land South upon the Lands Caled Timothy Clarkes the other...Land Contains tenn Acres and bounded North by the hie-way, South by the Land of Christopher Sanders Easterly by the land of Nathaniell Hayman and Westerly upon the house Lotts And were both Purchassed by me...of John Walley of Bristoll... until the said William Brenton...shall...Pay...Thomas Ward...the said sum of Thirty Pounds...with lawfull Intrest and the Charge in Mannageing the said Lands...fift day of May...One Thousand Six hundred Eighty and six.
Wit.   Wim Brenton.

   William Hiscox
   Gilbert Magick
   William Brenton Acknowlidged above...May 5th 1686 Before Walter Clarke Det Govr.
   Hanah Brenton the wife of...William Brenton did...consent to the...Sale...May 5th 1686
                                  Walter Clarke Dept. Go.

[298]   Nathanaell Coddington to Noell Mew.
...Nathanael Coddington of Newport...Merchat. and Susan-

nah his wife...for...four hundred Pounds Currant Silver mony of New England...Paid...by Noell Mew of Newport ...Merchant...Have Granted...a certain Parcell of Land Called Rocky Farme lying...in the Precincts off Newport... Containing...three hundred Acres...bounded...Southerly by the Sea Easterly by the Cove and Marshes of John Coggeshall Northerly Partly by John Coggeshalls land and Partly the Comon Runing on a line till it comes to a small Cove, and from thence Westerly bounded by the Comon Called Cherry Neck, and so Runs to the Sea...with all...houses Gardens Orchards woods...Ponds Creeks Coves...Thirteenth day of Aprill...One Thousand six hundred Eighty and Six,...
Wit.   Nathall. Coddington
  William Allen   Susannah Coddington
  Tho. Rodman

Newport Aprill 13th 1686 Nathll and Susannah Coddington ...declared...

                           Walter Clarke Dep Govr.

[299] Tacommonan to Randall Howldon & Ezechill Hollyman
...Tacommonan Right owner of all the medows and Mowable land upon a Neck of ground Comonly Called by the English ...Petawhomett neck Scittuate and being upon the great River Called...Nanhygansett bay lying over against the South end of that neck...Called Shawomett, which Bay is the east bounder, and that River Comonly Called by the English Potowomett River being the Southw [torn] bounder, and Coeassett Bay being the Northward bounder for the space or length of four miles according to the English Account up by the Said Potowomett River westward from the...Nanhigansett Bay, which Percell of Land as above-said with all the Rights...by water land wood...I...have...sold...unto Randall Howldon and Ezechill Hollyman both of Warwick...for the Just sum or fifteen Pounds...in wampum Peag Only I am to Recive the Vallue of one Coat of such Cloth as the Indians do now Comonly use to wear Annually as a gratuety here after... according to the Custom of the English dated the thirteenth

day of July...1654:
Wit.
   jeremiah Westcott.
   William Baker
   Samuell Edsall.

Tocommonon **X** his marke.
Awassuocitt **X** his marke
   Eldist son to him
above Wawnunockshaw **X** his marke an other Son.

[300] John Allis to Henry Neales.

...William Allis some times of Brantree in the Massathusetts Colony...deceassed did formerly grant unto Henry Neale senr. of said Town three quarters of One Sixteenth part of ...Block-Island now under the Government of Rhode-Island Excepting and Reserveing the Island Called foart Island and five and twenty Acres more to be taken out of the said three quarters of said sixteenth part, Butt...as no deed for Confirmation of the said Land Passed from William Allis I John Allis the heir...of William Allis...Do...Release...unto... Henry Neales...the said three quarters of one Sixtenth part of Block-Island...Excepting...foart Island and twenty five Acres to be taken out of the said three quarters of one sixteenth part neer the harbour according to mr Alcocks Reserve in his Release of said land,...24th of June 1685:
Wit.   John Allis
  Arthur Mason
  John Williams
  John Allis acknowlidged this...24th June 1686
                                        Bradstreet Governor

[301] Phillip Jones to Rebecca Tailer & John Nelson (Mortgage).

...fifteenth day of June...one Thousand six hundred Eighty & three...Between Phillip Jones of New Yorke merchant on the one Part, and Rebeckah Tailer Relict, Widow, of William Tailer late of Boston...Merchant deceassed, And John Nelson of Boston...Merchant, Administratrix and Administrator, to the Estate of...William Tailer decd. on the other Part,... Phillip Jones for...two hundred Pounds of Currant mony of New-England...by...Rebecca Tailer and John Nelson... paid...Hath...sold,...all that his Messuage or Tenement...

in the Town of Newport...with all the land belonging to the same (excepting the buriall place of John Gard and his wife) being upwards of Three quarters of an Acre of Land... bounded on the South by the land late in the Possession of William Brenton mercht decd. and bounded on the North by Lands...of Capt Peleg Sanford abutting upon the East on the hie-way that Extends North and South in the said Town, And so the sd Land Extendith Twelve foot in bredth down into the sea &c...with all...houses Outhouses...buildings... if...Philip Jones his heires...shall...pay...Rebecca Tailer and John Nelson...the sum of two hundred and four pounds of Currant mony of New-England...one hundred pounds... before the first day of Septembr...And the sum of One hundred and four Pounds more...before the first day of March next insueing...then this present...Indenture...shall...be voyd...

Wit.   Phillip Jones.
  John Hayward Not. Pub.   Boston...Octob 16th 1685
  Eliezer Moody: ...Bradstreet Governor.
                                       Sam Sewall Assistant.

[302] Rebecca Tailer & John Nelson to Mary Jones.
...Rebecca Tailer Relict widow of William Taylor late of Boston...Merct. and John Nelson of Boston...Mercht.... whereas Phillip Jones late of New Yorke Mercht. decd. by an Indenture of Morgage...bearing date the fifteenth day of June...One Thowsand six hundred Eighty and three the sum of two hundred Pounds mony to him...paid by the sd Rebecca Tailer and John Nelson did give...unto them...all his Messuage or Tenement Scittuate...in the Town of Newport ...with the land belonging to the same (Excepting the buriing place of John Gard and his wife) beinge upwards of three quarters of an Acre of Land...bounded on the south by the land late...of Peleg Sanford, and on the west by the hie way ...Extends North and South in the said Town, And so the said land Extendeth twelve foot in bredth down into the sea ...with all...houses Outhouses...a Provission...contained for the Redemption of the Premises upon the payment of the

sum of Two hundred and four Pounds of Currant mony of New-England...And yett a Considerable part...remaineth unpaid...whereof...the same became forfitted unto Rebecca Tailer and John Nelson,...be it...known That the sd Rebecca Tailer and John Nelson for.,..Sixty two pounds Currant mony of New England...paid by Mary Jones Relict widow of the sd Phillip Jones,...have Given...the afore-sd Messuage or tenement with all the Land belonging...bounded as afore-sd...Twenty ninth day of October...One Thousand six hundred Eighty & five...

Wit.   Rebekah Tailer—
  Edw. Perry ju.   J Nelson
  Zacheriah Shute.

[304] Daniell Wilcocks to Jacob Mott.

...Daniell Wilcocks of Namquck neer Punckatest Neck... for...thirty Pounds Sterling Currant mony of New England ...by Jacob Mott of Portsmouth...Planter...paid;...Have sold...one Compleat...halfe of a Share...or Sixteenth part of all that tract of land at Pocassett and places Adjacent bounded...Northward and Westward by the freemens Lotts neer the fall River and westward by the Bay or Sound that Runneth between the said Land and Rhode Island Southward partly by a line that is sett at a great Rock on which is a seader bush marked Neer the way that leadith to punckatest Eastward neer to a pond at Dartmouth Town bounds and westward to Suppowett Creeks mouth, And Northward up into the woods to Midleburough Town bounds and Quitquissett pond (always Excepting out of this Bargain...Sapowett Neck of Land and Medow thereunto belonging, and the land formerly granted by the Court of Plymouth to Captn Richard Morris, and soe much of the land as shall be allotted and appointed for the use of the ministry)...which...Land I... with...others lately purchassed of severall Gentlemen Agents of the Colony of New Plymouth, as may appear by one Deed ...bearing date March 5th. 1679-80...Thirteeth day of January...one Thousand six hundred & Eighty two.

Wit.   Daniell X Wilcocks
  Caleb Arnold   his marke
  George Brownell
  Zurill X Hall
    his marke.
Daniell Wilcocks...did...acknowlidge this...26 of September 1684

                            John Albro Assistant

[305]   William Wodell to Jacob Mott.
...William Wodell jun. of Portsmouth...for...Ninty pounds in Mony...paid...by Jacob Mott of Portsmouth... have...Sold,...one full third Part of a Share of Land in the Township of Dartmouth...as the said Township in the whole of it containeth...Thirty five shares of Land...devided and in part undevided, that part of a share alredy devided which belongeth to the said third part of a share hereby sold...is that Tract of Land which was the late Dwelling place of John Cornell of sd Dartmouth and is at or neer the place Called Coaxett in...Dartmouth and Consisteth of upland marsh and Medowland all which said devided part belonging unto the said third part of a share of Land as also the undevided part of the said third part of a share as...is sold unto ...Jacob Mott...(Excepting...Only one Acre and a halfe ...of medowland which lyeth on the south side of the Creek Called Chuestkeest Creek and is in the Posession of Peleg Tripp)...Twenty Eight day of November...one Thousand six hundred Eighty four—:
Wit.   William Wodell junio
  Thomas Eaton   Ruth Wodell—
  William Wodell
  John Anthony.
                ...3rd day of December...1684...
                William Wodell did...give...unto
                ...Jacob Mott...the lands...
                                    Peleg Slocum.
                                    John Anthony
William Wodell and Ruth Wodell his wife...acknowlidge this...Deed...10 of March 1684-5 Before me
                            John Albro Assistant

[306] John Hoskins to John Borden.
...John Hoskins of Tanton...for...Eight pounds & tenn shillings of Currant mony of New-England...paid by John Borden of Portsmouth...hath...sold...a Certain Tract of land Comonly...Called...the South Purchass lying southerly from Tanton three mile river and Scittuated in the Township of Tanton...the said Lott great being the fifty six lott as by the Records of...Tanton...more plainly appear... Scittuated neer to Rocky-Nook bounded on the North by the land formerly in the posession of Samuell Smeth, and southerly by the land of Jarat Talbut Easterly by the great river and westerly on the Comon or undevided lands of the aforesaid land the said lott being sixteen pole or pearch wide... Extending it selfe West and by north two miles...Containing seventy Acres...with a small lott Called the small lotts devission On the south side of the three mile river afore-said with an Equall Intrest in all the undevided Land belonging to the ...Tract of Land...thirteen day of January...1680
Wit. John Hoskins
  John Richmond
  John Macumber senr.
  Henry Hodges.
  John Hoskins acknowlidged this...2d of June 1684
                        Daniell Smith Assistant

[307] Mallachy Holloway to John Borden.
...Mallachy Holloway of Tanton...for...Eight Pounds of Currant mony of New England...paid by John Borden of Portsmouth...doth...sell...a Certain tract of Land...Called ...the South Purchass lying southerly from Tanton three miles River and...in the Township of Tanton...The great Lott being the Twenty ninth Lott lying at or Neer a Cove Called Muddy Cove bounded on the south by the land of Thomas Lenkon and of the North side by the Lands of Henry Hodges and the east end bounding of the said Cove and main River and the Wester end on the Comon or undevided land of the fore-sd tract the sd lott being sixteen Poles or pearch wide...Extending it selfe for length two miles westward by

north...Containing seventy Acres...with a small Lott Called the small Lotts of the south side of the thre mile river... with an Equall intrest in all the undevided lands belonging to ...Purchass of land...fourteen day of January...1680.

Wit.   Mallachy Holloway.

  John Richmond.
  John Macumber senr.
  The marke **X** of William Paull.

                        ...Acknowlidged by Mallachy Holloway...first day of November 1681.

                                  Daniell Smith Assistant

[308]   Henry Hodges to John Borden.
...Henry Hodges of Tanton...for...Eight Pounds in Currant mony of New England...Paid...by John Borden of Portsmouth...Henry Hodges with the free Consent of Heaster his wife have...sold,...Lott of Land lying...in Tantons Purchass Called the South Purchass being Southerly from Tanton three mile River...being the thirty lott as by the Records of the sd Town...more plainly appear, bounded on the South side by the lands of the sd John Borden and on the North by the land that was in the Posession of James Burt, the easter end on Tanton great river and the west end on the Comon or undevided lands of the said purchass, being sixteen Rods or Pearch wide...Extending its length two miles westward by North...being seventy Acres...with an equal Intrest in all the undevided lands belonging to the sd Purchass,...fourteen day of January...1680-81

Wit.   Henry Hodges.
  John Macumber senr.   The marke **X** of Easter Hodges.
  William **X** Paule
      his marke.
  John Richmond.
...acknowlidged by Henry Hodges...and his wife Easter Hodges first of November 1681

                                     Daniell Smith Assistant

[309]   Samuel Chandler to William Earle.
...Samuel Chandler of the Town duxbery of plimoth...for Twenty pounds by William Erle of...Portsmouth...yeoman ...have...sold...The one halfe of my Lot...lying...at Acushenah & Coakset & places Adjacent Comonly Called The purchase Land...with All...medows woods Timbers watters ...to be holden as of his Majesty...his Manor of East Greenwich...Thirtyth day of November...1660...

Wit.   The mark **X** of
   Nathanill Morton   Samuel Chandler
   James Cole senior

[311]   Phillip Delano to William Earle.
...Phillip Delano of...Duxbery...planter...for...Twenty pounds...paid by William Earle of...portsmouth...doe...sell...my Lott...at acushenah & Coakset & places adjacent Comonly Called the purchas Land...with all...medows woods watters...To be holden of his Majesty...as of his maner of East greenwich...thirtyth day of November 1660...

Wit.   Phillip delano
   Nathanill Morton
   James Cole senior

[312]   John Cobb to Willilam Earle.
...John Cobb of the Town of Plimoth...Yeoman...for... Thirtene pounds six shillings & eight pence...paid by William Earle of the Town of portsmouth...yeoman...with ye Consent of marthah my wife...doe...sell...one Third part or one prt of Three of my share of Land Lying at...asheushena Cookset & places adjacent...known by the name of the purchass Land...Both upland & medow with all...woods watters...To be holden as of his Majesty...his Manor of East Greenwich...twenty sixth day of September...1662

Wit.   Jno Cobb
   Nathanill Morton
   The marke of Stephen bryant
              X

[313]   Samuel Chandler to William Earle & Danil Wilcockes.

...Samuel Chandler of...Duxbery...planter...for... Twenty pounds...paid by William Earle & Danil Wilcockes of...portsmouth...yeoman...have...sould...one halfe of a share Lott...of Land Comonly Called the purchas Land... ascushana Coockset & places Adjoyning...Being the one halfe of a share Lott...which I...Bought of Christopher of marshfield in the Jurisdiction of plimoth & by him Bought of Jno Sprague of Duxbery...which was given unto...Jno Sprague by his Father Francis Sprague of...Duxbery both Upland & medow with all...woods Timber watters...To be holdon as of his Majesty his Manor of East greenwich... twenty sixt of septb...1662...

Wit.   the marke **X** of
  Nathanil Morton   Samull Chandler
  Jno Richard

[314] James Sands to William Earle.
...James of portsmouth...yeoman...I...James Sands for ...full sattisfaction...paid...in the Exchange of a parcell of Land by William Earle of Coackset in the Jurisdiction of new plimoth...yeoman...have...Bargained...(with the Consent of Sarah my wife...one halfe of a share of Land... at Accushnet & Coackset & places adjacent Comonly Called the purchas Land

                                         (Incomplete)

[315] Benedict Arnold to Newport.
...Benedict Arnold senr dwelling in the town of Newport... having bought about fifteen years sence two small Islands Called nomtussmuck or Goate Island And weenachsett or Coststers harber Lying in Narrowgansett bay neare...to Newport...as by Awrighting Date. May 22th 1658...under the hand of Cachonaquant Cheyfe Sacham of Narrowgansett ...I...for...ten pounds Cuntry pay...recived of the town of Newport...first day of may...1673

Wit.   Benedict Arnold senr
  Richard Bajly
  Joziah Arnold.

[316] John Cranston & Caleb Carr to Benedict Arnold.
...seventh Day of february...one Thousand six hundred fifty nine...John Cranston and Caleb Carr both of newport hath...sould unto Benedict Arnold of newport...one fourth part of the Islands Caled by the Indians Aquebinockutt and Canagonockutt and by the English Round Island and Rose Island being...in the Narraganset Bay and between Rhode Island and Quononaqutt Island...

Wit.   John Cranston
  Thomas Baker   Caleb Carr
  Ralph Earll

[317] Edward Robinson to Edward and francis Robinson.
...Edward Robinson off Newport...yeoman,...to my two Children Edward and francis Robinson which I had by Margrett Hall and because they are under Age I have Chosen as Feffees...for my...two Children, Edward Greenman, Clement Weaver senio and Thomas Burge of...Newport...Yeomen...doe give,...in trust and on the behalfe of my said Children all that my manshion House and Land In the Towneship of Newport...about fourty acres...bounded Northerly by the Land of Jno: Parker & John Allen, Easterly by the common Southerly by the Land of John Wood and Westerly by the common or highway...the same...shall be the...Estate...of my two sons...and the surviver of them if any one dyes before the Other Comes to the age of twenty one yeares ...Eighteenth day of may 1686

                                            the marke
Wit.   of Edward **X** Robenson.
  John Hulme
  the marke of
John **X** Benett
    Edward Robenson...acknowledged...above...
                                          Walter Clarke Govr.

[318] William Read to Thomas Brookes.
...William Read of Newport...for...sixty five pounds currant Silver money of New England...Paid...by Thomas Brookes of newport...marriner...doe...sell...one mansion

house and all...the Lands...belonging...in breadth Southeast and Northwest Sixty foot and Southwest and northeast fourty foot...Lyeing...in newport...Bounded Southeast, Northeast and Northwest by the Streets of the...Towne and Southwest by Land in the possession of Thomas Paine...fift day of July...1687

Wit.
   John Ward
   Richard X Hasleton
     his marke
   Thomas Ward

Will: Read
the marke of
Judy. X Read

...William Read & Judy his wife...acknowledged this...
...Walter Newbery one of the Council

[320] George Vaughan to Daniell Vaughan.
...George Vaughan of...East Greenwith...for...A Sertaine Parcell...of Land...Within the Towneship of East Greenwitch...and Twenty Pounds in money...Delivered to mee...by...my Brother Daniell Vaughan Now of...Newport...and Doe...Release...A certaine Parcell of Land...within...Newport...Thirty acres...bounded...on the North ...by Land in the Possession of Joshuah Coggeshall by the West...by the Sea or Salt Water, by the South...by the Highway by the East...by my Father John Vaughan his farme being formerly Part thereof...With all...Houseing ...woods...ninteenth day of March...one Thousand Six hundred Eighty and Six—

Wit.
   Thomas Fry
   Henry Timberlake

George Vaughan

March 20th 1686 George Vaughan...Owned this...Deed
                                Caleb Carr Assistant

[321] John Vaughan to Daniell Vaughan.
...John Vaughan of Newport...unto my son Daniell Vaughan of Newport...have Given...my farme or Mansion house with all the Land...belonging where now I dwell in the

Towneship of Newport...about fifty acres...Bounded, Northwardly by Land now...in the Possession of Joshua Coggeshall in part...by the Common westwardly by Land of ...Daniell Vaughan, Southwardly and Eastwardly by the Common, or highwayes and Common,...with all...Buildings, Gardens, Orchards,...three and twentieth day of... July...one Thousand six hundred Eighty seven—

Wit. John Gould   John Vaughan
   Bartholomew Hunt   his **X** marke
   William Wodell

John Vaughan...acknowledged...Walter Clarke one of the Councill

[322] John Vaughan of Newport...whereas my son Daniell Vaughan of Newport...is...Possesed of a certaine Tract... of Land in the Towneship of Newport...Containing about thirty acres...Bounded Westerly by the Sea or Salt water, Southwardly by a common Lane or highway Northerly by Land now in the possession of Joshua Coggeshall and Easterly by Land of mee...which...Land...Daniell did purchase of his Brother George Vaughan as by...writing...bearing date the ninteenth day of march...one Thousand Six hundred Eighty Six...and...was formerly mine...being part of my farme...three and twentieth day of...July...one Thousand Six hundred Eighty seven

Wit.   John Vaughan
   John Gould   his **X** marke
   Bartholomew Hunt
   William Wodell—

John Vaughan...acknowledged above...Walter Clarke one of the Councile

[323] John Alcock to John Rodman.
...John Alcock of Boston...Merchant...for...Two Hundred Pounds Currant mony of New England...paid...by John Rodman of Newport...mercht:...Have...Sold...One Sixteenth Part of...Newshorum als Block-Island...knowne by the name of Mr Bellinghams part...Formerly in the Occupation of Robert Guthridge and Lately in the Possession of

Thomas Mitchell decd. with twenty Five acres of Land thereto belonging Laid Out to that Share or farme Out of Land Sometime belonging to Henry Neale and...all... Buildings standing thereon, Lands...Feedings meadows Marshes...Trees...(Fort Island Only Excepted)...and... Doe...appoint my...friend Robert Guthridge of Block Isld ...my...Attorney...to...Deliver unto the sd John Rodman ...twenty Seaven day of August...One Thousand Six hundred Eighty and Seaven...

Wit.   John Alcock
Thomas Jackson
  Edmond Browne
  Eliezer Moody sen

                           Boston...Augt. 27th 1687
                           John Alcock...acknowledged this...
                                              Jon Usher
memorandum...1687...possession...was given...by Robert Guthridge the Attorney of...John Alcock to John Rodman
[326] John Alcock to Phillip Wharton.
...John Alcock of Boston...Merchant sonn & heire of John Alcock Late of Roxbury...Physitian Deceased...Doe...Release...unto Phillip Wharton...of Block Island...and now of...Boston Tobacconest...One Sixteenth Part of Block Island...which...Phillip Wharton formerly possessed... and to One Sixteenth Part...of Block Island that was in the Possession of John Glover Sometime of sd Boston & now of Swansey in New England...Lands...meadowes Marshes... Trees...(Excepting only out of the prmises Fort Island... Twentieth day of July...one Thousand Six hundred Eighty and Six...

Wit.   John Alcocke
  John Cooke
  Christopher Kilby   Boston July 21-1686
  Eliezer Moody sen   John Alcock...acknowledged the Within...
                                               Wait Winthrop

[328] Phillip Wharton to John Rodman.
...Phillip Wharton and Nathaniell Briggs both now of Block Island...Tobacconist...for...four hundred Pounds Currant Silver money of New England...paid...by John Rodman of Newport...Have Granted...Land...upon Block Island one Lott of two hundred acres and tenn, East Butting on the pond & South upon the Land Now...of Nathall. Dickins & West upon the Sea & North upon John Acres Land and five, five acre Lots Butting upon the Salt Pond, and in the neck three four acre Lots & one Eight part of meadow Land fresh and salt and one meadow Lott Containeing five acres and the Eight part of the Lots Commonly Called by the name of the ministr Lotts with the Eight part of all the Commonage in the neck & out of the neck Except six acres of Land... alredy Disposed of being...Late in the possession of... Nathall: Brigs, John Dodge, William Dodge, & Trustrum Doge with all the woods...twenty fift of July one Thousand six hundred Eighty & four)

Wit.   Philip wharton.
  Robert Little   Nathaniell Briggs.
  Henry Timberlake
  Nathall: Coddington

Phillip Wharton and Nathaniell Brigs...acknowledged the above written...

                        Walter Clarke Dept Gouvr.

[330] Daniell Gould to John Sirkitt.
...Daniell Gould of Newport...for...thirty pounds formerly Received and now forty pounds of currant silver Money of New England...paid by John Sirkitt of Newport...doe ...sell...Land Lyeing...in the Precincts of Newport...containeing...twenty acres and Bounded on the South by Edward Greenemans Land on the West by the highway or Common on the North and East by the Lands of...Daniell Gould...with all...Edefices...twelfe Day of September... 1687

Wit.   Peleg Tripp   Danll: Gould
      Thomas Ward, Scr:

Daniell Gould...acknowledged the above written...

            Walter Clarke

[332] William Allen to John Sirkett.
...William Allen and John Rathborne both of Newport... haveing been...in possession of...Land Lyeing...in the precincts of...Newport...containeing...ten acres and bounded on the South by Edward Greenemans. Land on the West by the Highway or Common on the North and East by the Land of Daniell Gould and...in consideration of...Sattisfaction ...received...for Our...Trobles, . . . Buildings...and... costs...concerneing the...Lands of John Sirkett of Newport ...Currier...wee...be fully sattisfied...doe...Quitclaime Unto...John Sirkett...the above mentioned Lands...tenth day of October...1687

Wit.   William Allen
 John Ward   John **X** Rathborne
 Thomas Ward   his mark

 William Allen and John Rathborne...acknowledged... above...

            Walter Clark

[334] John Strainge Senior to John Strainge Juni.
...John Strainge Senior of Portsmouth...for...Sufficient maintenance to mee and his Beloved mother in Meat Drink and Lodgeing...fitt for such ancient people as wee...doe... confirme, unto my sonn John Strainge A Parcell of Land containeing twenty acres...bounded Northerly and Westerly by the common, Southerly and Easterly by the Land of Daniell Lawton with my Now Dwelling House...and all Moveables therein, with all the Stock...fifteenth day of October...one Thousand six hundred eighty Seven

Wit.   the mark of
 Latham Clarke   John **X** Strainge Sen:
 John yelthro

...John Strainge Senor: Declared...this...Deed in Newport...Seventeenth day of October 1687

       Walter Newberry one of the Councill...

[335] Samuell Dyre to Charles Dyre.
...Samuell Dyre of Boston...Carpenter...for...two hun-

dred pounds New England Money...paid...by Charles Dyre of Newport...Husbandman...Have...sold...Land Lyeing ...In Newport...boundeth...on the East...partly by certaine Land...Late in the possession of mr Francis Brinley & Left: Collo: Peleg Sanford on the South...by Land...Late ...of mr Nicholas Easton & mr John Clarke on the West... by the sea & on the north...by Land...of Henry Dyre...with the Dwelling House...Orchards Gardens meadowes...woods ...Swamps...Comon of Pasture...(Excepting One Entire third part thereof Layed out unto mis Katharin Dyre by... the Towne Councill of Newport in...1681 as her Right of Dower) All...the Premises...are...in Newport...and now or Late in the Tenure of...Charles Dyre...fift day of October...one Thowsand six hundred Eighty and seven...

Wit.   West. Clarke   Samuell Dyre
      Robert Little.
      Daniell Vernon.

                      ...Samuell Dyre...acknowledged this...
                Peleg Sanford Justice of the peace

[337]   Ann Vernon & Daniell Vernon assent to Deed.

Ann Vernon Mother unto...Samuell Dyre and with the Consent of my Husband, doe allow...the above...Sale Relinquishing my Right...of Dower or thirds...18th day Octobr. 1687

                                                  Ann Vernon

...Daniell Vernon...acknowledged...assent...made by Ann Vernon his wife...march 12th 1687-8 Newport...Caleb Carr Justice

    Andrew Bowne to George Lawton.

...Andrew Bowne of new yorke...merchant and Elizabeth his wife...for...five hundred twenty five pounds...currant money of new England...by George Lawton Junr: of Portsmouth now Resident in freetowne...Husbandman...paid... Have...sold...A certaine Farme Parcell...being part...in the Towne of Newport...& part...in...Portsmouth...containing Two hundred & fourty Acres...now or Late in the holding...of Robert Allen...is bounded on the South by Jonathan Hulme his Land on the West by the Comon on the North by Lands in the possession of Samuell Sanford & on the East by the sea or salt water And...all...Houses Edefices Gardens Orchards...tenth day of may...one Thousand six hundred Eighty and seven...

Wit.
  John Thurber
  Saul Browne
  Joseph Browne
    Winton

Andrew Bowne
Elizabeth Bowne
...Andrew...& Elizabeth his wife...
acknowledged...

Tho Dongan

[339] Peleg Withington Letter of Attorney to Weston Clarke & John Greene

Barbados...Peleg Withington of the Island of Barbados... resident in the Towne and Parrish of St. michalls...doe... make my...friends Weston Clarke Secretary & Jno Greene mercht: both of...Newport...my True and Lawfull Attorneys...to Demand...any sums of money Percells of Land Houseing...due...unto me...Dated in Barbados the 24th Day of...february...1686...

Wit.
  Henry Beer
  James Hart
  Edward Archer

Peleg Withington.

...before mee
Richard Smith. Novber: 17, 1687.

[340] William Stoughton to John Walley.

...William Stoughton Esqr...have...received By Order of John Walley Esqr:...five hundred Fifty two pounds Tenn Shillings Currant Money of New England in...Condition of ...Deed of Mortgage for Redemption of the...Premisses,... do...Release...Unto...John Walley...all Right...which I ...have...to the Lands...therein mentioned to be Granted ...Unto...John Walley...as Though this...Bargaine...had never beene...Twenty fift day of November...one Thousand six hundred Eighty seven...

Wit.   William Stoughton
  Jsa. Addington
  Thomas Dudley

                        Boston 30th Novemb. 1687
                        William Stoughton Esqr...
                        acknowledged...
                                    Jno. Usher

[341] John Walley to Stephen Mumford & Robert Ayres. ...six and Twentith day of November...One Thousand six hundred Eighty seven...Between John Walley of Bristoll on the one part:—And Steephen Mumford of James Towne yeoman and Robert Ayres of Newport...yeoman;...on the Other part...John Walley for...six hundred and Twenty pounds in Currant money of New England...by...Stephen Mumford and Robert Ayres...paid...Hath...sould...his farme containeing about Two hundred and fourty acres of Land...in the Towneship of Newport...called...Braces farme Late in the Occupation of Richard Allison now in the actuall possession...of...Robert Ayres being the whole of that farme and Lands upland Meadows and swamps...given by William Brenton Esqr: in...his Last will...unto his sonn Willam Brenton...bounded Westerly by the Land...of Henry Bull and Jirah Bull, Southerly by the Land of Major John Coggeshall, Easterly by the sea, Northerly by the Land of John Easton Senr: in part...by the Common...with all houses Barnes...Buildings Wood, Trees and Stones...upon request...of...Stephen Mumford and Robert Ayres...and at their Cost...will...performe such Other act...for further Confirmation of the above granted...so as...John Walley...be not compelled to travill more than twenty Miles from his ...home...Also Sarah wife of...John Walley doth...confirme...premises...

Wit.   John Walley
  Jsa: Addington   Sarah Walley
  Thomas Dudley

Boston 30th Novembr 1687 John Walley Esqr:...acknowledged this...   ....william stoughton

[344] John Throckmorton to Jahleel Brenton and others.
...John Throckmorton...of middletowne in the County of Munmouth in East Jersey...whereas my father John Throckmorton formerly...of Providence...Deceased Did Owe... unto William Brenton of Newport...Deceased and to Alexander Bryant of milford in...Conecticot Deceased the...Sum of one hundred pounds currant pay of New England...doe ...Release...unto Jahleel Brenton and Peleg Sanford both of newport...Executors to...William Brenton Deceased and Richard Bryant of Milford son to...Alexander Bryant Deceased...the Lands...belonging...formerly unto my... father John Throckmorton Deceased Lyeing...in Providence ...Both upland and meadow...20th day of may 1687
Wit.   John Throckmorton
 Jonathan Marsh
 Grace Lippencott
...Newport...June the 15th 1687
 Acknowledged before mee John
 Coggeshall one of the Councill

[345] Debts Released unto John Throckmorton.
...John Throckmorton...of Middletowne in the County of munmouth in East Newjersey and Eldest sonn of John Throckmorton Late of Providence...Deceased Did Remise ...unto Jahleel Brenton and Peleg Sanford Both of Newport ...Executos. to William Brenton Late of Newport...Deceased and Richard Bryant of Milford...son to Alexander Bryant of...Milford Deceased...the Lands That Did belong Unto his...Father John Throckmorton of Providence Deceased Lyeing...in...Towne of Providence...Dated the twentieth day of may one Thousand six hundred Eighty and seven...And alsoe two mortgages formerly made Under the hand...of...John Throctmorton...Deceased Unto...William Brenton Deceased and...Alexander Bryant Deceased... one of the...mortgages being Dated the Twentieth day of Aprill one Thousand Six hundred fifty and three, the other ...Dated the thirtieth day of September one Thousand six hundred fifty five...wee Caleb Carr of newport...Attorney

for...Richard Bryant and...Peleg Sanford have...Released
...Richard Bryant his heires,...and the heires...of...William Brenton Deceased and the heires...of Alexander Bryant
...Release,...unto...John Throckmorton of middletowne...
all...Debts...Eleventh day of January...1687-8

Wit.   Peleg Sanford
  John Ward   Caleb Carr
  Thomas Ward

Peleg Sanford and Caleb Carr...the 15th day of January 1687-8...acknowledged...

                        Attest John Coggeshall
                            one of the Councill...

[347]   John Baily to John Briggs.

...John Baily of Newport...for...one hundred fourty and Six pounds Currant silver money of New England...paid...by John Briggs of Portsmouth...Junior...have...sould...farme of Land...Scittuate at and near Pachit Brooke in the Lands called Puncatest Lands in the County of Bristoll...Bounded Southwardly by the North line of Little Compton and West by Pachit brooke...and the highway Northerly by maj: Gouldings Land and is in breadth fifty poles...and is A mile in Length...Containeing one hundred Acres...alsoe the one Eight part of A Share in Deale of all...Undevided Lands Lyeing...in the Precincts of the...Towne of Little Compton...with the Dwelling house on the said Land being where Lately David Lake Dwelt with all...Edefecis Gardens Orchards...fourteenth Day of february...1687

Wit.   John **X** Baily
  Henry Dyre   his marke
  Thomas Ward

                ...Sutton Baily the wife of...
                John Baily doe...Release...Lands
                ...unto John Brigs...

                            Sutton **X** Baily
                Henry Dyre   her marke
                Thomas Ward
                John Baily and Sutton Baily his

wife...acknowledged...before me
Peleg Sanford Justice

[349]   Thomas Fish to Preserved Fish.
...Thomas Fish of Portsmouth...unto my...Grandson Preserved Fish the sonn and heire of my Sonn Thomas Fish Late of Portsmouth...Deceased...have Given...to be by him... Possessed...after the terme of Sixteene years...which will be in the year one Thousand Seven hundred the Late Dwelling house of my...Sonn Thomas Fish Deceased...with all... Lands Orchards, Gardens, and Out houses...in Portsmouth ...containeing...fifteene Acres...Bounded on the North by Stephen Cornells Land on the East by Land Lately belonging to Thomas Cooke Deceased on the South and West by the Highwayes or common of the said Towne...second day of may...one Thousand six hundred Eighty and four

Wit.   Thomas fish
  Thomas Ward
  Ammy Ward
  Mary Billing
  Thomas Fish...2: day of may 1684...Did...acknowledge this...   John Albro: Assistant

[350]   Jeremiah Browne to John Cooke.
...Jeremiah Browne & Mary Browne wife to...Jeremiah of Newport,...for...Thirty & nine Pounds Currant Silver money...paid...by John Cooke of Portsmouth...Have... sould...Land...in the Towne Ship of Portsmouth...tenn Acres...Bounded...On the East by Land now in the possession of George Sisson On the north by Land of Stephen Cornall On the West by Land formerly belonging to Thomas Fish of Portsmouth Deceased On the South Partly by Land of sd. John Cooke Sen & part by the Common...twenty Ninth day of march...1688

Wit.   Jeremiah Browne
  Robert Little   Mary Brown
  Weston Clarke
Jeremiah Browne and Mary Browne his wife...Did acknowledge...   Peleg Sanford

[352]   Joseph Barker to Lawrence Turner.
...Joseph Barker of Newport...Talor...for...Eighty Eight Pounds of currant Silver money of New England...paid...by Lawrence Turner Junior of Newport...husbandman...have...sold...Land...in the Precincts of Newport...Twenty-nine acres and Sixty-Seven pole...bounded...on the East by Land now in the Possession of Joseph Barker, Northerly by Lands of Henry Bull, Nochelas Evens and Andrew Langworthy Westerly by Land of Andrew Langworthy and the high-way and Southerly by Land Andrew Langworthy and the high Way...with all...the Woods, fences Wayes...Vacant Lands, Commons...Eight day of march...1688

Wit.   Joseph Barker
 Walter Roades   Sarah Barker
 William Weeden
 Elias Williams
 Joseph Barker...acknowledged this...
      Walter Newbery of the Councell...

[355]   William Browning to Robert Fish.
...William Browning of portsmouth...Planter...for...seventy pounds Starll: currant money of New England...paid...by Robert Fish of Portsmouth...Smith...have...sold...Land which was Given to mee by my Deceased Grandfather William Freeborne cittuate...in the Towneship of Portsmouth...Bounded...Northerly by Undevided Land or common Eastwardly by the Highway which goeth towards Newport Sotherly by the Land of Richard Cadmone. Westwardly by the Land of Giddian Freeborne...by Estimation twenty Acres...12th month caled february...1687-8 and alsoe Rebeckah Browning wife unto...William Browning...free consent to...Premisses...

Wit.   his marke and seal
 Christopher Almy   William **X** Browning
The marke of   his mark & seale
 Zurall Hall   Gidian **X** Freeborn
          her marke & seale
          Rebeckah **X** Browning

Gidian Freeborne and William Browning & Rebeckah his wife...acknowledged...

John Coggeshall Justice of the Peace

[357] Stephen Mumford & Robert Ayres to Sr. William Phips.

...Twenty ninth day of Novemb...one Thousand Six hundred Eighty seven...Between Stephen Mumford of James Towne...yeoman and Robert Ayres of Newport...yeoman of the one Part, and Sr. William Phips Knight late of Boston...on the Other Part...Stephen Mumford and Robert Ayres for ...three Hundred pounds in currant money of New England ...by...Sr. William Phips or his agent...paid...Have given ...their Farme containing about Two hundred and fourty acres...Lyeing...within the Towneship of Newport... Knowne by the name of Braces Farme Late in the occupation of Richard Allison now in the actuall Possession and Tenure of...Robert Ayres...upland Meadows and Swamps which they...purchased of John Walley of Bristoll Esq...bounded Westerly by the Land now or late of Henry Bull and Irah Bull Sotherly by the Land of major John Coggeshall Eastwardly by the sea northerly by the Land of John Easton Sen: ...and partly by the Common...With all houses Barnes... Trees...

Wit.
  Nathal. Byfield
  Samll. Crowley

Stephen Mumford
Robert Ayars
Signum
Anne X Mumford
Esther Ayars

Boston 30th November 1687

Stephen Mumford and Robert Ayers...before me one of his majesties Councill...acknowledged

John Walley

Ann Mumford & Ester Ayres...acknowledged before me one of the Councill...the fourth day of May 1688

Walter Newberry

[361] Agreement betweene John Vaughan & Joshua Coggeshall.

...John Vaughan Senior Liveing in the Bounds of Newport and Joshuah Coggeshall Dwelling Within the Bounds of Portsmouth...John Vaughan...to make...a part of the fenceing...betweene the Lands of...Josuah Coggeshall and ...John Vaughan...is to begin at the Beech Tree being the Corner Tree of...Joshuah's Land next towards the Common or high way which Leadeth from John Goulds towards George Laitons water mill: and soe to fence from that beech Tree towards the sea Unto a certaine Great Red Oake now Standing in the Line which...fence is measured to be forty and six Pole and all the rest of the fence in the said Line from the Red Oake downe to the Sea the said Joshuah Coggeshall...is...to make...Dated the 20th day of may 1671

Wit.   Joshuah Coggeshall

  George Hamond
  Thomas **X** nichols
     his marke

[362] George Lawton to Robert Lawton.

...George Lawton of Portsmouth...unto my son Robert Lawton of...Portsmouth have given...my fourty acres of Land...being in two...Parcells at or near the River Called the Wading River in the Towneship of Portsmouth where now I Dwell...bounded mostly by highways,...With all... Dwelling Houses...and mills, gardens, Orchards...second Day of...June...one Thousand six hundred Eighty Eight,

Wit.   George Lawton

  Thomas Durfie
  William Wodell
  George Lawton acknowledged this...

                    John Albro one of his majesties Councill

[363] Samuell Wilson to John Holmes.

...Samuell Wilson of Rochester in the Narrowganset Country...for...Thirty pounds Currant silver money of New England...paid...by John Holmes of Newport..Cordwinder ...doe...grant...unto...John Holmes...one halfe of A share it being the fourteenth Part of all the Lands and

meadowes in Point Juda Neck in Pettacomscott purchase...
with all...woods...Twenty fourth day of may...1687...
Wit.   Samuell Wilson
   Samll: Cranston
   Robert Little
   Weston Clarke
   Samuell Wilson...owned...24th day of may 1687 in Newport...
                                            Peleg Sanford
                                            Justice of Peace

[365] Samuell Wilson of...Rochester...doe...owne my selfe...to be...Indebted Unto John Holmes of Newport... in the full...Sum of one hundred pound Currant money of New England...Twenty fourth day of may...1687
The Condition of the above...is...that if...Samuell Wilson shall make Good...the above...John Holmes...in the quiet ...possession of A certaine peace...of Land being the one halfe of a Share or the fourteenth part of all the Land and meados...Lyeing in point Juda Neck which...holmes purchased of...Wilson...by A deed...bareing Date Even with These presents then the above...obligation to be Void...
Wit.   Samuell Wilson
   Samll: Cranston
   Robert Little
   Weston Clarke
   Samuell Wilson...owned the above written...Newport... 24th day of May 1687
                              Peleg Sanford Justice of Peace

[366] Samuell Wilson to Robert Hana.
...Samuell Wilson of...Rochester...in New England...for ...my Deceased fathers Last will...as also the Love...I ow to my Brother & Sister Robert & Mary Hana Have Given... Unto Robert Hana...one Equall halfe share of what was my fathers...In all that Parcell of Land...in the Towneship of Rochester...Called by the name of the Thousand Acres Near Robert Hasards farm he now Dwells on In Rochestr...26th day of June one Thousand six hundred Eighty & Eight...

Wit.   Samuell Wilson
  Jirah Bull
  Ezechiell Bull
  Henry Bull Jun
Samuell Wilson...before me one of the Councill...acknowl-
  edged this...the twenty seventh of June 1688
                                    Walter Newberry

[367]   Wanuemaching to Robert Stanton etc.
...whereas there was A perciell of Land Containing five miles in Length And one And halfe in breadth the bounds of it Lyeth on the One Side to A River Called westotowtucket & to the other Side to A river Called Ashuniunck or Else Adjoyning to mr Samuell Wilbors Line & mr John porters, ...I Wannemaching have sold to Robert Stanton & George Gardner...I...doe bind my Selfe...to maintaine the Right & title of the...Land Above...upon forfiture of All the Rest of my Land on the Narrogansett Cuntry...22th day of August...1662

Wit.   the marke of
  George Webb   X
  Hugh Moger   Wanuemathen
     the marke of
          X
  to wesecom Indian

[368]   David Lake to John Baily.
...David Lake Inhabitant at A place Called Pachit in... Puncatest and near Adjoineing to the northward part of the Lands of Little Compton in the County of Bristoll...for... one hundred and fourty pounds Currant Silver money of New England...paid...by John Baily of Newport...doe... sell...A...farme of Land...at and near Pachit Brooke... Bounded Southwardly by the north Line of the said Towne of Little Compton and Westward by Pachitt Brooke and the Highway, Northerly by maj: Goldings Land and is in Breadth fifty poles...and is A mile in Length...Containeing one hundred Acres...and also the one Eight part of A share...of all...Undevided Lands...in...Little Compton...

with the Dwelling house on the...Land being where now... David Lake Dwelleth with all...Edefeces, Gardens, Orchards,...seventeenth Day of January...1687-8
Wit. David Lake
  Joseph Timberlake
  William fobes —

        ...Sarah Lake the wife of...David Lake Doe...Release...the Right...I ...have in...Lands...

                    Sarah X Lake
  Joseph Timberlake
  William fobes
...David Lake and Sarah his wife Acknowledged this...
          John Coggeshall Justice of Peace

[371] Caleb Carr to Thomas Paine.
...Caleb Carr of James Towne Alias Cononicut Island... Junior...for...fifty pounds Currant Silver money of New England...paid...by Thomas Paine of Newport...marriner ...have Granted...A house Lot With A Dwelling house thereon...wherein Thomas Paine Now Dwelleth...in Newport...Containeing...fourty foot Square and Bounded on the South East by the Street of the said Towne and Southwest, Northwest, and Northeast by Other Lands or Lots...of... Thomas Paine...first day of August...1688
Wit. Caleb Carr Juni:
  John Ward
  paule Stephens

[373] Richard Smith to John Hull.
...Richard Smith of Rochester...for...five hundred pounds of...money of New England...by John Hull now Residing at Newport...marriner...paid...Have...Sold...Land...in the Island Quononaqut Als: James Towne...three hundred and Seventy acres...Bounded Southerly Upon the Land of Joseph mory, Westerly Upon the Sea or Narragansit Bay, Northerly by a highway and Easterly by a highway...now in the possession...of Richard Peirce...with all Woods... swamps...Richard Smith and Ester his wife...doe...Grant

...And also...Richard Smith and Easter his Wife have... Given...unto...John Hull...all...their...Portion in a small Island near...Island of Quononaqut called...Dutch Island and Purchased of the Indian Sachems with the Island Quononaqut...as may appear more at Large by Instruments under their hands...wee...doe...sell...for...the sum above mentioned...and...doe...appoint Joseph Mory of Jamestowne als: Quononaqut yeoman...their...Attorney... twentieth day of January...one Thousand six hundred Eighty & seven...

Wit.   Richd Smith
  Lodowick Updick   Ester Smith
  William **X** Knowles
     his marke
  Ephraim More
  Jno: Fones —
Richard Smith Esquire...before mee one of the Councill ...did acknowledg...

                               Walter Clarke

Quononqut the twenty one day of January one thousand six hundred & eighty seven or Eight

...Lands...taken by...Joseph mory...and...Delivered to ...John Hull...

Wit.
  Nicholas Carr
  John Wood
  Richard **X** Beare Tenant
     his marke

[376]   Michael Perry Recd: of John Easton
                         Boston 14th march 1687-8

Recd: of John Easton Constab: of Newport...seventy five pounds Thirteen shills: & 10d...for the Country Rate of that Towne, Nine pounds Two shill: & 6d of which...was a receit Given for before Recd: for the Use of John Usher Esqr: Treasurer:

                               X Michael Perry

£75—13s—10d

[378]   Francis Brinley Received of John Easton.
Received of John Easton Constable of Newport twenty Pence in money for accot: of mr Edward Randolph of Boston, and five Bush and one halfe of Barley and three peckes Wheat he has put on Board the Sloop Desire for...Mr: Randolphs accot: being in part of Payment for Copies of Laws & Commissions due to...Randolph...26th January 1687
                                            Francis Brinley
   Richard Cadman to Isaac Lawton.
...Richard Cadman of Portsmouth...weaver...for...Thirty pounds Sterling Currant Money of New England...Paid... By Isaac Lawton of Portsmouth...Yeman,...have...sold,... ten Acres...cittuate...in the...Towneship of Portsmouth Bounded...Northerly upon the Lane or highway Easterly by the Undevided Land or Commond Southerly and westwardly by the Lands of...Isaac Lawton and Robert Hodgson,... Eighteenth day of October...one Thousand Six hundred Eighty and Eight...
Wit.   Richard Cadman
   Robert Fish   Sarah Cadman
   Mathew X Greenhill
        his marke
     ...Richard Cadman and Sarah his wife...Acknowledged ...Deed...
                        John Coggeshall Justice of Peace
[380]   Richard Cadman to Robert Fish.
...Richard Cadman of Portsmouth...for...one hundred & forty pounds in money...paid by Robert Fish of Portsmouth ...have...sold...Land...in the Towneship of Portsmouth ...twenty Eight acres...Bounded Easterly by the highway Southerly by a Lane that goes to Robert Houchins and the Comon Westerly by Land of Nicholas Browne Northerly by Land of...Robert Fish and Giddion Freeborne...with all... Houses, Barns, Kribs, Orchards...to be holden as of the mannour of East Greenwich...Elizabeth Cadman my mother and Sarah the wife of mee...consent...Two and twentieth day of September...one Thousand six hundred eighty eight—

Wit.   Richard Cadman
  Christopher Almy   Sarah Cadman
  John yelthro   Elizabeth X Cadman
                                              her marke

Richard Cadman came with his wife Sarah...and did Acknowledge...deed...24th of September 1688
                        John Albro one of...Councill

Elizabeth Cadman...25 day of October 1688 acknowledged...
                        John Albro one of...Councill

[382] Daniell Greenhill to Henry Brightman.
......Daniell Greenhill of...Portsmouth...Maulster...for ...one hundred and twenty four pounds of Currant money of New England by Henry Brightman of...Portsmouth... paid...Have...sould,...Land...in the Towneship of Portsmouth...Containeing Twenty three Acres...bounded north by a highway, East by the Land of Majo John Albro South Esterly and South by Land Lately belonging to the Late deceased Icobod Potter and partly by a hieway West by (Land) belonging to mr George Lawton...with all...houses ...buildings, fences, Gardens, Orchards,...one and thirtith day of December...one Thousand six hundred Eighty three—
Wit.   Daniell Grennell
  John Sanford
  Mary Sanford

Daniell Grenell...28 day of Aprell 1684 did acknowledge...
                        John Albro: Assistant

...Mary Greenell the wife of Daniell Greenell...do...consent unto...sale...one and thirtieth day of December one Thousand Six hundred Eighty three
Wit.   Mary X Greenell
  John Sanford   her marke
  Mary Sanford

Mary Greenell...16 day of December 1684...owed this... hur...Deed
                        George Lawton Assistant

...William Woddell of Portsmouth...Doe...Release...unto

...Henry Brightman...my Right...in...the above...premisses...one and thirtieth day of December...one Thousand six hundred Eighty three

Wit.   William Wodell
  John Sanford
  Mary Sanford
  William Wodell...28th day of Aprill 1684...Did acknowledge...

                                      John Albro Assistant

[384]   Samuell Utly to John Maxson

...Samuell Utly of Stoneingtone...for...ten Pounds Currant Silver money of New England...paid by John Maxson of feversham...Have...Sould...one hundred acres of Land ...Lyeing as was formerly Deemed within the Precincts of Stoneingtone, but now in feversham...Butted...beginning at A White Oake tree Marked on four sides standing on the East side of Ashaawage River Joyneing to Land Laid out to George Cooke from thence Runeing Southwardly and Joyneing to Ashuwage River Thirty Rhods to a white Oake tree marked on four sides, from thence Eastwardly thirty Rhods to a white Oake tree marked on four sides from thence Runing one hundred and thirty Rods Southward to A white Oake tree marked on four sides standing by a Little Run of water from thence Runing Easterly one hundred Rods to A white Oake Tree marked on fower sides from thence Runing upon A direct Line to the Southeast Corner tree of Land Layd Out to George Cooke which Tree is a black Oake tree marked on four sides and soe Joyning to the said Cookes Land to the Tree first mentioned...two and twentieth day of february... one Thousand six hundred Eighty seven or Eight

Wit.   Samuell Utley
  John Brown
  Thomas Browne
...Acknowledged by Samuell Utley thirty one day of December 1688

                        James Pendleton Justice of the peace

[386]   Weston Clarke to Daniell King.

...Weston Clarke of Newport...for...fourty shillings Currant money...paid by Daniell King of Prudence Island Shipwright Have...Sould...one quarter part of my share of the Purchase of Westconayett Lands...22th day of Sept: 1687

              West: Clarke
...it is...understood...A Quarter part of a hole share of Land...
Wit.   West. Clarke
 Samll: Gardiner
 Robert Little
Weston Clarke before me acknowledged the above written...
         Walter Clark of the Counsell

[387] Eseck Carr to Robert Carr.
...Esecke Carr and Susanah his Wife of Little Compton... for...Twenty pounds Currant silver money of New England ...paid...By Robart Carr of Newport...Have...sold... halfe an acre...in...Newport...Bounded...East on the Land of Majo. Peleg Sanford South on Land now in the possession of mr Francis Brinley & mr Caleb Carr Sen: North on the Land of...Robert Carr & Land now or Late in the Possession of Samuell Gardner West on the highway or Common Road Leading through Newport Towne Into the necke...first day of August...1687
Wit.   Eseck Carr
 Samll: Gardner   Susanah Carr
 John Tillinghast   her **X** mark
 Weston Clarke
Eseck Car and Susannah Carr his wife acknowledged this ...thirteth day of November 1687
        Joseph Church Justice of the Peace

[388] John Parker to George Sisson.
...John Parker of Newport...Husbandman...and Esther his Wife for...one hundred twenty five pounds ten shillings of currant Silver money of New England...paid...by George Sison of Portsmouth...Husbandman...Have...sold...Land ...in...Newport...one and Thirty acres and bounded... Easterly on Lands of John Allin, Southerly on Lands formerly of Edward Robinson, Westerly and Northerly on the

Common,...with all...Dwelling Houses Out houses, Woods, ...twenty eight day of february...1688
Wit.   his marke
  Peleg Tripp   John **X** Parker
  John Sanford   her marke
  Elias Williams   Esther **X** Parker

  John Parker and Esther his wife did on the fourth day of March...1688 acknowledge...

                        John Albro one of...Councill

[390] James Man to Phillip Smith.

...James Man of Newport...for...one hundred and sixty pounds currant Silver money of New England...Paid...by Phillip Smith of Newport...have...sould...A certaine farm ...Containeing fourty Acres...in Newport...Bounded Southerly by the Lands of Jonathan Hulmes,...Phillip Smith, Thomas Ward, and Samuell Baily, Westerly by James Barkers Land and the highway Northerly by the Land of... Phillip Smith and Eastwardly by the Land of...Jonathan Hulmes...with all...Houses...Barnes Orchards, Gardens Woods...Thirteenth day of march...1688
Wit.   James Man
  John Ward
  John **X** Pebody
    his marke
  Thomas Ward

  ...James Man acknowledged Deed Before mee Francis Brinley one of his Majties: Justices

[392] George Lawton to Robert Lawton.

...George Lawton of Portsmouth...Unto my son Robert Lawton of...Portsmouth have Given...my Goods Chattells, Utensils,...Debts to me Oweing, Bills, Bonds, Specialties,... all other things...in whatsoever place...they...may be found ...second day of...June...one Thousand six hundred Eighty eight
Wit.   George Lawton
  Isaac Lawton
  Thomas Durfie

William Wodell
George Lawton did...acknowledge this...
John Albro one of his Majestyes Counciell
[393] William Wodell to Robert Lawton.
...William Wodell of Portsmouth...for...four hundred pounds in money...paid by Robert Lawton of...Portsmouth, have...Sould...Land...Within the Bounds of...Portsmouth...one hundred and ten acres...bounded Northwardly by Land now in the Possession of Robert Dennis in part and ...by Land in the possession of William Burrington Eastwardly by the Sea or Salt water Southwardly by Land now... of Peleg Shearman and Westward by the Common high way ...with all...Buildings, gardens, Orchards,...twelfth day of the moneth Called february...1688-9
Wit.   William Wodell
Joseph Timberlake
John Norcut
John Anthony
William Wodell Junor
Portsmouth february the 18th 1688-9...William Wodell... acknowledged...Deed...
John Albro one of...Councill
[395] Attest of John & Jeffery Christophers.
...We John Christophers Master, Jeffery Christophers Mate &c. belonging to the good barque Reserve of New London,... bound from Barbados to Newport...being at Sea, On tuesday the Twentie Ninth Day of October Last past, In the Latitude of Thirtie Nine Degrees and thirtie five Minits by dead reckoning...Mett with a most violent and Tempestuous storm,...that wee were forced to Lye by or a Hull, wind being at South East. On Wednesday...the thirtith day we were forced to Scudd with bare poles in a most Violent and great Sea breaking over us and...bareing away...all hogsheads and Casque from off our deck...Wee...do...Protest and exclaim against the Seas according to Custome...thirtieth day of November One thousand Six Hundred Eighty and nine...
...John Christophers   John Christophers

Geffery Christophers & Benjamin Waters...the Last day of Novemb 1689 & swore...to the truth...
John Coggeshall Depty Gov:

Jeffrey Christophers the marke and seall of
X
Benjamin Waters

[396] James Case to Joseph Carde.
...James Case of Seconett alias Little-comtowne)...Husbandman and Anna his Wife...for...fourty pounds of Currant money of New-england...paid...to Joseph Carde of Newport...Husbandman...do...Sell...land being in thy Precints of Newport...twelve acres...bounded...Notherly on the undevided Lands or common, Easterly on the highway partly, and...on Land or Orchard wch: formerly was called Knight Orchard, Southerly partly on Sd: Orchard, partly on Land of John Greene and partly on Land of John Rogers, and Westerly on Lands of the Sd: Joseph Carde,...with all... Commons, Fences,...tenth day of January...1688-89...
Wit.
    his mark
  Larance **X** Turne
  Edward Greenman
  Elias Williams

Jeames Case
Anna Case

Jeames Case...with his wife Anna did acknowledg...11 day of january 1688-89 before me John Albro
one of his Majesties counsell

[398] Hugh Mosher to Henry Brightman.
...Hugh Mosher of portsmouth...Black Smith...for...two hundred And thirty pounds in mony...payd by henry Brightman of portsmouth...have given...Land...in the township of portsmouth...And part In newport bounds...thirty Eight Acres...bounded northward by Land of John Vahan Eastwardly partly by...Land of Daniell Lawton, Called hunting Swamps &...by the Common Southwardly partly by the Common & partly by Land of witherington, westwardly by the Common...with all the dwelling houses Barnes Orchards ...I...Hugh mosher...granted unto him...Rebeckah Mosher

the wife of mee...Consent...twenty eight Day of January ...One thousand six hundred Eighty nine

Wit. Hugh Mosher
  Peleg Trip the mark of
  Thomas Cornell Rebeckah **X** Mosher
  John Yelthro:

Hugh & Rebeckah Mosher...the 30th day of January 1689 ...owned the above written

                             John Coggeshall Depty Genr

[400] John Hart to Ralph Chapman.

...Tenth day of Desemb...1688 Betwene John Hart of... Newport...Marrino & Ralph Chapman of said Island... shipwright for...Eighty pound Currant mony of new England ...have...sold...unto the said Ralph Chapman...Land...in the Narragansett Cuntry...qtaining five hundred Acres... Lying About foure miles from Pitticomquott Rock Southwest being neare the place Called Durty Swamp on the west partly by A highway tenn Rods wide betwene the said Land & the greatt pond & partly by other Lands Not as yett Layd out & one north & Easterly by Other Lands yett Layd out...

Wit. John Hart
  Robart Little Jeames Hart
  Thomas Gould Mary Cranston
  Roger Goulding Samll Cranston
                Walter Clark
                freeborne Clark

...Samuell Cranston the husband of...mary Cranston... Consented to...sale... Giles Slocome Ast

  Newport...Jun 13th: 1698 Walter Clarke & freeborne Clarke...Acknowledgment of...sale

Wit. Samll Cranston Govr
  Ebenezer Slocom
  Benjamin Barton

[401] Frances Brinly to William Mays.

...Frances Brinly of Newport...for...mony...payd...by William Mays of...Newport...Have...sold...unto William Maise...one quarter of An Acre...now fenced with Pailes with the hous & housing share on building & buildings which said Peace of Land being bounded on the north by Land of my sister Ann Coddington on the west by Land Given to my Cozen William Coddington on the South & East by the Streatt Lane...Newport...Fabuary the nineteenth 1673-4

Wit.   Frances Brinly
 Jeames Loyd   Hannah Brinly
 John **X** Wood
  his marke
 Thomas Brinly

[402] Robart Evers to William Edwards.

...Robart Ewer Marcht. & Elizabeth his wife of philadelph for...mony...payd to us from William Edwards of Newport...mercht...have...sold...Land...in the Township of Newport...Eighty foott frount to the Streatt & so...by the Land of William Mays sen & William mays Jun on the East & west & on the North by Land of Nathall Coddington who Is to make halfe the fence of that Line:...Second of July 1692

Wit.   Robert Ewer
 Nathanll Coddington
 George Allin.
 John Tuker

[403] Henry Hall to Jeames Ray.

...Henry Hall of westerly weaver...for...five pounds of mony of New England...payd...by Jeames Ray of Kings town...planta...doe...sell...one hundred Acres of Land... northwest from John Sheldons dwelling hous bounded... East side on the fresh pond on the north by the pine swampe & on the west on John Cottrall & John Crandalls Easterly on the South End of the Ceader Swampe, that I have under the hand...of Coianaquante as Appeareth more Largly upon the Genll records of Rhoad Island,...forth day of July... one thousand six hundred ninty & three

Wit.   the marke of
 the marke of   Henry **X** Hall
Frances **X** Culegrove

the marke of
Daniell **X** Wilcocks
...Acknowleg by Henry Hall...before me Joseph Clarke Consurvator of the peace Westerly the 7th Day of septembr 1693

[404] Henry Hall to William Tannor

...Henry Hall of westerly weaver...for...five pounds of mony of New England...payd...by William Tanno of Kins town plantter...have...sold...one hundred Acres of Land...Lying westerly from John Sheldings Dwelling hous bounde...begining at the brooke of John Sheldings bounds & So up his bounds Sixcore poles...to A white Oake tree marked on three sides & from thenc south & be west nearest sixscore poles to A walnutt bush & from thence west nearest to the river to An Ash tree marked on foure sides & so up Streame to the furthest that I have under the hand...of Coianaquant...forth day of July...one thousand six hundred ninty & thre

Wit.

the marke of
Frances **X** Colegrove

the marke of
Danll **X** Wilcock,

the marke of
Henry **X** Hall

...Acknowle by Henry hall...before mee Joseph Clark Consr of the peace westerly this 7th day of Sept 1693

[405] Henry Hall to peter wells.

...Henry Hall of westerly...for...five pounds of Mony of New England...payd...by peter wells of Kings town...plant...Have...sold...one hundred Acres of Land...westerly from John Sheldens dwelling hous bounded...Lying twelve Score pole in Length North west & South, East bounded on petticomcott Line & in breadth three score & tenn pole & the same Length on the west side Joyning to the Land whare Jobe badcock Liveth & at the Corner of Jobe badcock fence A Little bush marked & from thence Northerly to A small tree marked on foure sides foure pole from John

Sheldens that I have under the hand...of Coganaquant...
forth day of July...one thousand six hundred Ninty & three
Wit. the marke of
  the marke of Henry X Hall
Frances X Colegrove
  the marke of
Danll X Willcock
...Ackleg by...Henry hall before mee Joseph Clarke Consy of the peace Westerly the 7th of Sept 1693

[405]   Henry Hall to John Crandall.

...Henry Hall of westerly wever...for...five pounds of mony of New England...payd...by John Crandall of warwick...have...sold...one hundred & fourescore Acres... north west from John Sheldens dwelling hous bounded... begining at A greatt white Oake tree & so Runs Northerly to A stake & from thence upon A straitt Course to the head & from the greatt whitt oake tree to Anohter whitt Oake tree marked from thence Adirect Line to the river with Adrift way in the Olde path tht I have under hand...of Coganiquante...fourth day of July. one thousand Six hundred Ninty & three:
Wit. The marke of
  The marke of Henry X Hall
Frances X Colegrouve
  the marke of
Daniell X Willcock
...Acknowledge by...Henry hall...before me Joseph Clarke Consr of the peace Westerly the 7th of Sept 1693

[407]   Henry hall to John Shelden.

...Henry hall of Westerly...weaver...for...tenn pounds of mony of New England...payd...by John Shelden of Kings town...planter...have...sold...two hundred Acres ...northwest from...John Sheldins dwelling hous bounded ...at Awhitt oake tree marked on foure sides at the South east Corner & from thence North & by west nearest to Alittle brooke tenn score pole...to Astake & so the brook is the bounds westerly Eight Score poles...the line Coms west &

be south nearest to Atree marked by the broke & from thence tenn score poles...South & by East to Asmall whitt oake tree marked on foure sides & so from thence to the Afore mentioned tree on Astraight Line Eight Score...that I have under hand...of Coganaquant...forth Day of July...one thousand Six hundred Ninty & three.

Wit.   The marke of
  the marke of   Henry X Hall
Francis X Colegrove
  the marke of
Danll X Wilcock

...Acknowledged by...Henry hall...before mee Joseph Clark Consurvator of the peace

      Westerly this 7th day of Sept 1693.

[408] Benjamin Condon to John Sheldon.

...Benjamin Condon Late of the town of portsmouth... plantr...for...seven pounds...pd by John Shelldon of the Narroganset Cuntry...planter...have...sold...thirty & three Acres...being in the...narrowgansett Cuntrey neare pety-quomsett it being part of Aparciell...Containing two hundred & thirty Acres to mee granted by William Brenton, Benedict Arnold John Hull John Porter Samll wilbor Samll wilson & Thomas mumford as...by Adeed...Baring date the two & twentyeth day of Septembr in the year one thousand six hundred Seventy & One...six & twentieth Day of Octobr...1683

Wit. Edwd Richmond   the marke of
        George Hamonde   Benjamin X Congdon

Acknowledged by Benjamin Congdon Joseph Clarke Consurvot of the peace

[409] Henry Hull to Johnathan Knight.

...Henry Hull of Westerly Wever...for...twelve pounds & tenn shillings of moeny of New England...payd...by Johnathan Knight of Warwick...mason...have...sold... two hundred Acres...northwest from John Sheldons dwelling hous with A skirt of Land to pitticomcott Line—Resering Ahigh Way:...bounded...begining at Aread Oake tree marked on foure sides standing at the south Corner eight pole from John Sheldons Corner & so from thence east & benorth ten score pole to Awhitt Oacke bush marked on foure sides & from thence eight score poles to Astake standing north & by west in the plaine which belongs unto John Crandall & so from thence west & be south ten score poles to Astake marked on foure sides Eight pole from John Sheldons Line & so on Astraight Line to the first mentioned tree, that I have under hand...of Coganaquant...forth day of July... one thousand Six hundred Ninty & three

Wit.   the marke of
    the marke of   Henry F Hall
Frances C Colegrove
    the marke of
Danll X Wilcock

...Acknowledge by...Henry hall...before mee Joseph Clark Consr of the peace Westerly the 7th of Septr 1693

[410]   Peleg Sanford to Peleg Slocom.

...Peleg Sanford of Newport...for...One hundred & fifty pounds Currant Silver mony of New England...payd by Peleg Slocom of the township of Darkmouth in the County of new Bristoll in...New plymouth...have...sold...the one half of the westermost Island Commonly Called...Elizabeth Island Alis Cuttohunken...being in the Govr ment of new yorke qt 224 Acres...nineteenth day of Apriell...One thousand six hundred ninty three

Wit.   Peleg X Sanford
  Epharim Turner   his marke
  John Yelthro:—

                     Coronell Peleg Sanford & his wife
                     Mary   Acknowledged...deed...
                     the 19th of Apriell 1693
                            Benedict Arnold Ast:

[412]   Ezekiell Bull to Joseph Case.

...Ezekiell Bull of kingstown, Alis Rochester...Cordwinder ...for...Ninty pounds Currant mony of new Engand... payd by Joseph Case kings town...yeoman,...all my farme

...in the Pettyquamscutt purchase...qt:...two hundred & sixty Acres...bounded on the South by Land of my Brother Epharin Bull, Easterly & northerly by highways westerly by Undevided Lands...which...Land I had of my brother Jireth bull as...by a sale baring date the twenty third day of January 1691...with all timbr woods stones waters... herbage pastures buildings fencings orchards Gardens...one & twentieth day of November 1693...
Wit.   Ezekiel Bull
   Thomas Starr
          his
   Benjamin **X** Clark
          mark
   John Smith

[414] Samuell & Henry Dyre bind them selfes.
...Samuell Dyre & Henry Dyre boath of Newport...doe bind or selves...in the...sume of three hundred pounds starling unto our father William Dyre of Newport...to be levied of our Lands goods & Chattiells
The Condition of this...obligation is such yt if...Samuell Dyre & Henry Dyre Shall pay...unto their Sister Mary Dyre the Eldest Daughter of...William Dyre Aportion of One hundred pounds starling in marchantable pay within three years After the death of...William Provided...houshold goods...William shall order...unto her...shall...be...Deducted from the...one hundred pounds further...obledge themselves...to pay...fourty pounds Starling unto Elizabeth Dyre the second Daughter of...William Dyre when shee cometh to the Age of Eighteen years...25th day of July 1670...
Wit.   George whittman   Samuell Dyre
      George Brown   Henry Dyre

[415] Share in pitticomcutt to William Heffernon.
...John Hull Esq Late of boston...William Brenton & Benedict Arnold Esq John porter Samll Wilbor Samll. Wilson & Thomas Mumford Late of Rhoad Island purchased...Land ...Called...pitticomcott purchas which purchasers granted

...unto severall parsons...Whare fore wee Samuell Sewell And hanah his wife as heir: & in the Right of sd John Hull Jaleel Brenton & Peleg Sanford Executors...in the Right of...William Brenton Benedict Arnold & Josah Arnold Exccecutors...in the Right of sd benedj Arnold Henry Gardner in behalfe of him selfe Brothers & Sisters & in Right of sd John porter John Wilbor...in Right of said Samll Wilbor Thomas Mumford...in Right of sd Thomas Mumford & as Gardian to Jeames wilson heire to sd Samll Wilson Wee... doe declare...that...as share was granted unto William Hefternon then of pitticomcott three hundred Acres of Land by the first purchasers Above named for...seventeen pounds ...payd...for...the same, Bounded northerly by the Lands of Capt John fones Easterly partly by Land of William Agers or Assignes & Stephen Northup or his Assignes Southerly & westerly by the highway which three hundred Acres...wee ...Alow...unto...William Heffernon...twelth day of May ...one thousand six hundred & ninty two
Wit.

John Green	Sam: Sewall
John Pococke	Hannah Sewall
Boston N E Novemb	Jahleel Brenton
28th 1693 Signed...	Josiah Arnold
by Samuell Sewall &	Thomas Mumford
hanah his wife...	Peleg Sanford
Benjamin Gilliam	Benedict Arnold
Elizabeth Sewall	Henry X Gardner
	his marke
	Thomas mumford
	as Garden to the heir
	of Samll Wilson
	John Wilbor

[416] Thomas & Stephen Cornell to George Sison.
...Thomas And Stephen Cornell of Portsmouth...for... ninty pounds of Currant silver mony of new England...payd ...by George Sisson of portsmouth...Have...sold...Land ...in the township of portsmouth...twelve Acres...bounded

...Southerly partly by Land of John Cooke And Partly by Land now in the possestion of Lott Strange westerly by the highway Notherly by Land of Anthony Shaws Easterly by Land of...George Sissons...with all...dwelling houses out houses woods...Commons...second day of Apriell...1691
Wit.
            Thomas Cornell
 Isack Lawton
 Giles Slocom   the marke of
 John Yelthro   Stephen X Cornell
            Hannah X Cornell
             hir marke

[417] ...Thomas Cornell & Stephen Cornell And hannah the wife of Stephen...Acknowledg this...
          Isaat Lawton Astant.

[418] John Greene to George Sisson.
...John Greene...of Warwicke...In the year 1654 did sell unto mr Thomas Lawton then of portsmouth...six hundred Acres of upland at or About Coweeset which...hee hath...by A deed baring date Jun the 5th 1674 to George Sisson & his wife Sarah Sisson both of portsmoth...And George Sisson being Willing...to Exchange the same for Aquarter shear of farme Lands & to Allowe fourty shillings in mony...I majo John Greene...in Consideration of the surrender of the sd deeds & upland of six hundred Acres & fourty shillings ...New England silver mony payd...have...sold unto George Sisson...one quarter shear of farme...six hundred Acres...being one eight And twentieth part of seven hole shears Ordered by the purchasers of Warwick...baring date the 5th of March 1673 said seven hole sheares bounded Easterly by the farmes of Nachick & wequickaconuke southerly by the north Line of Cowesett plantation & northerly by the north Line of Warwick purchas onely seven shears of meadow Land...Layd out the sd quarter shear being pt of Awhole quarter Sheare...given mee by my father mr John Green Sen...Eleventh day of may...one thousand six hundred ninty & three...

Wit.   John Greene
   Joseph Cooke
   Garsham Smith
Major John Green did...Acknowledge...deed
                     Before me Giles Slocum Aste
[420]   Joseph Allin to Joseph Hull.
...Joseph Allin of Darkmouth in the County of bristoll...yeoman...for...two hundred seventeen pounds fifteen shillings...payd of Currant mony of New England by Joseph Hull Late of Socomesett...but now of Kings town Alis Rochester...yeoman...have...sold...my right...in the pittiquamsett purchas...that is...two thirds of Atract...six hundred & twelve Acres...Lying on the back side of the ponds so Called...Alls two thirds of Atract of Land in motonuk neck in the purchas Aforesaid Containing three hundred & twelve Ackers...boath which...I bought of Henry Gardner & John Watson...deed of sale in parchment...baring date the twentieth day of July 1692 Allso all...Land...Lying to the westward of the second Sugr lofe hill In sd pitticomcott purchas which containes five hundred Acres...which...I bought of Christopher Allin of Little Compton by Adeed of Sale in parchment Doth...Appeare...Eleventh day of Novembr 1693
Wit.   Joseph Allin.
   Abraham Anthony
   Thomas Wait
   John Smith
The Seaventh of Novembr 1693...Joseph Allin...Newport ...owned...deed...
                              Caleb Carr Ajt
[422]   John Watson & Henry Gardner to Joseph Allin.
...John Watson & Henry Gardner of Kings town alis Rochester,...yeomen...for...seventy seven pounds fifteen shillings Currant mony of New England...by Joseph Allin of Darkmouth in the province of the Mattetucetts...yeoman...Have...sold...two thirds of Atract of Land in pittiguamscott purchas in Kingstown...Lying on the back side the

ponds, so Called,...six hundred And twelve Akers...& is in width one hundred seventy & seven Rod...bounded Eastwardly by Land of Thomas Mumford...Southward by the pond & Westward by Land belonging to the heires...of Samuell Willson notherly by undevided Lands...with the beach And ponds to the southward...as Allso two thirds of... Lands In Motonuck Neck...which qt: three hundred & twelve Acres...bounded Eastward by Land of Benedict Arnold &c Southward on Point Judeth ponds so Called westward by Lands of Capt Samuell Sowell Northward partly by Land Layd out & partly by Lands undevided...with all... trees Swamps beaches...twenty Eight day of July one thousand six hundred ninty two...

Wit.
   William X Gardner
      his marke
   George X Gardner
      his marke
   Ephram X Gardner
      his marke

John Watson
Henry Gardner

Christopher Allin to Joseph Allin

Christopher Allin of Little Comton...yeoman...for...One hundred & fourty pounds...payd of Currant mony of new England by Joseph Allin of Darkmouth...yeoman...have ...sold...all yt his farme...in the pittquomcott purchas on the westward of the second suger hill so Called qt five hundred Acres...Bounded...westward partly by A high way of tenn Rod wide betwene sd Land & the Greatt pond & partly by Land not yett Layd out Northward by Land formerly Layd out to John Gould Eastward by Lands Layd out Southward partly by A pond & partly by undevided Lands...Christopher Allin is Cabable to grant by...deed...from Ralph Chapman baring date the 24th day of May 1693 said Chapman having bought the said Land of John hart marrino...baring date the 10th day of Desemb 1688...which Land John hart had... of his mother Freeborn hart who purchased the some of the first proprieters of sd pittquomscott Lands...by...A deed...

baring date the 20 day of Apriell 1674...19th day of Septemb 1693...
Wit.   Christopher Allin
  William Fleetwood
  Joseph Devell
  John Smith

[425] William Brenton etc. to freeborn hart.
...three & twentieth day of (torn)...1674 Betwene William Brenton John Hull Benedict Arnold John Porter Samll Wilbor Samll Wilson & Thomas mumford of the one part & freeborn hart Executrix & widdow of Thomas hart Late of newport...deceased...for...six & twenty pounds starling... payd...by freeborn hart...wee...have granted...five hundred Acres...of which wee...are Joynt purchassers...Lying About foure miles from pittiquamscott Rock south west being near the place Called the durty swampe bounded...on the west partly by Ahighway tenn Rods wide betwene the sd Land heareby granted & the greatt pond & partly by other Land not...yett Layd out & on the north by Other Land not Layd Out...onely Exsepted that if at Any time heare After Any mineralls...be dyscovered in...the...Land... minerall shall be devided Into Eight equall sheers...which sd Land...was granted to...Thomas hart...in his Last will ...Disposed of...unto hir...freeborn hart...& After hir Deceas to...thomas hart son of the sd thomas harte...
Wit.   Benedict Arnold
  Jireth Bull   John Hull
  Richard baily   John Porter
  Joseph mory   Samll Wilbor
  Samuell holmes   Samll Wilson
  William Coldman   Thomas mumford

      The first bounds south in the Above... being omitted...that is...partly by Apond & partly by A seader swampe.

[426] Nathll Coddington to William Edwards.
...nathaniell Coddington of newport...doe...release... title unto the Land...sold unto William Edwards...my hand & seall this 13 of August 1694

Wit.   Nathll Coddington
   George Lawton
   Joseph Nicholson
   John Smith
Newport...Novembr 6th 1694...Nathll Codding Acknowledged...deed...

                           Benedict Arnold Ast:
   William Edwards to Robert Ayres.
...William Edwards...In consideration of thirty pounds... recived of Robert Ayres of Newport...Carpenter doe... make over the with in mentioned deed with all the Lands... thirteenth of August 1694...   The marke of
...deed of sale   William **X** Edwards
   Recorded in the
   402 page of this
   book signed by
   Robert Euers.

[427] John Williams Acquitts John Rathbon.
...John Williams Attorney to John Green Attorney to the Gardians of the Children of the Late mr John Alcock of Roxbury...And as An Executor to the Estate...by marrying Eldest Daughter of the sd Alcock...doe Acquitt...John Rathbon...from the payment of thirty pounds which hath bene Recived Eleven pounds five shillings of the sd Alcock ...And the Rest by thomas Terry & myselfe...is in full payment of Atwo And thirtieth part of Block Island And twelve Acres & Ahalfe of Land which was to be Deducted out of the two And thirtieth part...Above sd which...John Rathbon bought of my father mr John Alcock...as by an Account upon the block Island book of Accounts 5th day of June 1672...
Wit.   Emanull Woolley   John Williams
       John **X** Guniell
          his marke
New shoram Octobr 10th 1682
John Gunniell Attested to the Above...
                                     Jeames Sands
                                     Simon Ray

[428] Thomas Mumford to Samson Batty.
...Thomas mumford of kings town...for...fourty two pounds Currant mony of new England...payd...by Samson Batty of Jeames town...have sold...Land...in the...pitticomcott purchas...And is the Eight Lott in the Plott...three hundred Acres...bounded...East...by Land...of John Thomas South...by undevided Lands westerly by the...Line of the sd pitticomcott purchas North...by Land...of John Wilbore...twentieth forth day of Octobr...one thousand six hundred ninity & three

Wit.   Thomas Mumford
  his marke   Abigall mumford
 John X Thomas   her X marke
 John Pocock
 Nathll Crockford

...Thomas mumford...Acknowledged...deed this 25th 8 mo 1693

                                  John Easton Gover

[429] Thomas Mumford to John Thomas.
...Thomas Mumford of Kingstown...for...fourty two pounds new England Currant mony...payd by John Thomas of Jeames Town...Have...solde...Land...in the...pitticomcott purchas...And is the tenth Lott...three hundred Acres...bounded...north...by the Greatt pond East...by undevided Lands & Southerly And westerly by Samson Batties Land...twenty forth day of Octob...one thousand six hundred ninty & three

Wit.   Thomas Mumford
  the marke of   Abigall X mumford
 Samson X Batty   marke
 John Pococke
 Nathll Crockford

...thomas mumford...Acknowledged...deed this 25th day of October 1695

                                  John Easton Gover

[432] Ralph Chapman to Christopher Allin.
...twenty forth Day of may...1693...Ralph Chapman of

Newport...shipwright for...One hundred & ten pounds Currant mony of New England...payd by Christopher Allin of Little Cumpton...yewman...hath...sold....all...his farme & tract of Land...in pitticomcott purchas on the westward of Suger Lofe hill Containing five hundred Acres... bounded West ward partly by Ahigh way of tenn Rod wide yt Lyeth betwene sd Land & the Greatt pond & partly by Lands Not yett Layd Out northerly by Lands formerly Layd out to John Gould Eastward by Lands Layd Out Southward partly by Apond & partly by undevided Lands...Ralph Chapman is Capable to grant by...Adeed...from John hart... date the tenth day of Desember in...1688...Except which is Reserved in the Originall deed from the proprieters to freeborn hart Mother of the sd John hart...baring Date...20th day of Apriell...1674...

Wit.
  Rog Goulding
  James Larkin
  John Smith

Ralph Chapman
Abigall **X** Chapman
  hir marke

The 24 of May 1693...Ralph Chapman Owned...deed before mee   Caleb Carr Ast.

[434] Ralph Chapman to Giles Slocom.

...Ralph Chapman of newport...Shipwright...for...foure hundred & five pounds Currant mony of New England... payd by Giles Slocom of the township of Portsmouth...Gent. ...Have...sold...my Farme...known by the name of withington's Farme...in the township of Newport...One hundred And twenty Acres...bounded...Begining at A markt Maple tree at the pen fold gapp & so Extending south Easterly to wards the highway that Leads from Newport to portsmouth About One hundred rode And from thence Allmost paralell to the sd highway to the petetion Line betwene sd Newport and the town of portsmouth Ninty Nine Rode to A marked stake which is with in Sixteen Rode of An Oake tree in Said petition Line Marked ─────── And so from sd stake Along sd petition Line till it meets with Lott Stranges Line One hundred & thirty Rode & so Along to his Corner tree in the swampe Sixty Rodes And from thence fourty foure rods to the highway that Leads to George Lawtons Mill & from thence south southwest to wards Richard Dunes One hundred And three rodds to A small Oake markt not far from the highway & from thence Along by sd way to the first markt maple tree sixty six rods...wch...Land so bounded was Layd out to William Withington Deceased by Order of the Quarter meetting of...town of Newport the seventh day of October one thousand six hundred seventy foure: And... Confirmed to him by the town Clerke...6th day of August 1675...with all...trees...salts...buildings Orchards gardens...thirteenth day of January 1693-4...

Wit.   Ralph Chapman
  Nicholas Carr   Abigaill Chapman
  George Bradly
Fabuary 24th 1693-4

...Ralph Chapman And Abigall his wife...Owned the Above...

                                            Caleb Carr Ast

[436] John Wood to Thomas Fry.

...John wood...of Est greenwich...for...twenty five pounds Currant mony of new England...payd...by thomas Fry...of Above sd town...have...sold...my Dwelling hous & hous Lott of Land...in the Above sd town of Est greenwich...being in number the ninteenth Lott in the first devition...it being tenn Acres...bounded...on the southwest Corner being Abuttenwood tree & from thence twenty rod west an by north to A walnutt bush from thence Eighty rodd to Ablack Oake tree And from thence twenty rodd to An Oake tree And from thence Eighty Rod to the first mentioned boundree being Abutton wood tree...twenty second day of march...one thousand six hundred Ninty three or foure

Wit.   John X Wood
  Thomas Green Junr   his marke
  John Spencer   Alse X Wood
                                             hir marke

[437] Thomas Fry to Thomas Fry.
...Thomas Fry of Newport...Glausier...unto my Eldest son Thomas Fry Glaiessur Living in Debtford Alis Este Greenwith...have Granted...my Right...unto Land in the township of sd deptford...which...Came to mee by petition And purchas...by the Genll Assembley of Rhoad-Island... two hundred Acres...Eleventh Day of March...1688-9
Wit.   Thomas Fry
  Mikell **X** Spencer
    his mark
  Mars **X** Wascoatt
    hir mark
  John Heath

[438] Pettaquamscet Lands to Samuell Sewall.
...Jahleel Brenton and Peleg Sanford Esq Benedict Arnold Esq Henry Gardner John Wilbor & Thomas Mumford as will on his owne behalfe as Gardian to Jeames Wilson, heires ...of Wiliam Brenton & Benedict Arnold Esqr John porter Samuell Wilbor Samuell Wilson & thomas Mumford Late of Rhoad Island Deceased...whereas John Hull Esq Late of boston...Deceased...with william Brenton Benedict Arnold John Porter Samuell Wilbor Samuell Wilson & Thomas Mumford did purchas...Land...Called...Pettaquamscet purchas And whereas A hows Lott of fourty Acres...And A farme Adjoining thare to: saving the highway, of foure hundred & sixty Acres...runing to Socatuckett River with A Certain quantie: of March near Or Adjoining to the sd hous Lott Lately in the Occupation of Robert Hanna was Layd Out & Assigned to...John Hull Esq...And whereas A Lott in the tract of Land...Called the thousand Acres qt two hundred Acres No. two: And two Lotts in point Judeth Neck Lying together In the most Southerly part of sd neck Containing six hundred Acres...No. six & seven, And A Lott at Mattonuck Neck Containing three hundred Acres No. six, And A lott of six hundred Acres...Lying to the westward of point Judeth ponds & said Mattonuck neck No. two, And A Lott qt one thousd Acres...Lying at the north west

part of the purchas Adjoyning to the Land of Samuell Albrough No. foure, And two more Lotts qt three hundred Acres Apeace Adjoyning unto And neare the greatt Pond in the westermost part of the purchas No. foure & six, & Another Lott of march An Beach Lying to the westward of point Judeth Breach No. one, begining as sd Breach And A lott...on An Island In point Judeth Ponds...Called Mumfords Island being A seventh part of sd Island No. foure, Recking from the north to South whard In Like mannoer... Assigned...to Samuell Sewall of Boston And Hannah his wife Daughter & heire of...John Hull Late purchasser...of John porter as by A plott under the hand of John Smith Surveyar of sd Lands...Jahleel Brenton Peleg Sanford Benedict Arnold Henry Gardner John Wilbor & Thomas Mumford doe ...Confirm...unto...Samuell Sewall & hannah his wife... seventh day of September...One Thousand six hundred Ninty & three...
Wit.

Ephraim Turner	Benedict Arnold Ast:
John Smith	Peleg Sanford
Newport...September 7th 1693	Benedict Arnold
Peleg Sanford Esqr John Wilbor	John Wilbor
Thomas Mumford & Henry Gardener Acknowledged...	Thomas Mumford as Gardian to Jeames Wilson
	Thomas Mumford
	Henry X Gardner
	his marke

[440] Nathanaell Niles to Samuell Sewall.
...twenty Third day of July...one thousand six hundred ninty & two...Betwene Nathaniell Niles of Block Island... yeoman on the One part And Samuell Sewall of Boston... Esq of the Other part...Nathaniell Niles for...One hundred & twenty five pounds Currant mony of new England Recived of...Samuell Sewall...Hath...sold...parciell of upland... in block Island...Sixty foure Acres...bounded westerly by the high way southerly upon the Land of John Rodman East-

erly upon A frech pond...Called...Neales Pond Northerly with Land of Robart Guttridge...Allso One Other peice...of Land...in Block Island...at A place...Called Corne Neck qt upwards of fifty Acres Bounded Southerly with Land of Joshua Raymant Easterly & Northerly with A ditch partly with the Breach, And partly with ponds westerly

Wit.   Nathanaell Niles

 Isa: Addington
 Addington Davenport
 Edward Turfrey
 John Wally.

Boston July 23th 1692
...Nathaniell Niles...Acknowledged this...

          John Joylife
          Peter Sergant

[442]   Elizabeth Winslow to Nathaniell Coddington.
...Elizabeth Winslow of boston...widdow...whareas my father Edward Hutchinson of boston...Gent: deceased & in ...his Last will...date the ninteenth day of August 1675... did...bequeath in the words following Item...unto my son Elisha my Daughters Elizabeth Winslow Ann Dyre & Susanna Hutchinson...all the rest of my Lands boath at Narrogansett as Also my Island...Called Round Island or Hutchinsons Island And All Other Lands goods debts Hous hold Stufe plate...I...Elizabeth Winslow for...sixty five pounds Currant mony of New England...payd by Nathaniell Coddington of Newport...marcht...Have...sold...my...share of Land...in...boston neck...Butted Easterly on A cove westerly on Pitticomcott Lands Northerly And Southerly on the Lands given to the Executor of my fathers will...twenty seventh day of March 1694...

Wit.   Elizabeth Winslow

 Mary Dill
 Mary Dill Junr.

Newport...28th March 1694 Elizabeth Winslow of Boston Acknowledged...

          Giles Slocum Ast:

[444] Mary Phips to Stephen Mumford & Robert Ayares. ...Dame Mary phips wife And Attorney of...Sr. William phips have...received of the...Mortgagers Stephen mumford And Robart Ayares...One hundred And fifty pounds Currant mony of New England...to the use of my...husband wch with former payments...dos Compleatt...the... sume of three hundred pounds...doe...release...unto... Stephen Mumford & Robart Ayres...the farme & Lands... thirtyeth day of November 1694...

Wit.   Mary Phips
 John White   The Lady mary Phips...
 Tho: Hutchinson   Acknowledged...
            John Forster

Above...hath Referance to A deed of Mortgage...in this book in the 357: 358-359 & 360 pages...

[445] John Surkett to Thomas Gould. ...John Surkett for...Valluable Consideration...payd by Thomas Gould of newport...doe...Assigne...all the Lands ...with all the housses out houses & barnes & buildings... One And thirtieth day of...July...one thousand six hundred ninty six

Wit.   the marke of
 William Greenman   John **X** Surkett
 John Yelthro:

John Surkett Acknowledged...Newport first day August 1696
           Walter Clarke Gover

The Above...hath Reference to A deed from Daniell Gould to John Surkett...330 & 331 pages of this boak...

ERRATA

Page Line
17 19 and 24 read "Will" instead of "Witt."
47 27 read "1658" instead of "1608."
49 22 read "Sacconet" instead of "Sarronet."
66 7 add date "1665".
73 28 add name "Peleg Sanford."
127 20 read "past" instead of "part."
230 31 and 32 read "Hall" instead of "Hull."
113 9 read "myantanamy" instead of "myaptanamy."

INDEX

Acres, John from Perry, Thomas Deed-1670	23
Acres, John to Williams, John Receipt-1672	23
Albro, John & Lawton, George from Clarke, Capt. Thomas Deed-1677	109
Alcock, John Inventory-1677	122
Alcock, John heirs of to Rathbon, John Receipt-1672	238
Alcock, John to Rodman, John Deed-1687	202
Alcock, John to Wharton, Philip Deed-1686	203
Alcock, John to Williams, John Power of Attorney-1668	23
Alderman from Mamamutt Deed-1683	175
Allen, Matthew to Hudlestone, Valentine Deed-1679	132
Allen, William & Rathbon, John to Sirkett, John Deed-1687	205
Allin, Christopher to Allin, Joseph Deed-1674	236
Allin, Christopher from Chapman, Ralph Deed-1693	239
Allin, Joseph from Allin, Christopher Deed-1674	236
Allin, Joseph to Hull, Joseph Deed-1693	235
Allin, Joseph from Watson, John & Gardner, Henry Deed-1692	235
Allin, Jedidiah from Almy, Job Deed-1683	174
Allis, John to Neales, Henry Deed-1685	192
Almy, Christopher, to Ward, Thomas Deed-1681	155
Almy, Job to Allin, Jedidiah Deed-1683	174
Almy, Job to Ward, Thomas Deed-1681	154
Almy, John from Dunham, Samuel Deed-1668	36
Almy, John to Lawton, Thomas Assignment of deed-1671	34
Almy, John to Lawton, Thomas Deed-1671	35
Almy, John to Lawton, Thomas Deed-1671	36
Almy, John to Lawton, Thomas Deed-1671	37
Almy, John to Lawton, Thomas Deed-1671	38
Almy, John & Lawton, Thomas Agreement-1673	46
Almy, John from Morton, Thomas Deed-1668	34
Almy, John from Richard, John Deed-1671	37
Almy, John from Ringe, Andrew Deed-1668	35
Almy, John from Southworth, Thomas Deed-1668	34
Almy, John to Ward, Thomas Deed-1675	107
Almy, William Will-1676	103
Andrews, Samuel Protest-1677	101
Anthony, Joseph from Bulger, Richard Deed-1674	116
Anthony, John to Tew, Richard Deed-1642	64
Appleton, Samuel from Paine, John Deed-1663	110
Aquinaumpau to Gould, Thomas, Deed-1660	29

Arnold, Benedict from Cachanaquoant   Deed-1658 67
Arnold, Benedict et al. from Kaskottape   Deed-1659............ 68
Arnold, Benedict et al. to Clarke, William   Deed-1674......... 111
Arnold, Benedict & Coddington, William from Cagananaquoant
    Deed-1657 67
Arnold, Benedict, from Cranston, John & Carr, Caleb   Deed-
    1659 200
Arnold, Benedict to Goulding, Roger & Penelope   Deed-1676... 105
Arnold, Benedict et al. to Hart, Freeborn   Deed-1674.......... 237
Arnold, Benedict et al. to Hazard, Robert   Deed-1671.......... 12
Arnold, Benedict et al. to Heffernon, William   Deed-1692...... 232
Arnold, Benedict to Newport, town of   Deed-1673............. 86
Arnold, Benedict, Governor, versus Newport, town of   1671.... 85
Arnold, Benedict to Newport, town of   Deed-1673............. 199
Arnold, Benedict et al. from Quisaquance   Deed-1659.......... 68
Arnold, Benedict et al. to Sewall, Samuel   Deed-1693.......... 242
Arnold, Josiah et al. to Heffernon, William   Deed-1692........ 232
Arnold, Stephen from Arnold, William   Deed-1663............. 77
Arnold, Stephen from Carpenter, Joseph   Deed-1674........... 50
Arnold, Stephen from Naw-naw-nanten-new   Deed-1674........ 78
Arnold, Stephen from Rhodes, Zachary   Deed-1663............. 78
Arnold, Stephen from Sayles, John   Deed-1659................ 77
Arnold, William to Arnold, Stephen   Deed-1663............... 77
Atherton, Jonathan to Smith, Richard   Deed-1673............. 31
Awawsunks et al. to Barker, James & Carr, Caleb   Deed-1674..49, 53
Ayres, Robert from Edwards, William   Deed-1694............. 238
Ayres, Robert & Mumford, Stephen from Walley, John   Deed-
    1687 208
Ayres, Robert & Mumford, Stephen to Phips, Sir William   Deed-
    1687 213

Badcocke, James   Will-1679 136
Baily, John to Briggs, John   Deed-1687....................... 210
Baily, John from Lake, David   Deed-1687/8................... 216
Baily, Richard & Terry, Joseph from Smith, Richard   Deed-
    1671/2 31
Barker, Wm. from Loveday, Thomas   Power of attorney-1671.. 19
Barker, James, Sr.   Land Recorded-1675...................... 83
Barker, James & Carr, Caleb from Awawsunks et al.   Deed-
    1674 ....49, 53
Barker, James from Easton, Nicholas   Deed-1674.............. 79
Barker, James from Newport, town of   Deed-1662............ 16
Barker, James & Smith, Elisha   Agreement-1675 92
Barker, James & Smith, Edward   Bounds changed-1657........ 48
Barker, James to Tew, Richard   Deed-1665.................... 66

Barker, Joseph to Turner, Lawrence Deed-1688............... 212
Barnes, John et al. from Ousamequen et al. Deed-1657.......... 145
Bartlett, Benjamin from Nash, Samuel Deed-1666...........-.. 146
Bartlett, Robert to Burge, Thomas Deed-1670................ 140
Barton, Benjamin et al. from Gorton, Samuel Deed-1677....... 134
Barton, Susanah et al. from Gorton, Samuel Deed-1677........ 134
Batty, Samson from Mumford, Thomas Deed-1693............ 239
Billing, Samuel from Robinson, Edward Deed-1658............ 47
Billing, Seaborn from Tew, Richard Deed-................... 84
Blackmor, James & Bukman, John from Inman, Edward Deed-
  1672... 21
Blackmor, James & Bukman, John from Inman, Edward & Mowry,
  John Deed-1672..................................... 21, 22
Boomer, Matthew Land Recorded-1676....................... 95
Boomer, Matthew to Browne, George Deed-1676.............. 96
Boomer, Matthew from Brightman, Henry Deed-1676/7....... 122
Boomer, Matthew to Reade, John Deed-1677................. 122
Boomer, Matthew from Stevens, Henry Deed-1676............ 96
Boomer, Matthew from Williams, Owen Indenture-1658....... 76
Borden, John from Hodges, Henry Deed-1680-81.............. 197
Borden, John from Holloway, Malachi Deed-1680............ 196
Borden, John from Hoskins, John Deed-1680................ 196
Borden, Matthew from Manchester, Thomas Deed-1682........ 170
Bourne, Thomas et al. from Ousamequen et al. Deed-1657...... 145
Bowne, Andrew to Lawton, George Deed-1687................ 206
Bradford, Alice to Lawton, Thomas Deed-1668.............,.. 33
Brayton, Francis from Burton, Stephen Deed-1671............ 52
Brayton, Francis from Brenton, William Deed-1650........... 116
Brenton, Jahleel to Browne, Joseph Deed-1676............... 91
Brenton, Jahleel et al. to Heffernon, William Deed-1692...... 232
Brenton, Jahleel et al. to Sewall, Samuel Deed-1693........... 242
Brenton, Jahleel et al. from Throckmorton, John Deed-1687... 209
Brenton, William Will-1674................................ 60
Brenton, William to Brayton, Francis Deed-1650 116
Brenton, William to Browne, Joseph Deed-1674 59
Brenton, William et al. from Kaskottape Deed-1659........... 68
Brenton, William from Clarke, Walter Deed-1657............. 70
Brenton, William et al. to Clarke, William Deed-1674......... 111
Brenton, William to Ginings, Thomas Deed-1659.............. 48
Brenton, William from Gould, Thomas Deed-1675............ 83
Brenton, William et al. to Hart, Freeborn Deed-1674.......... 237
Brenton, William et al. to Hazard, Robert Deed-1671......... 12
Brenton, William from Hutchinson, Elisha & Hannah Deed-
  1670... 135

Brenton, William et al. from Quisaquance Deed-1659	68
Brenton, William to Sanford, Peleg Deed-1670	72
Brenton, William to Sanford, Peleg Deed-1674	74
Brenton, William to Sanford, Peleg Deed-1679	136
Brenton, William from Sanford, Peleg Deed-1685	186
Brenton, William from Walley, John Deed-1685	186
Brenton, William to Walley, John Deed-1685	187
Brenton, William to Ward, Thomas Deed-1686	189
Brewster, Wrastlin to Durfee, Thomas Deed-1678	116
Brightman, Henry to Boomer, Mathew Deed-1676/7	122
Brightman, Henry to Greenhill, Daniel Deed-1683	220
Brightman, Henry from Mosher, Hugh Deed-1689	225
Brightman, Henry from Sisson, George Deed-1681	172
Briggs, Hannah from Fisher, Edward Deed-1677	157
Briggs, Nathaniel & Wharton, Phillip to Rodman, John Deed-1684	204
Brigs, John to Brigs, Thomas Deed-1678	121
Brigs, John from Dunham, John Deed-1662	176
Brigs, John Senr. to Brigs, John Junr. Deed-1670	140
Brigs, John from Baily, John Deed-1687	210
Brigs, John Senr. & Brigs, John Junr. Agreement-1679	143
Brigs, John to Lawton, Thomas Deed-1668	34
Brigs, John from Smith, Richard Deed-1672	49
Brigs, Thomas from Brigs, John Deed-1678	121
Brinley, Francis Land Recorded-1679	126
Brinley, Francis from Easton, John Receipt-1687	219
Brinley, Francis to Mays, William Deed-1673/4	226
Brinley, William & Coggeshall, John Orders of Council-1677	104
Brookes, Thomas from Read, William Deed-1687	200
Browne, George from Boomer, Matthew Deed-1676	96
Browne, Jeremiah & Mary to Cooke, John Deed-1688	211
Browne, Capt. John from Pocoke, John Deed-1683	171
Browne, Joseph from Brenton, Jahleel Deed-1676	91
Browne, Joseph from Brenton, William Deed-1674	59
Browne, Mary & Jeremiah to Cooke, John Deed-1688	211
Browne, William Land Recorded-1678	115
Browne, William from Rainbrow, Edward Deed-1672	91
Browne, William to Sisson, George Deed-1671/2	159
Brownell, George from Hazard, Robert Deed-1671	13
Brownell, Thomas from Warner, John Deed-1677	144
Browning, William to Manchester, Thomas Deed-1684/5	179
Browning, William to Fish, Robert Deed-1687/8	212
Brewster, Love et al. Ousamequen et al. Deed-1657	145

Bryant, Richard et al. from Throckmorton, John Deed-1687...	209
Buckland, Benjamin et al. from Inman, Edward Deed-1672....	22
Bucman, John & Blackmor, James from Inman, Edward Deed-1672	21
Bucman, John & Blackmor, James from Inman, Edward & Mowry, John Deed-1672..	21, 22
Bulger, Richard to Anthony, Joseph Deed-1674...............	116
Bull, Ephraim et al. from Bull, Jireh Deed-1685..............	183
Bull, Ezekiel et al. from Bull, Jireh Deed-1685..............	183
Bull, Ezekiel to Case, Joseph Deed-1693.....................	231
Bull, Henry et al. from Bull, Jireh Deed-1685.................	183
Bull, Jireh to Bull, Henry et al. Deed-1685...................	183
Burge, Thomas to Cooke, John Deed-1671....................	30
Burge, Thomas from Bartlett, Robert Deed-1670............	140
Burge, Thomas to Ward, Thomas Deed-1671	106
Burge, Thomas to Ward, Thomas Deed-1674	107
Burges, Thomas Land Recorded-1673	26
Burton, Stephen to Brayton, Francis Deed-1671..............	52
Busecot, Peter to Warner, John Deed Confirmed-1681/2......	176
Button, Henry to Easton, Nicholas Indenture-1616............	8
Butts, Thomas from Earle, Ralph Deed-1668.................	120
Cachanaquoant to Arnold, Benedict Deed-1658	67
Cachanaquant to Houldon, Randall & Gorton, Samuel Deed-1659	117
Cadman, Richard to Fish, Robert Deed-1688	219
Cadman, Richard to Lawton, Isaac Deed-1688	219
Cagananaquoant to Coddington, William & Arnold, Benedict Deed-1657	67
Cahoone, William to Hagbourne, Samuel Deed-1670..........	161
Calhoune, William from Terry, Thomas Deed-1662/3..........	161
Calverly, Edmund to Easton, Peter Receipt-1672.............	18
Canonicus & Miantunomu to Williams, Roger Deed-1637......	162
Canonicus to Sanford, Peleg Deed-1675.....................	80
Card, Joseph Land Recorded-1674	42
Card, Joseph from Case, James Deed-1688-9..................	225
Carder, Richard to Gorton, Samuel Deed-1650...............	137
Carder, Richard et al. from Miantonomi Deed-1642..........	113
Carpenter, Abijah from Carpenter, Joseph Deed-1673..........	47
Carpenter, Joseph to Arnold, Stephen Deed-1674	50
Carpenter, Joseph to Carpenter, Abijah Deed-1673	47
Carpenter, William from Greene, John, Jr. Deed-1658..........	52
Carr, Caleb & Barker, James from Awawsunks et al. Deed-1674	49, 53

Carr, Caleb & Cranston, John to Arnold, Benedict   Deed-1659.. 200
Carr, Caleb, from Cranston, John   Deed-1675................... 79
Carr, Caleb to Heffernan, Susanah.   Settlement-1680-81....... 139
Carr, Caleb to Paine, Thomas   Deed-1688..................... 217
Carr, Caleb et al. from Quisaquance   Deed-1659.............. 68
Carr, Caleb from Sanford, Peleg   Deed-1675.................. 84
Carr, Esek & Susannah to Carr, Robert   Deed-1687............ 222
Carr, Robert from Carr, Esek & Susannah   Deed-1687......... 222
Carr, Robert to Davis, Samuel   Deed-1676.................... 98
Carr, Susanna & Esek to Carr, Robert   Deed-1687............. 222
Case, James to Card, Joseph   Deed-1688-9 225
Case, Joseph from Bull, Ezekiel   Deed-1693................... 231
Chamberlin, Henry to Hudlestone, Valentine   Deed-1679-80.... 131
Champlin, Jeffery to Clarke, Walter   Deed-1669............... 92
Champlin, John to Salmerdore, Negro   Grant of Freedom..... 47
Champlin, John to Sanford, Peleg   Deed-1675................. 82
Chandler, Edmond et al. from Ousamequen et al.   Deed-1657... 145
Chandler, Samuel to Earle, William   Deed-1660 198
Chandler, Samuel to Earle, William & Wilcox, Daniel   Deed-1662 198
Chapman, Ralph to Allen, Christopher   Deed-1693............. 239
Chapman, Ralph from Hart, John   Deed-1688.................. 226
Chapman, Ralph to Slocom, Giles   Deed-1693-4............... 240
Christophers, Jeffrey & John   Ship Protest-1689.............. 224
Christophers, John & Jeffery   Ship Protest-1689.............. 224
Clarke, Carew to Ward, Thomas   Deed-1679................... 127
Clarke Hannah from Wilbur, Samuel   Deed-1666.............. 44
Clarke, John to Smith, Richard   Deed-1674 44
Clarke, John from Terry, Thomas   Deed-1663.................. 162
Clarke, John to Tew, Richard   Deed-1650..................... 180
Clarke, Latham from Wilbur, Samuel   Deed-1671.............. 45
Clarke, Thomas   Will-1674 56
Clarke, Capt. Thomas to Albro, John & Lawton, George   Deed-1677 109
Clarke, Walter   Land Recorded-1665 93
Clarke, Walter to Brenton, William   Deed-1657 70
Clarke, Walter from Champlin, Jeffery   Deed-1669............ 92
Clarke, Walter to Coggeshall, John   Deed-1674............... 87
Clarke, Walter & Vaughan, Mrs. Frances   Agreement-1656..... 43
Clarke, Weston & Greene, John from Withington, Peleg   Power of Attorney-1686 207
Clarke, Weston to King, Daniel   Deed-1687................... 221
Clarke, William   Appraisal of Land-1679...................... 129
Clarke, William   Land Recorded-1679 129

Clarke, William from Brenton, William et al.   Deed-1674....... 111
Clarke, William to Lay, Edward   Deed-1679 130
Clarke, William from Paine, John   Deed-1677.................. 128
Clarke, William to Pearce, John   Deed-1675.................... 112
Clarke, William from Tew, Henry   Marriage Indenture-1633.... 9
Cobb, Gersham to Lawton, Thomas   Deed-1668.................. 32
Cobb, John to Earle, William   Deed-1662...................... 198
Coddington, Nathaniel to Edwards, William   Deed-1694 237
Coddington, Nathaniel to Mew, Noel   Deed-1686 190
Coddington, Nathaniel from Winslow, Elizabeth   Deed-1694.... 244
Coddington, William   Deposition-1652 59
Coddington, William & Arnold, Benedict from Cagananaquoant
 Deed-1657 67
Coddington, William et al. from Kaskottape   Deed-1659........ 68
Coddington, William & Coggeshall, John   Agreement-1668...... 88
Coddington, William to Greenman, David & Edward   Deed-1642 104
Coddington, William et ux. to Easton, Nicholas   Deed-1672.... 19
Coddington, William et al. from Quisaquance   Deed-1659....... 68
Cogamaquoant to Knight, Richard & Halls, Henry   Deed-1664.. 6
Coggeshall, John   Land Recorded-1665 89
Coggeshall, John & Brinley, William   Orders of Council-1677.. 104
Coggeshall, John from Clarke, Walter   Deed-1674.............. 87
Coggeshall, John & Coddington, William   Agreement-1668...... 88
Coggeshall, John from Coggeshall, Elizabeth Baulston   Divorce-
 1654... 89
Coggeshall, Elizabeth Baulston from Coggeshall, John   Divorce-
 1654... 89
Coggeshall, John & William to Manchester, John   Deed-1678... 130
Coggeshall, Joshua to Cunagrave, Walter   Deed-1651.......... 185
Coggeshall, Joshua & Vaughan, John   Agreement-1671......... 213
Coggeshall, William to Goulding, Roger   Deed-1681.......... 153
Coggeshall, William & John to Manchester, John   Deed-1678... 130
Coggeshall, William to Pearce, John   Deed-1681.............. 158
Coles, Daniel et al. from Gorton, Samuel   Deed-1677.......... 134
Coles, Maher et al. from Gorton, Samuel   Deed-1677.......... 134
Collins, Lieutenant Elizur to Green, Thomas   Indenture-1664.... 102
Colson, Nathaniel & Cooke, Stephen   Testimony-1678.......... 114
Colson, Nathaniel   Survey-1678 114
Congdon, Benjamin to Sheldon, John   Deed-1683.............. 230
Cooke, John from Browne, Jeremiah & Mary   Deed-1688...... 211
Cooke, John from Burge, Thomas   Deed-1671 30
Cooke, John to Gibbs, Robert   Deed-1673..................... 30
Cooke, John from Gibbs, Robert   Deed Returned-1674......... 30
Cooke, John from Manchester, William   Deed-1680 138

Cooke, John from Manchester, William   Deed-1680 139
Cooke, John from Sisson, George   Deed-1683................. 169
Cooke, John to Ward, Thomas   Deed-1680.................... 134
Cooke, Stephen & Colson, Nathaniel   Testimony-1678......... 114
Cornell, Richard to Wodell, Gersham   Receipt-1672........... 20
Cornell, Stephen & Thomas to Sisson, George   Deed-1691...... 233
Cornell, Thomas   Land Recorded-1675 84
Cornell, Thomas & Stephen to Sisson, George   Deed-1691...... 233
Correy, William from Earle, William   Deed-1669.............. 155
Correy, Capt. William from Manchester, William   Deed-1681... 156
Costin, William   Will-1679 159
Council, Orders of to Coggeshall, John & Brinley, William   1677 104
Crandall, Elizabeth et al. from Gorton, Samuel   Deed-1677..... 134
Crandall, Heber & Jeremiah from Crandall, John   Deed-1678.... 115
Crandall, Jeremiah & Heber from Crandall, John   Deed-1678.. 115
Crandall, John, Senr. to Crandall, John, Junr.   Assignment-1670 69
Crandall, John to Crandell, Jeremiah & Heber   Deed-1678...... 115
Crandall, John Junr. from Crandall, John Senr.   Assignment-1670 69
Crandall, John et al. from Gorton, Samuel   Deed-1677......... 134
Crandall, John from Hall, Henry   Deed-1693................. 229
Cranston, Capt. John   Ratification of deed-1673............... 30
Cranston, John   Land Recorded-1674 42
Cranston, John to Carr, Caleb   Deed-1675.................... 79
Cranston, John & Carr, Caleb to Arnold, Benedict   Deed-1659.. 200
Cranston, John from Gould, Thomas   Deed-1673.............. 29
Cranston, John from Gould, Thomas   Deed-1674.............. 41
Crow, William to Lawton, Thomas   Deed-1668................. 33
Cudworth, James et al. from Ousamequen et al.   Deed-1657 145
Cunagrave, Walter from Coggeshall, Joshua   Deed-1651........ 185
Cunagrave, Walter to Green, John   Deed-1651................. 185

Damon, John et al. from Ousamequen et al.   Deed-1657........ 145
Davis, Aaron to Sanford, Peleg   Deed-1672-73................. 73
Davis, Samuel from Carr, Robert   Deed-1676.................. 98
Deane, Thomas to Sisson, George   Deed-1683................. 171
Delano, Philip to Earle, William   Deed-1660.................. 198
Derin, Samuel to Rathbone, John   Deed-1671................. 11
Dering, Mary to Sands, James   Deed-1671................... 12
Devell, Joseph to Ward, Thomas   Deed-1679.................. 130
Devell, Joseph from Wilcox, Daniel   Deed-1672............... 133
Dodge, Tristram to George, Peter   Deed-1666................ 15
Dunham, John to Brigs, John   Deed-1662..................... 176

Dunham, Samuel to Almy, John   Deed-1668................... 36
Durfee, Thomas from Brewster, Wrastlin   Deed-1678 116
Durfee, Thomas from Manchester, William   Deed-1681........ 143
Durfee, Thomas from Talman, Peter   Deed-1683............... 169
Dyre, Charles from Dyre, Samuel   Deed-1687.................. 206
Dyre, Henry from Dyre, William   Deed-1670.................. 24
Dyre, Henry & Samuel to Dyre, William   Indenture-1670....... 232
Dyre, Samuel to Dyre, Charles   Deed-1687..................... 206
Dyre, Samuel & Henry to Dyre, William   Indenture-1670...... 232
Dyre, William Senr. to Dyre, William Junr.   Deed-1670........ 179
Dyre, William to Dyre, Henry   Deed-1670..................... 24
Dyre, William from Dyre, Samuel & Henry   Indenture-1670... 232
Dyre, William Junr. from Dyre, William Senr.   Deed-1670...... 179

Earle, Ralph to Butts, Thomas   Deed-1668..................... 120
Earle, William from Chandler, Samuel   Deed-1660 198
Earle, William from Cobb, John   Deed-1662 198
Earle, William to Correy, William   Deed-1669................. 155
Earle, William from Delano, Phillip   Deed-1660 198
Earle, William from Sands, James   Deed-   ...., 199
Earle, William & Wilcox, Daniel from Chandler, Samuel   Deed-1666 198
Easton, John to Brinley, Francis   Receipt-1687................ 219
Easton, John to Perry, Michael   Receipt-1687-8 218
Easton, Nicholas   Will-1676 120
Easton, Nicholas to Barker, James   Deed-1674................ 79
Easton, Nicholas from Button, Henry   Indenture-1616......... 8
Easton, Nicholas, from Coddington, William et ux.   Deed-1672 19
Easton, Nicholas to Greenman, David & Edward   Deed-1648.... 97
Easton, Nicholas from Newport, town of   Deed-1662.......... 15
Easton, Peter from Calverly, Edmund   Receipt-1672........... 18
Easton, Peter & Stevens, Henry   Agreement-1652.............. 76
Edwards, William to Ayres, Robert   Deed-1694................ 238
Edwards, William from Coddington, Nathaniel   Deed-1694..... 237
Edwards, William from Evers, Robert   Deed-1692............. 227
Eliott, Asaph from Gerrish, William   Deed-1682.............. 163
Evers, Robert to Edwards, William   Deed-1692............... 227

Fish, Preserved from Fish, Thomas   Deed-1684................ 211
Fish, Robert from Browning, William   Deed-1687-8........... 212
Fish, Robert from Cadman, Richard   Deed-1688............... 219
Fish, Thomas to Fish, Preserved   Deed-1684................... 211
Fisher, Edward to Briggs, Hannah   Deed-1677................ 157
Foster, Timothy et al. from Ousamequen et al.   Deed-1657..... 145

Freeborne, Gideon   Land Recorded-1639 58
Freeborne, Gideon from Hazard, Robert   Deed-1671........... 14
Freeborne, Gideon from Warner, John   Deed-1682............. 166
Freeborne, William   Land Recorded 58
Fry, Thomas Senr. to Fry, Thomas Junr.   Deed-1688-9........ 242
Fry, Thomas Junr, from Fry, Thomas Senr.   Deed-1688-9...... 242
Fry, Thomas from Newport, town of   Deed-1672.............. 108
Fry, Thomas from Wood, John   Deed-1693-4................... 241

Gardiner, George to Gardiner, Nicholas   Deed-1673............ 99
Gardiner, Nicholas from Gardiner, George   Deed-1673......... 99
Gardiner, Nicholas from Porter, John   Deed-1671............. 99
Gardiner, Nicholas from Porter, John   Deed-1673............. 99
Gardiner, William from Porter, John   Deed-1671.............. 95
Gardner, George & Stanton, Robert from Wanuemaching   Deed-1662 216
Gardner, Henry et al. to Heffernan, William   Deed-1692....... 232
Gardner, Henry et al. to Sewall, Samuel   Deed-1693.......... 242
Gardner, Henry & Watson, John to Allen, Joseph   Deed-1692   235
George, Mary from George, Peter   Deed-1679.................. 128
George, Peter from Dodge, Tristram   Deed-1666............... 15
George, Peter to George, Mary   Deed-1679.................... 128
George, Peter to George, Samuel   Deed-1678.................. 129
George, Peter to Williams, John   Deed-1668.................. 15
George, Samuel from George, Peter   Deed-1678................ 129
Gerrish, William to Eliott, Asaph   Deed-1682................ 163
Gibbs, Robert from Cooke, John   Deed-1673................... 30
Gibbs, Robert to Cooke, John   Deed Returned-1674............ 30
Gibbs, Robert from Springer, Lawrance   Deed-1679............ 126
Ginings, Thomas from Brenton, William   Deed-1659............ 48
Ginings, Thomas Sr. to Ginings, Thomas, Jr.   Deed-1674...... 48
Ginings, Thomas Jr. from Ginings, Thomas Sr.   Deed-1674.... 48
Gonzales, Lawrence to Hall, Will   Assignment of Deed-1672... 17
Gonzales, Lawrence from Kent, Thomas   Power of Attorney-1672 17
Goose, John   Protest-1677 100
Gorton, John from Gorton, Samuel   Deed-1677................. 119
Gorton, Samuel from Carder, Richard   Deed-1650............. 137
Gorton, Samuel to Coles, Daniel et al.   Deed-1677........... 134
Gorton, Samuel to Gorton, John   Deed-1677................... 119
Gorton, Samuel & Houldon, Randall from Cachanaquant   Deed-1695 117
Gorton, Samuel et al. from Miantonomi   Deed-1642........... 113
Gould, Daniel to Surkett, John   Deed-1687................... 204

Gould, Elizabeth   Testimony-1684 176
Gould, Thomas from Aquinaumpau   Deed-1660 29
Gould, Thomas to Cranston, John   Deed-1673................ 29
Gould, Thomas from Koshkotap   Deed-1657.................... 29
Gould, Thomas to Brenton, William   Deed-1675............... 83
Gould, Thomas to Cranston, John   Deed-1674................. 41
Gould, Thomas from Surkett, John   Deed-1696............... 245
Goulding, Penelope & Roger from Arnold, Benedict   Deed-1676 105
Goulding, Roger from Coggeshall, William   Deed-1681......... 153
Goulding, Roger & Penelope from Arnold, Benedict   Deed-1676 105
Green, James & Thomas from Green, John Sr.   Deed-1675..... 102
Green, John from Cunagrave, Walter   Deed-1651.............. 185
Green, John Sr. to Green, James & Thomas   Deed-1675........ 102
Green, John to Greene, James   Deed-1681-2.................... 173
Green, John from Greenman, Edward & David   Deed-1647..... 184
Green, Thomas from Collins, Lieutenant Elizur   Indenture-1664 102
Green, Thomas & James from Green, John Senr.   Deed-1675.... 102
Green, Thomas from Todd, Walter   Deed-1673-4.............. 101
Greene, James from Green, John   Deed-1681-2................. 173
Greene, John Jr. to Carpenter, William   Deed-1658............. 52
Greene, John & Clarke, Weston from Withington, Peleg   Power of Attorney-1686 207
Greene, John to Lawton, Thomas   Deed-1654.................. 46
Greene, John et al. from Miantonomi   Deed-1642.............. 113
Greene, John to Sisson, George   Deed-1693.................... 234
Greenell, Matthew to Manchester, Thomas   Deed-1681......... 153
Greenell, Matthew from Manchester, William   Deed-1681....... 142
Greenell, Matthew from Tripp, John   Deed-1651............... 145
Greenell, Mathew from Weeden, Rose   Deed-1673.............. 38
Greenhill, Daniel to Brightman, Henry   Deed-1683............. 220
Greenhill, Matthew & Manchester, William to Ward, Thomas   Deed-1682 167
Greenman, David   Land Recorded-1648 97
Greenman, David & Edward from Coddington, William   Deed-1642 104
Greenman, David & Edward from Easton, Nicholas   Deed-1648   97
Greenman, David & Edward to Green, John   Deed-1647....... 184
Greenman, Edward & David from Coddington, William   Deed-1642 104
Greenman, Edward & David from Easton, Nicholas   Deed-1648   97
Greenman, Edward & David to Green, John   Deed-1647....... 184

Hagbourne, Samuel from Cahoone, William   Deed-1670....... 161
Hall, Henry to Crandall, John   Deed-1693 229
Hall, Henry to Knight, Jonathan   Deed-1693 230
Hall, Henry to Ray, James   Deed-1693 227
Hall, Henry to Sheldon, John   Deed-1693 229
Hall, Henry to Tanner, William   Deed-1693 228
Hall, Margaret from Robinson, Edward   Deed-1684............ 184
Hall, Henry to Wells, Peter   Deed-1693...................... 228
Hall, Will from Gonzales, Lawrence   Assignment of Deed-1672 17
Hall, William to Sisson, Richard   Deed-1658.................. 71
Hall, Henry & Knight, Richard from Cogamaquoant   Deed-1664   6
Hanna, Mary & Robert from Wilson, Samuel   Deed-1688...... 215
Hanna, Robert & Mary from Wilson, Samuel   Deed-1688...... 215
Harris, Andrew from Westcott, Robert   Deed-1656............. 152
Hart, Freeborn from Brenton, William et al.   Deed-1674...... 237
Hart, John to Chapman, Ralph   Deed-1688.................... 226
Hazard, Robert from Brenton, William et al.   Deed-1671....... 12
Hazard, Robert to Brownell, George   Deed-1671............... 13
Hazard, Robert to Freeborne, Gideon   Deed-1671.............. 14
Hazard, Robert against Hazard, Thomas   Claim-1677......... 110
Hazard, Thomas   Will-1676 110
Hazard, Thomas from Hazard, Robert   Claim-1677............ 110
Hatch, Walter et al. from Ousamequen et al.   Deed-1657....... 145
Hatherly, Timothy et al. from Ousamequen et al.   Deed-1657... 145
Haviland, William to Malins, Robert   Deed-1675............... 81
Heffernan, Susannah from Carr, Caleb   Settlement-1680-81..... 139
Heffernan, William from Sewall, Samuel et al.   Deed-1692..... 232
Herbert, John   Protest-1676 95
Hicks, John to Sabeere, Stephen   Deed-1677................... 100
Hicks, Thomas to Springer, Lawrence   Deed-1679............. 126
Hicks, Samuel to Ward, Thomas   Deed-1672................... 151
Hicks, Samuel to Ward, Thomas   Deed-1682 167
Higgin, Seaborn   Land Recorded-1675 85
Hodges, Henry to Borden, John   Deed-1680-81................. 197
Holloway, Malachi to Borden, John   Deed-1680............... 196
Hollyman, Ezekiel & Holden, Randall from Tacommonan   Deed-1654 191
Holmes, John from Wilson, Samuel   Deed-1687............... 214
Holmes, John from Wilson, Samuel   Indenture-1687........... 215
Holden, Randall et al. from Kaskottape   Deed-1659............ 68
Holden, Randall & Gorton, Samuel from Cachanaquant   Deed-1695 117
Holden, Randall & Hollyman, Ezekiel from Tacommonan   Deed-1654 191

Holden, Randall et al. from Miantonomi   Deed-1642.......... 113
Holden, Randall to Paine, Anthony   Deed-1645................ 38
Holden, Capt. Randall & Williams, Roger   Testimony-1664..... 178
Hoskins, John to Borden, John   Deed-1680.................... 196
House, Samuel et al. from Ousamequen et al.   Deed-1657...... 145
Howland, Henry et al. from Ousamequen et al.   Deed-1657..... 145
Hubbard, Samuel   Land Recorded-1672 14
Hudlestone, Valentine from Allen, Matthew   Deed-1679........ 132
Hudlestone, Valentine from Chamberlin, Henry   Deed-1679-80.. 131
Hudlestone, Valentine from Manchester, John   Deed-1679...... 131
Hull, John et al. to Clarke, William   Deed-1674............. 111
Hull, John et al. to Hart, Freeborn   Deed-1674.............. 237
Hull, John et al. to Hazard, Robert   Deed-1671.............. 12
Hull, John from Smith, Richard   Deed-1687................... 217
Hull, Joseph from Allen, Joseph   Deed-1693.................. 235
Hutchinson, Elisha & Hannah to Brenton, William   Deed-1670.. 135
Hutchinson, Hannah & Elisha to Brenton, William   Deed-1670.. 135

Inman, Edward   Land Recorded-1675 80
Inman, Edward to Blackmore, James & Buckman, John   Deed-1672.. 21
Inman, Edward to Buckland, Banjamin et al.   Deed-1672..a & b 22
Inman, Edward from Manion, William   Deed-1669.............. 20
Inman, Edward & Mowry, John to Blackmore, James & Buckman, John   Deed-1672 ....21, 22
Inman Edward & Mowry, John   Land Recorded-1672.......... 24
Inman, Edward & Mowry, John from Mannion, William   Deed-1666 20
Inman, Edward from Philip, King of the Wampanoags et al.   Deed-1669. 21

Jackson, Samuel et al. from Ousamequen et al.   Deed-1657...... 145
Jeffery, William   Will-1674 66
Jeffery, William with Knight, Richard   Agreement-1650....... 5
Jeffery, William to Turner, Lawrence   Deed-1653-4........... 28
Jennings (See Ginings).
Jones, Mary from Taylor, Rebecca & Nelson, John   Deed-1685.. 193
Jones, Philip to Taylor, Rebecca & Nelson, John   Mortgage-1683 192
Jourdaine, John to Lawton, Thomas   Deed-1668............... 36

Kashotap to Coddington, William et al.   Deed-1659............ 68
Kelly, Michael from Newport, town of   Deed-1673............ 108
Kendrick, George from Knight, Richard   Deed-1656........... 27
Kendrick, George to Turner, Lawrence   Deed-1663............ 27

Kent, Thomas to Gonzales, Lawrence   Power of Attorney-1672.. 17
Kent, Thomas from Portsmouth, town of   Ratification of holdings-1672 ... 17
King, Daniel from Clarke, Weston   Deed-1687 ... 221
Knight, Jonathan from Hall, Henry   Deed-1693 ... 230
Knight, Richard   Entail-1648 ... 6
Knight, Richard & Hall, Henry from Cogamaquoant   Deed-1664   6
Knight, Richard with Jeffery, William   Agreement-1650 ... 5
Knight, Richard to Kendrick, George   Deed-1656 ... 27
Knight, Richard from Rogers, James   Deed-1648 ... 5
Knight, Richard to Turner, Lawrence   Deed-1658 ... 26
Koshkotap to Gould, Thomas   Deed-1657 ... 29

Lake, David to Bailey, John   Deed-1687-8 ... 216
Lamb, Caleb & Williams, Stephen from Wise, Joseph, Sr.   Deed-1673 ... 81
Lawton, Daniel from Lawton, Thomas   Power of Attorney-1674   57
Lawton, George & Albro, John from Clarke, Capt. Thomas   Deed-1677 ... 109
Lawton, George, from Bowne, Andrew   Deed-1687 ... 206
Lawton, George to Lawton, Robert   Deed-1688 ... 214
Lawton, George to Lawton, Robert   Assignment-1688 ... 223
Lawton, Isaac from Cadman, Richard   Deed-1688 ... 219
Lawton, Robert from Lawton, George   Deed-1688 ... 214
Lawton, Robert from Lawton, George   Assignment-1688 ... 223
Lawton, Robert from Wodell, William   Deed-1688-9 ... 224
Lawton, Thomas from Almy, John   Assignment of deed-1671.. 34
Lawton, Thomas from Almy, John   Deed-1671 ... 35
Lawton, Thomas from Almy, John   Deed-1671 ... 36
Lawton, Thomas from Almy, John   Deed-1671 ... 37
Lawton, Thomas from Almy, John   Deed-1671 ... 38
Lawton, Thomas & Almy, John   Agreement-1673 ... 46
Lawton, Thomas from Bradford, Alice   Deed-1668 ... 33
Lawton, Thomas to Briggs, John   Deed-1668 ... 34
Lawton, Thomas from Cobb, Gersham   Deed-1668 ... 32
Lawton, Thomas from Crow, William   Deed-1668 ... 33
Lawton, Thomas from Greene, John   Deed-1654 ... 46
Lawton, Thomas from Jourdaine, John   Deed-1668 ... 36
Lawton, Thomas to Lawton, Daniel   Power of Attorney-1674.. 57
Lawton, Thomas from Nelson, William   Deed-1668 ... 32
Lay, Edward from Clarke, William   Deed-1679 ... 130
Layton, John to Tew, Richard   Deed-1643 ... 65
Leonard, James to Sheffield, Icabod   Deed-1681 ... 182
Lloyd, James from Sylvester, Nathaniel   Deed-1678 ... 172

Long, Philip   Land Bounded-1680-81 165
Long, Philip & Vaughan, Daniel   Agreement-1682............. 164
Loveday, Thomas to Barker, William   Power of Attorney-1671.. 19
Lynch, Sir Thomas to Paine, Capt. Thomas   Order-1682........ 170

Makepeace, William to Ward, Thomas   Deed-1680.............. 149
Makepeace, William to Ward, Thomas   Deed-1681.............. 150
Malins, Robert from Haviland, William   Deed-1675............ 81
Mamamutt to Alderman   Deed-1683 175
Mamamutt to Wilcox, Daniel   Deed-1683 174
Man, James to Smith, Philip   Deed-1688..................... 223
Manchester, John from Coggeshall, John & William   Deed-1678 130
Manchester, John to Hudlestone, Valentine   Deed-1679........ 131
Manchester, Thomas to Borden, Matthew   Deed-1682........... 170
Manchester, Thomas from Browning, William   Deed-1684-5.... 179
Manchester, Thomas from Grenell, Matthew   Deed-1681....... 153
Manchester, Thomas to Pearce, John   Deed-1681.............. 144
Manchester, Thomas to Pearce, John   Deed-1681.............. 157
Manchester, Thomas to Sisson, Richard   Deed-1658 71
Manchester, William to Cooke, John   Deed-1680............... 138
Manchester, William to Cooke, John   Deed-1680............... 139
Manchester, William to Correy, Capt. William   Deed-1681..... 156
Manchester, William to Durfee, Thomas   Deed-1681........... 143
Manchester, William & Greenhill, Matthew to Ward, Thomas
    Deed-1682 167
Manchester, William to Grenell, Matthew   Deed-1681......... 142
Manchester, William to Pearce, John   Deed-1681............. 141
Manion, William to Inman, Edward   Deed-1669................ 20
Manion, William to Inman, Edward & Mowry, John   Deed-1666 :20
Maxson, John from Utley, Samuel   Deed-1687-8............... 221
Mayhew, Matthew to Sanford, Peleg et al.   Deed-1674......... 108
Mays, Sarah et al. from Gorton, Samuel   Deed-1677........... 134
Mays, William from Brinley, Frances   Deed-1673-4............ 226
Mays, William et al. from Gorton, Samuel   Deed-1677......... 134
Mew, Noel from Coddington, Nathaniel   Deed-1686............ 190
Miantonomi & Cannonicus to Williams, Roger   Deed-1637.... 162
Miantonomi to Holden, Randall et al.   Deed-1642............. 113
Mirick, William to Ward, Thomas   Deed-1673................. 106
Moore, Richard et al. from Ousamequen et al.   Deed-1657..... 145
Morton, Nathaniel et al. from Ousamequen et al.   Deed-1657.... 145
Morton, Thomas to Almy, John   Deed-1668................... 34
Mosher, Hugh to Brightman, Henry   Deed-1689............... 225
Mott, Jacob, from Wilcox, Daniel   Deed-1682................. 194

Mott, Jacob, from Wodell, William   Deed-1684............... 195
Mowry, Joseph from Wilcox, Daniel   Deed-1682............... 160
Mowry, John & Inman, Edward to Blackmore, James & Buckman, John   Deed-1672 ....21, 22
Mowry, John & Inman, Edward   Land Recorded-1672......... 24
Mowry, John & Inman, Edward from Minnion, William   Deed-1666 20
Mumford, Stephen & Ayres, Robert from Phips, Mary   Receipt-1694 245
Mumford, Stephen & Ayres, Robert to Phips, Sir William   Deed-1687 213
Mumford, Stephen & Ayres, Robert from Walley, John   Deed-1687 208
Mumford, Thomas to Battey, Samson   Deed-1693 239
Mumford, Thomas et al. to Clarke, William   Deed-1674...... 111
Mumford, Thomas et al. to Hart, Freeborn   Deed-1674....... 237
Mumford, Thomas et al. to Hazard, Robert   Deed-1671...... 12
Mumford, Thomas et al. to Heffernan, William   Deed-1692.... 232
Mumford, Thomas to Sanford, Peleg   Deed-1667............. 72
Mumford, Thomas et al. to Sewall, Samuel   Deed-1693........ 242
Mumford, Thomas to Thomas, John   Deed-1693.............. 239

Nash, Samuel to Bartlett, Benjamin   Deed-1666............... 146
Nash, Samuel et al. from Ousamequen et al.   Deed-1657....... 145
Naw-naw-nanten-new to Arnold, Stephen   Deed-1674.......... 78
Neales, Henry, from Allis, John   Deed-1685................... 192
Nelson, John & Taylor, Rebecca from Jones, Philip   Mortgage-1683 192
Nelson, John & Taylor, Rebecca to Jones, Mary   Deed-1685.... 193
Nelson, William to Lawton, Thomas   Deed-1668............... 32
Newbery, Walter from Richardson, William   Deed-1674........ 94
Newport, town of versus Arnold, Benedict   1671.............. 85
Newport, town of from Arnold, Benedict   Deed-1673.......... 86
Newport, town of from Arnold, Benedict   Deed-1673.......... 199
Newport, town of to Barker, James   Deed-1662............... 16
Newport, town of to Easton, Nicholas   Deed-1662............. 15
Newport, town of to Fry, Thomas   Deed-1672................. 108
Newport, town of   Highways-1654 54
Newport, town of to Kelly, Michael   Deed-1673............... 108
Newport, town of to Sanford, John   Deed-1674............... 74
Newport, town of to Sanford, Peleg   Deed-1674............... 75
Nicholson, Joseph to Nicholson, Samuel   Power of Attorney-1672 18

Nicholson, Samuel from Nicholson, Joseph   Power of Attorney-
    1672 18
Niles, Nathaniel to Sewall, Samuel   Deed-1692................. 243

Ousamequen et al. to Chandler, Edmond et al.   Deed-1657....... 145

Paine, Anthony from Holden, Randall   Deed-1645............. 38
Paine, John to Appleton, Samuel   Deed-1663................... 110
Paine, John to Clarke, William   Deed-1677..................... 128
Paine, John to Taynter, Joseph   Trust Deed-1669.............. 39
Paine, Thomas from Carr, Caleb   Deed-1688................... 217
Paine, Capt. Thomas from Lynch, Sir Thomas   Order-1682..... 170
Painter, Thomas to Tew, Richard   Deed-1663-4................,66
Palmer, Henry to Sabeere, Stephen   Award-1672.............. 25
Park, William from Wise, Joseph   Deed-1671.................. 40
Parker, John   Land Recorded-1676 96
Parker, Richard from Williams, Roger   Deed-1678............. 113
Parker, John to Sisson, George   Deed-1688..................... 222
Parker, Richard from Throckmorton, John   Deed-1654......... 163
Partridge, Ralph et al. from Ousamequen et al.   Deed-1657..... 145
Pawtuxet, Purchasers of to Westcott, Stukely   Deed-1648...... 151
Peabody, William et al. from Ousamequen et al.   Deed-1657.... 145
Pearce, John from Clarke, William   Deed-1675................. 112
Pearce, John from Coggeshall, William   Deed-1681............. 158
Pearce, John from Manchester, Thomas   Deed-1681............ 144
Pearce, John from Manchester, Thomas   Deed-1681............ 157
Pearce, John from Manchester, William   Deed-1681............ 141
Perry, Michael from Easton, John   Receipt-1687-8............. 218
Phillip, King of the Wampanoags et al. to Inman, Edward   Deed-
    1669 21
Phips, Mary to Mumford, Stephen & Ayres, Robert   Receipt-
    1694 245
Phips, Sir William from Mumford, Stephen & Ayres, Robert
    Deed-1687 213
Pocoke, John to Browne, Capt. John   Deed-1683............... 171
Porter, John et al to Clarke, William   Deed-1674............... 111
Porter, John to Gardiner, Nicholas   Deed-1671................. 99
Porter, John to Gardiner, Nicholas   Deed-1673................. 99
Porter, John to Gardiner, William   Deed-1671................. 95
Porter, John et al. to Hart, Freeborn,   Deed-1674.............. 237
Porter, John et al. to Hazard, Robert   Deed-1671.............. 12
Porter, John & Sanford, John   Testimony-1669................. 178
Porter, John to Smith, Richard   Deed-1671..................... 9
Portsmouth, town of to Kent, Thomas   Ratification of Holdings-
    1672 17

Potter, Robert et al. from Miantonomi   Deed-1642............ 113
Powell, Ralph to Simmons, John   Deed-1679.................. 147

Quisaquance to Brenton, William et al.   Deed-1659............. 68

Rainebrow, Edward to Browne, William   Deed-1672........... 91
Rathbon, John from Alcock, John heirs of   Receipt-1672...... 238
Rathbone, John from Dering, Samuel   Deed-1671............. 11
Rathbone, John & Allen, William to Sirkett, John   Deed-1687.. 205
Rathbone, John & Vose, Edward from Williams, John   Deed-1671 11
Ray, James from Hall, Henry   Deed-1693..................... 227
Read, John from Boomer, Mathew   Deed-1677................. 122
Read, William to Brookes, Thomas   Deed-1687............... 200
Reape, Joan to Rhodes, Zachariah   Deed-1676-7.............. 109
Reape, Sarah to Smith, Leonard   Deed-1674.................. 57
Reckes, John from Shivereck, Samuel   Deed-1680............. 152
Rhodes, Zachariah to Arnold, Stephen   Deed-1663............ 78
Rhodes, Zachariah from Reape, Joan   Deed-1676-7............ 109
Richard, John to Almy, John   Deed-1671..................... 37
Richardson, William to Newbery, Walter   Deed-1674.......... 94
Ringe, Andrew to Almy, John   Deed-1668.................... 35
Robinson, Edward to Billings, Samuel   Deed-1658............. 47
Robinson, Edward Junr. & Francis from Robinson, Edward Senr.   Deed-1686... 200
Robinson, Edward to Robinson, Edward Junr. & Francis   Deed-1686... 200
Robinson, Edward to Hall, Margaret   Deed-1684............... 184
Robinson, Francis & Edward Junr. from Robinson, Edward Senr.   Deed-1686... 200
Rodman, John from Alcock, John   Deed-1687................. 202
Rodman, John from Wharton, Philip to Briggs, Nathaniel   Deed-1684... 204
Rogers, James to Knight, Richard   Deed-1648................. 5
Rogers, James from Sanford, John   Deed-1659............... 90

Sabeere, Stephen from Hicks, John   Deed-1677 100
Sabeere, Stephen from Smith, John   Deed-1676 90
Sabeere, Stephen to Palmer, Henry   Award-1672............. 25
Salmerdore (Negro) from Champlin, John   Grant of Freedom.. 47
Sands, James from Dering, Mary   Deed-1671 12
Sands, James to Earle, William   Deed...................... 199
Sanford, John et al. from Gorton, Samuel   Deed-1677........ 134
Sanford, John from Newport, town of   Deed-1674............ 74
Sanford, John & Porter, John   Testimony-1669.............. 178

Sanford, John to Rogers, James   Deed-1659.................... 90
Sanford, John to Sanford, Peleg   Deed-1674................... 75
Sanford, Mary et al. from Gorton, Samuel   Deed-1677........ 134
Sanford, Peleg from Brenton, William   Deed-1670............ 72
Sanford, Peleg from Brenton, William   Deed-1674............ 74
Sanford, Peleg, from Brenton, William   Deed-1679............ 136
Sanford, Peleg to Brenton, William   Deed-1685.............. 186
Sanford, Peleg to Carr, Caleb   Deed-1675..................... 84
Sanford, Peleg from Champlin, John   Deed-1675.............. 82
Sanford, Peleg from Cananicus   Deed-1675 80
Sanford, Peleg from Davis, Aaron   Deed-1672-73............. 73
Sanford, Peleg et al. to Heffernan, William   Deed-1692........ 232
Sanford, Peleg et al. from Mayhew, Matthew   Deed-1674...... 108
Sanford, Peleg from Mumford, Thomas   Deed-1667.......... 72
Sanford, Peleg from Newport, town of   Deed-1674........... 75
Sanford, Peleg from Sanford, John   Deed-1674............... 75
Sanford, Peleg et al. to Sewall, Samuel   Deed-1693........... 242
Sanford, Peleg from Sisson, Richard   Deed-1660.............. 71
Sanford, Peleg to Slocom, Peleg   Deed-1693.................. 231
Sanford, Peleg et al. from Throckmorton, John   Deed-1687... 209
Sanford, Peleg, from Waterman, Thomas   Deed-1672-73....... 73
Saunders, Tobias & Turner, Lawrence   Land Recorded-1673.... 28
Sayles, John to Arnold, Stephen   Deed-1659................... 77
Sewall, Hannah et al. to Heffernan, William   Deed-1692........ 232
Sewall, Samuel from Brenton, Jahleel et al.   Deed-1693........ 242
Sewall, Samuel et al. to Heffernan, William   Deed-1692........ 232
Sewall, Samuel from Niles, Nathaniel   Deed-1692............. 243
Sheffield, Icabod from Leonard, James   Deed-1681............ 182
Sheldon, John from Congdon, Benjamin   Deed-1683.......... 230
Sheldon, John from Hall, Henry   Deed-1693.................. 229
Shivereck, Samuel to Reckes, John   Deed-1680................ 152
Shotton, Samson et al. from Miantonomi   Deed-1642.......... 113
Simmons, John   Will-1678-9 121
Simmons, John from Powell, Ralph   Deed-1679............... 147
Simmons, John to Ward, Thomas   Deed-1679.................. 133
Simmons, John to Ward, Thomas   Deed-1680.................. 148
Sirkett, John from Allen, William & Rathbone, John   Deed-1687.. 205
Sirkett, John from Gould, Daniel   Deed-1687................. 204
Sisson, George   Land Bounded-1682-3......................... 166
Sisson, George to Brighton, Henry   Deed-1681................ 172
Sisson, George from Browne, William   Deed-1681-2........... 159
Sisson, George to Cooke, John   Deed-1683.................... 169

Sisson, George from Cornell, Thomas & Stephen Deed-1691...	233
Sisson, George from Deane, Thomas Deed-1683..............	171
Sisson, George from Greene, John Deed-1693.................	234
Sisson, George from Parker, John Deed-1688.................	222
Sisson, George from Tripp, Peleg Deed-1677.................	105
Sisson, Richard from Hall, William Deed-1658...............	71
Sisson, Richard from Manchester, Thomas Deed-1658........	71
Sisson, Richard to Sanford, Peleg Deed-1660................	71
Slocum, Giles from Chapman, Ralph Deed-1693-4............	240
Slocum, Peleg from Sanford, Peleg Deed-1693..............	231
Smith, Edward & Barker, James Bounds changed-1657........	48
Smith, Elisha & Barker, James Agreement-1675..............	92
Smith, John to Sabeere, Stephen Deed-1676...................	90
Smith, Leonard from Reape, Sarah Deed-1674...............	57
Smith, Philip from Man, James Deed-1688....................	223
Smith, Philip et al. from Mayhew, Matthew Deed-1674.......	108
Smith, Richard from Atherton, Jonathan Deed-1673..........	31
Smith, Richard to Briggs, John Deed-1672...................	49
Smith, Richard from Clarke, John Deed-1674................	44
Smith, Richard to Hull, John Deed-1687......................	217
Smith, Richard from Porter, John Deed-1671.................	9
Smith, Richard to Terry, Joseph & Bailey, Richard Deed-1671-2	31
Smith, Richard et al. from Quisaquance Deed-1659............	68
Southworth, Constant et al. from Ousamequen et al. Deed-1657	145
Southworth, Thomas to Almy, John Deed-1668...............	34
Southworth, Thomas et al. from Ousamequen et al. Deed-1657	145
Springer, Lawrence to Gibbs, Robert Deed-1679.............	126
Springer, Lawrence from Hicks, Thomas Deed-1679..........	126
Stafford, Thomas to Warner, John Deed-1684-5...............	181
Stafford, Thomas from Warner, John Deed-1684-5............	181
Stanton, Robert & Gardner, George from Wanuemaching, Deed-1662	216
Stevens, Henry to Boomer, Matthew Deed-1676..............	96
Stevens, Henry to Easton, Peter Agreement-1652.............	76
Stoughton, William from Walley, John Mortgage-1685........	188
Stoughton, William to Walley, John Deed-1687...............	207
Strainge, John Senr. to Strainge, John Junr. Deed-1687........	205
Strainge, John Junr. to Strainge, John Senr. Deed-1687.......	205
Surkett, John to Gould, Thomas Deed-1696....................	245
Sweet, Philip to Warner, John Deed-1684.....................	177
Sylvester, Nathaniel to Lloyd, James Deed-1678...............	172
Tacommonan to Holden, Randall & Hollyman, Ezekiel Deed-1654	191

Talman, Peter to Durfee, Thomas   Deed-1683................. 169
Talman, Peter from Wamsetta   Deed-1661.................... 188
Tanner, William from Hall, Henry   Deed-1693............... 228
Tatapanum et al. to Cudworth, James et al.   Deed-1657......... 145
Taylor, Rebecca & Nelson, John to Jones, Mary   Deed-1685.... 193
Taylor, Rebecca & Nelson, John from Jones, Philip   Mortgage-1683.. 192
Taynter, Joseph from Paine, John   Trust Deed-1669........... 39
Terry, Joseph & Bailey, Richard from Smith, Richard   Deed-1671-2.. 31
Terry, Thomas to Acres, John   Deed-1670..................... 23
Terry, Thomas, to Administrators of John Hull's Estate   Deed-1683.. 183
Terry, Thomas to Calhoane, William   Deed-1662-3............. 161
Terry, Thomas to Clarke, John   Deed-1663.................... 162
Terry, Thomas from Williams, John   Receipt-1677............. 173
Tew, Henry   Land Recorded-1674 65
Tew, Henry to Clarke, William   Marriage Indenture-1663...... 9
Tew, Richard from Anthony, John   Deed-1642................ 64
Tew, Richard from Barker, James   Deed-1665................. 66
Tew, Richard to Billing, Seaborne   Deed-   84
Tew, Richard from Clarke, John   Deed-1650................... 180
Tew, Richard from Layton, John   Deed-1643.................. 65
Tew, Richard from Painter, Thomas   Deed-1663 or 4.......... 66
Tew, Richard from Wood, Thomas   Deed-1657............... 85
Thomas, John from Mumford, Thomas   Deed-1693............. 239
Throckmorton, John to Brenton, Jahleel et al.   Deed-1687...... 209
Throckmorton, John to Parker, Richard   Deed-1654............ 163
Tibbitts, Henry to Ward, Thomas   Deed-1672.................. 132
Tift, John   Will-1674 165
Tisdale, John et al. from Ousamequen et al.   Deed-1657......... 145
Todd, Walter to Green, Thomas   Deed-1673-4................. 101
Tripp, John to Grenell, Matthew   Deed-1651................... 145
Tripp, John to Tripp, Joseph   Deed-1671..................... 16
Tripp, John to Tripp, Peleg   Deed-1665...................... 19
Tripp, John from Weeden, Rose   Receipt-1650................. 144
Tripp, Joseph from Tripp, John   Deed-1671................... 16
Tripp, Peleg to Sisson, George,   Deed-1677.................... 105
Tripp, Peleg from Tripp, John   Deed-1665.................... 19
Tulie, John to Vaughan, Daniel   Deed-1682................... 164
Turner, Humphry et al. from Ousamequen et al.   Deed-1657   145
Turner, Lawrence   Land Recorded-1673 28
Turner, Lawrence from Barker, Joseph   Deed-1688............ 212
Turner, Lawrence from Jeffery, William   Deed-1653-4.......... 28

Turner, Lawrence from Kendrick, George   Deed-1663.......... 27
Turner, Lawrence from Knight, Richard   Deed-1658.......... 26
Turner, Lawrence & Saunders, Tobias   Land Recorded-1673... 28

Utley, Samuel to Maxson, John   Deed-1687-8................. 221

Vaughan, Daniel & Long, Philip   Agreement-1682............. 164
Vaughan, Daniel from Tulie, John   Deed-1682................ 164
Vaughan, Daniel from Vaughan, George   Deed-1686........... 201
Vaughan, Daniel from Vaughan, John,   Deed-1687............. 202
Vaughan, Mrs. Francis & Clarke, Walter   Agreement-1656..... 43
Vaughan, George to Vaughan, Daniel   Deed-1686.............. 201
Vaughan, John   Land Recorded-1675 81
Vaughan, John & Coggeshall, Joshua   Agreement-1671........ 213
Vaughan, John to Vaughan, Daniel   Deed-1687................ 202
Vaughan, John   Land Recorded-1673 25
Vaughan, John Sr. to Vaughan, John Jr.   Deed-1673........ 26
Vaughan, John Jr. from Vaughan, John Sr.   Deed-1673...... 26
Vaughan, William   Testimony-1671 180
Vose, Edward & Rathbone, John from Williams, John   Deed-1671... 11

Wadsworth, Christopher et al. from Ousamequen et al.   Deed-1657.. 145
Waite, Thomas to Ward, Thomas   Deed-1680.................. 149
Walley, John to Ayres, Robert & Mumford, Stephen   Deed-1687.. 208
Walley, John to Brenton, William   Deed-1685............... 186
Walley, John from Brenton, William   Deed-1685............. 188
Walley, John to Mumford, Stephen & Ayres, Robert   Deed-1687.. 208
Walley, John from Stoughton, William   Deed-1687........... 207
Walley, John, to Stoughton, William   Mortgage-1685......... 188
Wamsetta et al. to Cudworth, James et al.   Deed-1657....... 145
Wamsetta to Talman, Peter   Deed-1661..................... 188
Wanucmaching, to Stanton, Robert & Gardner, George   Deed-1662.. 216
Ward, Thomas   Land Recorded-1674 40
Ward, Thomas from Almy, Christopher   Deed-1681............ 155
Ward, Thomas from Almy, Job   Deed-1681.................... 154
Ward, Thomas from Almy, John   Deed-1675................... 107
Ward, Thomas from Brenton, William   Deed-1686............. 189
Ward, Thomas from Burge, Thomas   Deed-1671................ 106
Ward, Thomas from Burge, Thomas   Deed-1674................ 107
Ward, Thomas from Clarke, Carew   Deed-1679................ 127

Ward, Thomas from Cooke, John   Deed-1680.................. 134
Ward, Thomas from Devell, Joseph   Deed-1679............... 130
Ward, Thomas from Hicks, Samuel   Deed-1672................. 151
Ward, Thomas from Hicks, Samuel   Deed-1682................. 167
Ward, Thomas from Makepeace, William   Deed-1680.......... 149
Ward, Thomas from Makepeace, William   Deed-1681.......... 150
Ward, Thomas, from Manchester, William & Greenehill, Matthew
    Deed-1682 167
Ward, Thomas et al. from Mayhew, Matthew   Deed-1674....... 108
Ward, Thomas from Mirick, Thomas   Deed-1673............... 106
Ward, Thomas from Simmons, John   Deed-1679............... 133
Ward, Thomas from Simmons, John   Deed-1680............... 148
Ward, Thomas from Tibbitts, Henry   Deed-1672.............. 132
Ward, Thomas from Waite, Thomas   Deed-1680.............. 149
Ward, Thomas from Wilson, Samuel   Deed-1682.............. 168
Warner, Anna et al. from Gorton, Samuel   Deed-1677.......... 134
Warner, John to Brownell, Thomas   Deed-1677................ 144
Warner, John from Busecot, Peter   Deed Confirmed-1681-2... 176
Warner, John to Freeborne, Gideon   Deed-1682............... 166
Warner, John et al. from Gorton, Samuel   Deed-1677.......... 134
Warner, John et al. from Miantonomi   Deed-1642............. 113
Warner, John from Stafford, Thomas   Deed-1684-5............ 181
Warner, John, to Stafford, Thomas   Deed-1684-5.............. 181
Warner, John from Sweet, Philip   Deed-1684................. 177
Warner, John Senr. to Warner, John Junr.   Deed-1683........ 158
Warner, John Junr. from Warner, John Senr.   Deed-1683..... 158
Waterman, John et al. from Ousamequen et al.   Deed-1657..... 145
Waterman, Richard et al from Miantonomi   Deed-1642....... 113
Waterman, Thomas to Sanford, Peleg   Deed-1672-73.......... 73
Watson, George et al. from Ousamequen et al.   Deed-1657...... 145
Watson, John & Gardner, Henry to Allen, Joseph   Deed-1692.. 235
Weeden, Rose to Greenell, Matthew   Deed-1673............... 38
Weeden, Rose to Tripp, John   Receipt-1650................... 144
Weeden, William   Land Recorded-1674 42
Wells, Peter from Hall, Henry   Deed-1693.................... 228
West, Matthew   Land Recorded-1674 40
West, Matthew to West, Nathaniel   Deed-1676-7.............. 93
West, Nathaniel to West, Matthew   Deed-1676-7.............. 93
Westcott, Robert to Harris, Andrew   Deed-1656.............. 152
Westcott, Robert from Westcott, Stukely   Deed-1656.......... 152
Westcott, Stukely from Pawtuxet, Purchasers of   Deed-1648.. 151
Westcott, Stukely to Westcott, Robert   Deed-1656............ 152
Weston, Francis et al. from Miantonomi   Deed-1642.......... 113

Wharton, Philip from Alcock, John   Deed-1686............. 203
Wharton, Philip & Briggs, Nathaniel to Rodman, John   Deed-1684 204
Wicks, John et al. from Miantonomi   Deed-1642.............. 113
Wilbur, John et al. to Heffernan, William   Deed-1692......... 232
Wilbur, John et al. to Sewall, Samuel   Deed-1693............. 242
Wilbur, Samuel to Clarke, Latham   Deed-1671 45
Wilbur, Samuel to Clarke, Hannah   Deed-1666 44
Wilbur, Samuel et al. to Clarke, William   Deed-1674.......... 111
Wilbur, Samuel et al. to Hart, Freeborn   Deed-1674............ 237
Wilbur, Samuel et al. to Hazard, Robert   Deed-1671.......... 12
Wilcox, Daniel to Devell, Joseph   Deed-1672................... 133
Wilcox, Daniel & Earle, William from Chandler, Daniel   Deed-1662 198
Wilcox, Daniel from Mamanuett   Deed-1683 174
Wilcox, Daniel to Mott, Jacob   Deed-1682..................... 194
Wilcox, Daniel to Mowry, Joseph   Deed-1682.................. 160
Williams, John   Land Recorded-1679 125
Williams, John from Acre, John   Receipt-1672.................. 24
Williams, John from Alcock, John   Power of Attorney-1668..... 23
Williams, John from George, Peter   Deed-1668................ 15
Williams, John to Rathbone, John & Vose, Edward   Deed-1671 11
Williams, John to Terry, Thomas   Receipt-1677................ 173
Williams, Owin to Boomer, Matthew   Indenture-1658........... 76
Williams, Roger & Holden, Capt. Randall   Testimony-1664..... 178
Williams, Roger from Miantonomi & Canonicus   Deed-1637.... 162
Williams, Roger to Parker, Richard   Deed-1678................ 113
Williams, Stephen & Lamb, Caleb from Wise, Joseph Sr.   Deed-1673 81
Wilson, Samuel et al. to Clarke, William   Deed-1674.......... 111
Wilson, Samuel to Hanna, Robert & Mary   Deed-1688......... 215
Wilson, Samuel et al. to Hart, Freeborn   Deed-1674........... 237
Wilson, Samuel et al. to Hazard, Robert   Deed-1671.......... 12
Wilson, Samuel to Holmes, John   Deed-1687 214
Wilson, Samuel to Holmes, John   Indenture-1687 215
Wilson, Samuel to Ward, Thomas   Deed-1682.................. 168
Winslow, Elizabeth to Coddington, Nathaniel   Deed-1694...... 244
Winslow, Josiah senr. et al. from Ousamequen et al.   Deed-1657 145
Winslow, Kenelm et al. from Ousamequen et al.   Deed-1657.... 145
Wise, Joseph Sr. to Lamb, Caleb & Williams Stephen   Deed-1673 81
Wise, Joseph to Park, William   Deed-1671..................... 40
Withington, Peleg to Clarke, Weston & Greene, John   Power of Attorney-1686 207

Wodell, Gersham from Cornell, Richard Receipt-1672.......... 20
Wodell, William to Lawton, Robert Deed-1688-9.............. 224
Wodell, William et al. from Miantonomi Deed-1642.......... 113
Wodell, William to Mott, Jacob Deed-1684................... 195
Wood, John to Fry, Thomas Deed-1693-4..................... 241
Wood, Thomas to Tew, Richard Deed-1657................... 85

www.ingramcontent.com/pod-product-compliance
Lightning Source LLC
Chambersburg PA
CBHW030546080526
44585CB00012B/277